Crochet
One-Skein Wonders®
for Babies

Crochet One-Skein Wonders® for Babies

Edited by Judith Durant & Edie Eckman

Photography by Geneve Hoffman

Storey Publishing

The mission of Storey Publishing is to serve our customers by
publishing practical information that encourages
personal independence in harmony with the environment.

Edited by Melinda A. Slaving and Gwen Steege
Art direction and book design by Mary Winkelman Velgos
Text production by Liseann Karandisecky
Indexed by Christine R. Lindemer, Boston Road Communications

Cover and interior photography by © Geneve Hoffman Photography, except page 89 (left)
   by John Polak
Graphics by Mary Winkelman Velgos, 1, 9, 53, 75, 137, 151, 169, 205, 231
Diagrams and patterns by Karen Manthey
How-to illustrations by Alison Kolesar

Storey books are available for special premium and promotional uses and for customized editions. For further information, please call 1-800-793-9396.

Storey Publishing
210 MASS MoCA Way
North Adams, MA 01247
www.storey.com

Printed in China by R.R. Donnelley
10 9 8 7 6 5 4 3 2 1

Library of Congress Cataloging-in-Publication Data on file

CONTENTS

INTRODUCTION . . . 8

1 LITTLE Hats + Caps

Morgan Beanie . . . 10
Baby Ringle . . . 11
Pink Camouflage Cap . . . 13
Wee Little Hat and Mittens . . . 15
Spring Petals Bonnet . . . 17
Bunny Hat . . . 19
Snowflakes Hat . . . 22
Heart Squared Hat . . . 25
Crocodile Stitch Pixie Hat . . . 27
Shine Bright, Day or Night . . . 30
A Winter's Night Hat . . . 33
Hope Beanie . . . 34
Little Tam . . . 36
Baby Duomo Cap . . . 38
Braided Headband . . . 40
Toddler's Watch Cap . . . 42
Squiggle Twins . . . 44
Autumn Beanie . . . 46
Flower Power Beret . . . 48
Queen Anne's Lace Beanie . . . 50

2 LITTLE Socks + Bootees

Christening Bootees . . . 54
Pompom Bootees . . . 55
Baby Mocs . . . 58
Little Hearts Bootees . . . 60
Baby Crocs . . . 62
Monster Bootees . . . 64
Baby Mukluks . . . 66
Bumpy Bootees . . . 67
Teeny Tiny Socks . . . 69
Sunshine Boot Toppers . . . 71
Mommy & Me Leg Warmers . . . 73

③ LITTLE *Tops + Dresses*

Dad & Me Necktie Shirts . . . 76
The Back's Where It's At Bolero . . . 78
Tiny Tango Vest . . . 82
Summer Kisses Cardigan . . . 85
Reversible Sweater . . . 87
Pretty in Pink . . . 89
In the Woods Vest . . . 93
Handsome Boy's Vest . . . 95
Kimono Shell Sweater . . . 97
Prism Pinafore . . . 100
Vintage Bluebell Sacque . . . 102
Pinwheel Vest . . . 106
Boy's Cardigan . . . 110
Rosetta Cardigan . . . 113
Unforgettable Vest . . . 117
Six-Button Vest . . . 119
Floral Lace Cardigan . . . 123
April Showers Cape . . . 126
Jumper Top . . . 128
Pistachio Gelato Jacket . . . 130
Justin's Jacket . . . 134

④ LITTLE *Bottoms*

Ruffled Diaper Cover . . . 138
Buttoned-Up Diaper Cover . . . 141
Octagon Pants . . . 143
Drawstring Pants . . . 146
All Grow'd Up Skirt . . . 149

⑤ LITTLE *Bibs + Washcloths*

Little Star Bib and Washcloth . . . 152
Bib Trio . . . 154
Sweet Pea Bib . . . 158
Ribbed Baby Bib . . . 160
Baby's Bath Set . . . 162
Waves and Patchwork Washcloths . . . 164
Burp Cloth . . . 166

⑥ LITTLE *Toys*

Benjamin Bear . . . 170
Lil' Miss Lilly . . . 174
Kitty Kat Lovey . . . 175
Owl Puppet . . . 177
Ellie Bear . . . 180
Zip, Snap, and Button It! . . . 182
Effie Effalump . . . 186
Granny Bunny Buddy . . . 188
The Owl and the Pussycat . . . 191
Little Pegasus . . . 193
Cuddly Snuggly Elephant . . . 196
Goldie the Bouncing Fish . . . 200
Pocket Dolly . . . 202

7 LITTLE Blankets + Sacks

Zucchini Sleep Sack and Cap . . . 206

Snuggly Wave Cocoon . . . 209

Cotton Play Mat . . . 211

Christening Cloud . . . 213

Ivory Dreams Blanket . . . 216

Flouncy Edged Blanket . . . 218

Vaya con Dios Stroller Blanket . . . 221

Sweet Baby James . . . 224

Grey Coverlet . . . 226

Baptism Blanket . . . 229

8 LITTLE Bags + Accessories

Put-and-Take Purse . . . 232

Little Miss Felted Purse . . . 234

Max's Backpack . . . 236

Dad's Diaper Bag . . . 239

Cady's Cowl . . . 243

Dewdrop Flower Pin . . . 244

Diaper Stacker . . . 246

Bottle Cozies . . . 249

Pacifier Clip . . . 251

Little Bunny Mittens . . . 252

Baby's First Christmas Stocking . . . 254

Hyperbolic Mobile . . . 257

Ombré Wrap . . . 260

Mom's (or Dad's) Hot-or-Cold Pack . . . 263

APPENDIX

About the Designers . . . 266

Glossary . . . 272

Other Techniques . . . 275

Yarn Weights with Recommended Hook
    Sizes and Gauges . . . 277

Abbreviations . . . 278

Symbol Key . . . 279

INDEX . . . 280

Index to Projects by Yarn Weights . . . 286

INTRODUCTION

Welcome to the eighth wonder of the one-skein world, *Crochet One-Skein Wonders® for Babies*. It was such a joy to compile *One-Skein Wonders® for Babies*, we immediately launched into this crochet edition. Once again, we have included delightful items for infants, toddlers, small children, even moms and dads, and the projects were created by designers from near and far.

The projects are arranged by categories: hats and caps, socks and bootees, tops and dresses, bottoms, bibs and washcloths, toys, blankets and sacks, bags and accessories. And if you don't know what type of project you're looking for but have a particular yarn that you want to use, we've included an index on page 286 to projects by yarn weight.

Our contributors once again came through with some impossible-to-resist designs. Find the perfect hat among the twenty styles offered: Crocodile Stitch Pixie Hat by Anne-Michelle Phelan will make your little one stand out in a crowd; and Shine Bright Day or Night by Marcia Sommerkamp is knit with yarn that's hunter's orange by day and light reflective at night, ensuring that you and baby will not be missed.

If it's bootees you're looking for, check out the Christening Bootees by Pam Daley for your special day or the Baby Crocs by Gwen Steege for everyday style. Tiny Tango Vest by Kristen Stoltzfus will add some pizzazz to baby's moves, and In the Woods Vest by Justyna Kacprzak can change personality through yarn color choice.

You'll find a variety of bottom covers, from the Ruffled Diaper Cover by Corley Groves to Judith's full-length Drawstring Pants. Bibs and washcloths are both cute and handy: Little Star Bib and Washcloth by Donna Barranti, Bib Trio by Edie, and Sweet Pea Bib by Lorna Miser would all make great shower presents.

Crochet is the perfect craft for making baby toys, and any child will love Benjamin Bear by Ida Herter, Kitty Kat Lovey by Aurelia Mae Delaney, Effie Effalump by Melissa Morgan-Oakes, or Cuddly Snuggly Elephant by Kate Wood. Keep baby warm and cozy with an array of blankets and sacks, including Zucchini Sleep Sack and Cap by Reyna Thera Lorele and Sweet Baby James by Sharon Ballsmith. And be sure to visit the bags and accessories chapter for Max's Backpack by LeAnna Nocita-Lyons, Diaper Stacker by Deborah Bagley, and Little Bunny Mittens by Brenda K. B. Anderson.

Crocheting for little ones requires some special considerations, and you'll find tips for success and safety scattered throughout the book. And please keep in mind that babies come in all shapes and sizes; use the age specification included with each pattern as a general guideline, but be aware that a particular nine-month-old may fit into a garment intended for a three-to-six-month-old and vice versa.

We hope you enjoy this new collection. Happy hooking!

Judith Durant
Edie Eckman

CHAPTER ONE

LITTLE
Hats
+
Caps

Morgan Beanie

DESIGNED BY *Ashley Leither*

The Morgan Beanie uses basic stitches to create a beautiful textured pattern that grows from the half double crochet crown. Color options are endless.

SIZE AND FINISHED MEASUREMENTS
To fit 0–3 months: 12"/30.5 cm circumference

YARN
Lion Brand Vanna's Choice, 100% acrylic, 170 yds (156 m)/ 3.5 oz (100 g), Color 138 Pink Poodle (4)

CROCHET HOOK
US K/10½ (6.5 mm) *or size needed to obtain correct gauge*

GAUGE
Rounds 1–5 = 3½"/9 cm

OTHER SUPPLIES
Yarn needle

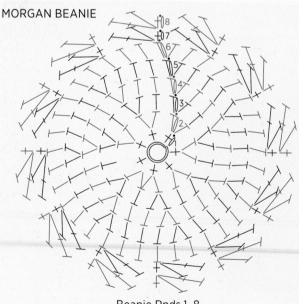

MORGAN BEANIE

Beanie Rnds 1–8

CROCHETING THE BEANIE

- Make an adjustable ring (see page 272).

- **Rnd 1:** Ch 1, 7 sc in ring, join with slip st to first sc. *You now have 7 sts.*

- **Rnd 2:** Ch 1 (does not count as st here and throughout), hdc in same st, 2 hdc in each st around, ending with hdc in same st as first hdc, join with slip st to first hdc. *You now have 14 hdc.*

- **Rnd 3:** Ch 1, hdc in same st, hdc in next st, *2 hdc in next st, hdc in next st; repeat from * around, ending with hdc in same st as first hdc, join with slip st to first hdc. *You now have 21 hdc.*

- **Rnd 4:** Ch 1, hdc in same st, hdc in next 2 sts, *2 hdc in next st, hdc in next 2 sts; repeat from * around, join with slip st to first hdc. *You now have 28 hdc.*

- **Rnd 5:** Ch 1, hdc in same st, hdc in next 3 sts, *2 hdc in next st, hdc in next 3 sts; repeat from *, ending with hdc in same st as first hdc, join with slip st to first hdc. *You now have 35 sts.*

- **Rnd 6:** Ch 1, hdc in same st, hdc in each st around, ending with hdc in same st as first hdc, join with slip st to first hdc. *You now have 36 sts.*

- **Rnd 7:** Ch 1, (sc, hdc, dc) in same st, skip next 2 sts, *(sc, hdc, dc) in next st, skip next 2 sts; repeat from * around, join with slip st to first sc.

- **Rnd 8:** Ch 1, (sc, hdc, dc) in same st, skip next (hdc, dc), *(sc, hdc, dc) in next sc, skip next (hdc, dc); repeat from * around, join with slip st to first sc.

- Repeat Rnd 8 until the beanie measures 5½"/14 cm tall.

- Fasten off. Weave in ends.

Baby Ringle

DESIGNED BY *Tanja Osswald, Osswald Design*

Slip stitches, when worked loosely with a large hook, make a drapey fabric and a wonderfully elastic ribbing. This hat is worked with sock yarn, making it the perfect weight for a newborn.

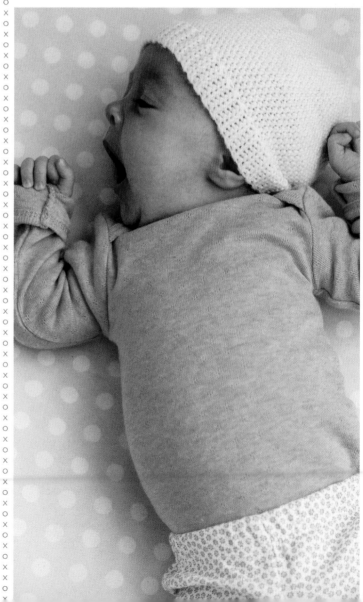

11

SIZE AND FINISHED MEASUREMENTS

To fit 0–3 months: 12"/30.5 cm circumference at ribbing, relaxed, stretching to 16"/40.5 cm

YARN

Lana Grossa Meilenweit Merino, 80% merino wool/20% nylon, 460 yds (420 m)/3.5 oz (100 g), Color 2009 raw white **❶**

CROCHET HOOK

US E/4 (3.5 mm) *or size needed to obtain correct gauge*

GAUGE

27 stitches and 26 rows = 4"/10 cm in pattern

OTHER SUPPLIES

Stitch marker, yarn needle

CROCHETING THE RIBBING

- Chain 7.
- Row 1: Working in back loop only of ch sts, slip st in 2nd ch from hook and in each ch across, turn. *You now have 6 slip sts.*
- Rows 2–88: Ch 1, BL slip st in each st across, turn. *You now have 44 ridges.*
- Fold the ribbing in half lengthwise with RS together to join beginning and end. Working through double thickness of the back bars of the foundation row and back loops of the row just worked, slip st in each st across. *Do not fasten off.*

CROCHETING THE BODY

- Turn ribbing so that the seam is on the inside.
- Rnd 1: Ch 1; working across side edge of ribbing, 2 FL slip sts in each ridge around, including working 2 FL slip sts in the seam. *You now have 90 sts. Do not join.* Pm in the first st of the rnd and move it up as you work the rnds.
- Rnds 2–16: Work FL slip st in each st around.

DECREASING FOR THE CROWN

Note: Six decreases are made in each round. To avoid straight decrease lines, the decreases are shifted. If you prefer decrease lines, work all decreases at the beginning of each repeat.

- Rnd 1: (FL slip st 2 tog, FL slip st in next 13 sts) six times. *You now have 84 sts.*
- Rnd 2: (FL slip st in next 12 sts, FL slip st 2 tog) six times. *You now have 78 sts.*

- **Rnd 3:** (FL slip st in next 5 sts, FL slip st 2 tog, FL slip st in next 6 sts) six times. *You now have* 72 sts.
- **Rnd 4:** (FL slip st 2 tog, FL slip st in next 10 sts) six times. *You now have* 66 sts.
- **Rnd 5:** (FL slip st in next 6 sts, FL slip st 2 tog, FL slip st in next 3 sts) six times. *You now have* 60 sts.
- **Rnd 6:** (FL slip st in next 2 sts, FL slip st 2 tog, FL slip st in next 6 sts) six times. *You now have* 54 sts.
- **Rnd 7:** (FL slip st 2 tog, FL slip st in next 7 sts) six times. *You now have* 48 sts.
- **Rnd 8:** (FL slip st in next 4 sts, FL slip st 2 tog, FL slip st in next 2 sts) six times. *You now have* 42 sts.
- **Rnd 9:** (FL slip st in next 5 sts, FL slip st 2 tog) six times. *You now have* 36 sts.
- **Rnd 10:** (FL slip st 2 tog, FL slip st in next 4 sts) six times. *You now have* 30 sts.
- **Rnd 11:** (FL slip st in next st, FL slip st 2 tog, FL slip st in next 2 sts) six times. *You now have* 24 sts.
- **Rnd 12:** (FL slip st in next 2 sts, FL slip st 2 tog) six times. *You now have* 18 sts.
- **Rnd 13:** (FL slip st 2 tog, FL slip st in next st) six times. *You now have* 12 sts.
- **Rnd 14:** (FL slip st 2 tog) six times. *You now have* 6 sts.
- Fasten off, leaving a long sewing length. With yarn needle, weave tail through remaining sts. Pull up snug and fasten off. Weave in ends.

Pink Camouflage Cap

DESIGNED BY *Elizabeth Garcia Kalka*

This military-style cap features straight sides and a brim. Alternating single crochet and double crochet stitches creates an interesting texture. There will be no hiding in this one!

SIZE AND FINISHED MEASUREMENTS
To fit newborn: 13"/33 cm circumference

YARN
Lily Sugar 'n Cream, 100% cotton, 150 yds (138 m)/3 oz (85 g), Color 19920 Pink Camo

CROCHET HOOK
US H/8 (5 mm) *or size needed to obtain correct gauge*

GAUGE
Rounds 1–4 = 3¾"/9.5 cm

OTHER SUPPLIES
Yarn needle

PATTERN ESSENTIALS

Exch (extended chain) Chain st pulled longer than usual, up to the height of the first st of the row or rnd.

CROCHETING THE TOP

- Ch 4, join with slip st to form a ring.

- Rnd 1 (RS): Exch (does not count as st), 10 hdc in ring, join with slip st to first hdc. *You now have* 10 hdc.

- Rnd 2: Exch, 2 hdc in each st around, join with slip st to first hdc. *You now have* 20 hdc.

- Rnd 3: Exch, *hdc in next st, 2 hdc in next st; repeat from * around, join with slip st to first hdc. *You now have* 30 hdc.

- Rnd 4: Exch, *hdc in next 2 sts, 2 hdc in next st; repeat from * around, join with slip st to first hdc. *You now have* 40 hdc.

CROCHETING THE SIDES

- Rnd 5: Ch 1, BLsc in each st around, join with slip st to first sc.

- Rnd 6: Ch 1, *sc in next st, dc in next st; repeat from * around, join with slip st to first sc.

- Rnd 7: Exch, *dc in next st, sc in next st; repeat from * around, join with slip st to first sc.

- Rnds 8–11: Repeat Rnds 6 and 7 twice.

- Rnd 12: Ch 1, sc in each st around, join with slip st to first sc.

CROCHETING THE BRIM

- Row 13: Ch 1, sc in first st, hdc in next st, *2 hdc in next st, hdc in next st; repeat from * four times, sc in next st, slip st in next st, turn. *You now have* 16 sts.

- Row 14: Ch 1, skip slip st, sc in next st, (hdc in next 2 sts, 2 hdc in next st, hdc in next 3 sts, 2 hdc in next st) twice, hdc in next 2 sts, sc in next st, slip st in next st (the first open st of Rnd 12). *You now have* 22 sts.

- Fasten off. Weave in ends.

PINK CAMOUFLAGE CAP

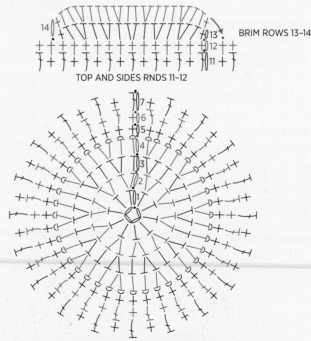

BRIM ROWS 13–14

TOP AND SIDES RNDS 11–12

TOP AND SIDES THROUGH RNDS 1–7

Wee Little Hat and Mittens

DESIGNED BY *Andrea Lyn Van Benschoten*

Newborns need hats to keep them warm. Subtly shaded baby alpaca does the trick with this one, and it's paired with tiny scratch mittens.

SIZE AND FINISHED MEASUREMENTS
To fit newborn: 12"/30.5 cm hat circumference, 4"/10 cm mitten circumference

YARN
Rowan Alpaca Colour, 100% baby alpaca, 131 yds (120 m)/1.75 oz (50 g), Color 134 Jasper (3)

CROCHET HOOK
US F/5 (3.75 mm) *or size needed to obtain correct gauge*

GAUGE
20 stitches and 16 rounds = 4"/10 cm in half double crochet
24 stitches and 28 rounds = 4"/10 cm in single crochet

OTHER SUPPLIES
Yarn needle

CROCHETING THE HAT

- **Rnd 1:** Ch 2, 10 hdc in 2nd ch from hook, join with slip st to top of ch-2. *You now have* 10 hdc.

- **Rnd 2:** Ch 2 (does not count as st throughout), 2 hdc in each hdc around, join with slip st to first hdc. *You now have* 20 hdc.

- **Rnd 3:** Ch 2, *hdc in next hdc, 2 hdc in next hdc; repeat from * around, join with slip st to top of first hdc. *You now have* 30 hdc.

- **Rnd 4:** Ch 2, *2 hdc in next hdc, hdc in next 2 hdc; repeat from * around, join with slip st to top of first hdc. *You now have* 40 hdc.

- **Rnd 5:** Ch 2, *2 hdc in next hdc, hdc in next 3 hdc; repeat from * around, join with slip st to top of first hdc. *You now have* 50 hdc.

- **Rnd 6:** Ch 2, *2 hdc in next hdc, hdc in next 4 hdc; repeat from * around, join with slip st to top of first hdc. *You now have* 60 hdc.
- **Rnd 7:** Ch 2, hdc in each hdc around, join with slip st to top of hdc.
- **Rnds 8–17:** Repeat Rnd 7 ten times.
- **Rnd 18:** Ch 2, *FPhdc in next st, BPhdc in next st; repeat from * around, join with slip st to top of first hdc.
- **Rnds 19–22:** Repeat Rnd 18 four times.
- Fasten off. Weave in ends.

CROCHETING THE SCRATCH MITTENS (MAKE 2)

- **Rnd 1:** Ch 2, 8 sc in 2nd ch from hook, join with slip st to first sc. *You now have* 8 sc.
- **Rnd 2:** Ch 1, 2 sc in each sc around, join with slip st to first sc. *You now have* 16 sc.
- **Rnd 3:** Ch 1, *2 sc in next sc, sc in next sc; repeat from * around, join with slip st to first sc. *You now have* 24 sc.
- **Rnd 4:** Ch 1, sc in each sc around, join with slip st to first sc.
- **Rnds 5–12:** Repeat Rnd 4 eight times.
- **Rnd 13:** Ch 1, sc2tog, sc in next 14 sc, sc2tog, sc in next 6 sc, join with slip st to first sc. *You now have* 22 sc.

- **Rnd 14:** Ch 1, sc2tog, sc in next 14 sc, sc2tog, sc in next 4 sc, join with slip st to first sc. *You now have* 20 sc.
- **Rnd 15:** Ch 1, sc in each sc around, join with slip st to first sc.
- **Rnd 16:** Repeat Rnd 14.
- **Rnd 17:** Ch 1, sc2tog, sc in next 10 sc, sc2tog, sc in next 6 sc, join with slip st to first sc. *You now have* 18 sc.
- **Rnd 18:** Ch 1, sc2tog, sc in next 8 sc, sc2tog, sc in next 6 sc, join with slip st to first sc. *You now have* 16 sc.
- **Rnd 19:** Ch 1, sc in each sc around, join with slip st to first sc.
- **Rnd 20:** Ch 2, hdc in each sc around, join with slip st to top of first hdc.
- **Rnd 21:** Ch 2, *FPhdc in next hdc, BPhdc in next hdc; repeat from * around, join with slip st to top of first FPhdc.
- **Rnd 22:** Repeat Rnd 21.
- Fasten off. Weave in ends.

WEE LITTLE HAT

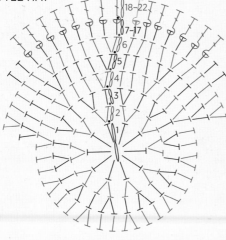

Abbreviated Hat Pattern

Spring Petals Bonnet

DESIGNED BY *Tamara Del Sonno, Clickity Sticks*

Even the most adorable baby will look cuter still with a face surrounded by delicate crocheted flower petals. The stretchy yarn used for the sample makes it fit a little longer than it may otherwise.

SIZES
To fit newborn (6 months, 12 months)

YARN
Patons Stretch Socks, 41% cotton/39% wool/13% nylon/7% elastic, 239 yds (219 m)/1.75 oz (50 g), Color 31444 Cherry Sours ①

CROCHET HOOK
US F/5 (3.75 mm) and US E/4 (3.5 mm) *or size needed to obtain correct gauge*

GAUGE
5 pattern repeats = 4"/10 cm in shell pattern on smaller hook

OTHER SUPPLIES
Yarn needle, 3 yds/3 m of ⅜"/9.5 mm ribbon, sewing needle and coordinating thread

PATTERN ESSENTIALS

Shell Pattern
(multiple of 4 stitches + 2)

Chain the desired number of sts.

Set-Up Row: Sc in 2nd ch from hook, *skip 1 ch, (2 dc, ch 1, 2 dc) in next ch, skip 1 ch, sc in next ch; repeat from * across, turn.

Row 1: Ch 2 (does not count as st), dc in first sc, *(2 dc, ch 1, 2 dc) in next ch space, dc in next sc; repeat from * across, turn.

Row 2: Ch 2, dc in first st, *(2 dc, ch 1, 2 dc) in next ch space, dc in next dc; repeat from * across, turn.

Repeat Row 2 for pattern.

CROCHETING THE PETAL BRIM

- With larger hook loosely chain 54 (58, 62).

- Change to smaller hook.

- **Set-Up Row:** Sc in 2nd ch from hook, *skip 1 ch, (2 dc, ch 1, 2 dc) in next ch, skip 1 ch, sc in next ch; repeat from * across, turn. *You now have* 13 (14, 15) pattern repeats.

- **Row 1:** Ch 1, sc in first sc, *(2 dc, ch 1, 2 dc) in next ch-space, sc in next sc; repeat from * across, turn.

- **Row 2:** Ch 1, sc in first sc, *7 dc in next ch-space, sc in next sc; repeat from * across. Fasten off, leaving a 6"/15 cm tail.

CROCHETING THE BONNET

- Working across the opposite side of starting chain with RS facing, join yarn with slip st at beginning of row.

- **Set-Up Row:** Ch 1, sc in first ch, *skip 1 ch, (2 dc, ch 1, 2 dc) in next ch, skip 1 ch, sc in next ch; repeat from * across, turn. *You now have* 13 (14, 15) pattern repeats.

- Beginning with Row 1 of Shell pattern, work even in pattern until piece measures 4 (4½, 5)"/10 (11.5, 12.5) cm from foundation ch.

- With larger hook, skipping all dcs, sc in each sc and ch-space across to gather back of bonnet, slip st to first sc to join into a circle. Fasten off.

FINISHING

- With RS facing and beginning at left front corner, sc evenly along the row ends to the right front corner. Tack top corner of each end "petal" to bottom edge of bonnet. Weave in ends. Weave ribbon through bottom edge of bonnet just above single crochet edging. With sewing needle and thread, tack ribbon down at center back to prevent baby from pulling it out. **Note:** The photographed sample used more ribbon for longer ties. However, we recommend keeping ties on items for young children to 6"/15 cm or less.

SPRING PETALS BONNET

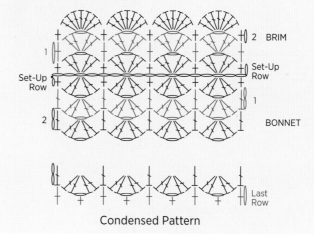

Condensed Pattern

Bunny Hat

DESIGNED BY *Laura Biondi, Black Sheep Crochet*

This cute bunny-eared hat is written for four sizes, taking your child from newborn to three years of age. And you may just get all four out of one skein!

SIZES AND FINISHED MEASUREMENTS

To fit XS (S, M, L)/0–6 (6–12, 12–18, 18–36) months: 12½ (15, 17, 18½)"/31.5 (38, 43, 47) cm hat circumference, 4"/10 cm hat depth, 5½"/14 cm ear length

YARN

Bernat Baby Coordinates, 75.2% acrylic/22.2% rayon/2.6% nylon, 431 yds (394 m)/5.6 oz (160 g), Color 46008 Natural

CROCHET HOOK

US H/8 (5 mm) *or size needed to obtain correct gauge*

GAUGE

13 stitches and 10 rounds = 4"/10 cm in double crochet

OTHER SUPPLIES

Two stitch markers, yarn needle

CROCHETING THE HAT

- Ch 3, join with slip st to form a ring.

- Place a st marker in the first st and move it up as you begin each rnd.

- **Rnd 1:** Ch 3 (counts as dc here and throughout), 7 dc in ring; do not join. *You now have* 8 dc.

- **Rnd 2:** 2 dc in each dc around. *You now have* 16 dc.

- **Rnd 3:** *Dc in next dc, 2 dc in next dc; repeat from * around. *You now have* 24 dc.

- **Rnd 4:** *Dc in next 2 dc, 2 dc in next dc; repeat from * around. *You now have* 32 dc.

BUNNY HAT

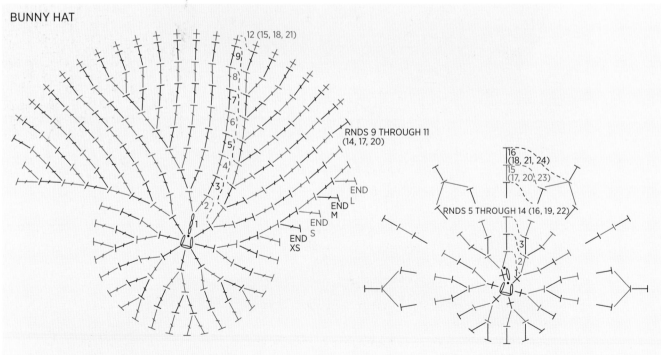

Abbreviated Hat Pattern

Abbreviated Ear Pattern

- **Rnd 5:** *Dc in next 3 dc, 2 dc in next dc; repeat from * around. *You now have* 40 dc.

Sizes 6–12, 12–18, and 18–36 months only

- **Rnd 6:** *Dc in next 4 dc, 2 dc in next dc; repeat from * around. *You now have* 48 dc.

Sizes 12–18 and 18–36 months only

- **Rnd 7:** *Dc in next 5 dc, 2 dc in next dc; repeat from * around. *You now have* 56 dc.

Size 18–36 months only

- **Rnd 8:** *Dc in next 6 dc, 2 dc in next dc; repeat from * around. *You now have* 60 dc.

All sizes

- Continuing to move first stitch marker up on each rnd, place second marker in first st and leave in place to make it easier to count rnds for the rest of the hat.
- Dc in each dc around for 6 (8, 10, 12) rnds.
- **Rnd 12 (15, 18, 21):** Sc in each st around; join with slip st to next st. Fasten off. Weave in ends.

CROCHETING THE EARS (MAKE 2)

- Ch 3, join with a slip st to form a ring.
- Place a st marker in the first st and move it up as you begin each rnd.
- **Rnd 1:** Ch 1, 6 sc in ring; *do not join. You now have* 6 sc.
- **Rnd 2:** 2 hdc in each sc around. *You now have* 12 hdc.
- **Rnd 3:** *Hdc in next hdc, 2 hdc in next hdc; repeat from * around. *You now have* 18 hdc.
- Continuing to move first stitch marker up on each rnd, place second marker in first st and leave in place to make it easier to count rnds for the rest of the ear.
- **Rnds 4–14 (16, 19, 22):** Hdc in each each hdc around.
- **Rnd 15 (17, 20, 23):** *Hdc in next hdc, hdc2tog; repeat from * around. *You now have* 12 sts.
- **Rnd 16 (18, 21, 24):** Hdc in each hdc around. Fasten off, leaving a long sewing length.

FINISHING

- Use yarn needle and tail to sew the tops of the ears shut, making sure to keep them flat. Place the ears opposite one another, approximately 2 rnds down from the top of the hat, and sew them to the hat. Make sure they are on securely, since children will tug on them! Weave in ends.

Hat Sizing

When in doubt, make a baby hat larger than you think ideal rather than smaller. A hat that's too big can be grown into, but one that's too small is useless. In general, you can estimate one to two inches of negative ease, meaning that a hat with a finished measurement of 14 inches will fit a 15- to 16-inch head — some stitch patterns and yarn will have more negative ease, some will have less.

Snowflakes Hat

DESIGNED BY *Justyna Kacprzak, Cute and Kaboodle*

Simply embroidered snowflakes adorn this cap of double and half double crochet. Earflaps add warmth, and the buttoned-up visor adds style.

SIZE AND FINISHED MEASUREMENTS
To fit 0–6 months: 14"/35.5 cm circumference

YARN
Patons Fairytale Soft DK, 55% Polyamide, 45% acrylic, 178 yds (163 m)/1.75 oz (50 g), Color 06309 Blue (3)

CROCHET HOOK
US size G/6 (4 mm) *or size needed to obtain correct gauge*

GAUGE
15 stitches and 11 rows = 4"/10 cm in double crochet

OTHER SUPPLIES
Two ⅝"/16 mm buttons, sewing needle and coordinating thread, yarn needle, scraps of white yarn for snowflakes

CROCHETING THE HAT

See chart on page 24.

- Chain 4.
- **Rnd 1:** 12 dc in 4th ch from the hook, join with slip st to first dc. *You now have 12 dc.*
- **Rnd 2:** Ch 2 (does not count as st here and throughout), 2 dc in each dc around, join with slip st to first dc. *You now have 24 dc.*
- **Rnd 3:** Ch 2, (2 dc in next dc, dc in next dc) around, join with slip st to first dc. *You now have 36 dc.*

- **Rnd 4:** Ch 2, (2 dc in next dc, dc in next 2 dc) around, join with slip st to first dc. *You now have* 48 dc.
- **Rnd 5:** Ch 2, (2 dc in next dc, dc in next 3 dc) around, join with slip st to first dc. *You now have* 60 dc.
- **Rnds 6–14:** Ch 2, dc in each dc around, join with slip st to first dc.
- Fasten off.

THE FIRST EARFLAP AND TIE

- With RS facing, skip first 8 dc and rejoin yarn to the next st.
- **Row 1:** Ch 1 (does not count as st here and throughout), hdc in next 12 dc, turn. *You now have* 12 hdc.
- **Row 2:** Ch 1, FLhdc2tog, (BLhdc in next st, FLhdc in next st) four times, BLhdc2tog, turn. *You now have* 10 hdc.
- **Row 3:** Ch 1, (FLhdc in next st, BLhdc in next st) five times, turn.
- **Row 4:** Ch 1, FLhdc2tog, (BLhdc in next st, FLhdc in next) three times, BLhdc2tog, turn. *You now have* 8 hdc.
- **Row 5:** Ch 1, (FLhdc in next st, BLhdc in next st) four times, turn.
- **Row 6:** Ch 1, FLhdc2tog, (BLhdc in next st, FLhdc in next st) twice, BLhdc2tog, turn. *You now have* 6 hdc.
- **Row 7:** Ch 1, FLhdc2tog, BLhdc in next st, FLhdc in next st, BLhdc2tog, turn. *You now have* 4 hdc.
- **Row 8:** Ch 1, FLhdc2tog, BLhdc2tog, turn. *You now have* 2 hdc.
- **Row 9:** Ch 1, sc2tog. *You now have* 1 st.
- **Tie:** Ch 40, 2-dc cluster in 3rd ch from the hook, ch 2, slip st in ch where the bobble was made, 1 slip st in each ch across. Fasten off. **Note:** The photographed sample used longer ties.

However, we recommend keeping ties on items for young children to 6"/15 cm or less.

THE VISOR

- With RS facing, join yarn with slip st to the next st after first earflap
- **Row 1:** Ch 1, FLhdc in next 20 dc, turn. *You now have* 20 hdc.
- **Rows 2–4:** Ch 1, (FLhdc in next st, BLhdc in next st) 10 times, turn.
- **Row 5:** Ch 1, FLhdc2tog, (BLhdc in next st, FLhdc in next st) eight times, BLhdc2tog, turn. *You now have* 18 hdc.
- **Row 6:** Ch 1, (FLhdc in next st, BLhdc in next st) nine times, turn.
- **Row 7:** Ch 1, FLhdc2tog, (BLhdc in next st, FLhdc in next st) seven times, BLhdc2tog, turn. *You now have* 16 hdc.
- **Row 8:** Ch 1, FLhdc2tog, (BLhdc in next st, FLhdc in next st) six times, BLhdc2tog, turn. *You now have* 14 hdc. Fasten off.

THE SECOND EARFLAP AND TIE

- With RS facing, join yarn with slip st to the next st after the visor. Repeat instructions for the first earflap.

FINISHING

- Fold visor up. Using sewing needle and thread, sew buttons at the top of the front flap, sewing the visor to the hat. Weave in ends. Using photo as a guide, use white yarn to embroider snowflakes to bottom border of hat.

Tie Length

To eliminate choking danger, we recommend keeping ties on items for young children to 6"/15 cm or less.

SNOWFLAKES HAT

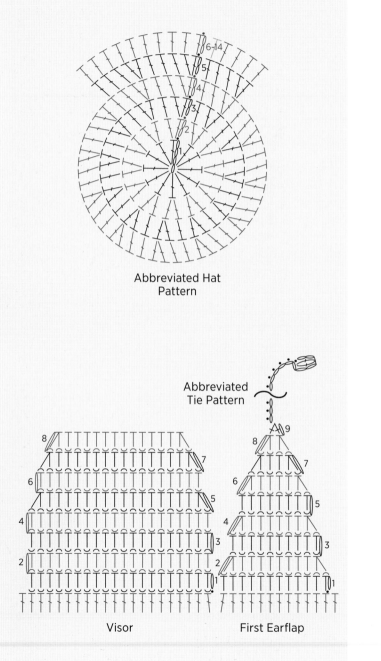

Abbreviated Hat
Pattern

Abbreviated
Tie Pattern

Visor   First Earflap

Heart Squared Hat

DESIGNED BY *Laura Hontz*

A small bit of contrasting yarn for the heart makes this a lovable hat for baby or toddler. Four granny squares are joined, topped off, and trimmed.

SIZE AND FINISHED MEASUREMENTS
To fit 0–6 months: 14"/35.5 cm circumference and 5½"/14 cm tall

YARN
Sirdar Spinning Snuggly DK, 55% nylon/45% acrylic, 179 yds (165 m)/1.75 oz (50 g), Color 303 Cream (MC)

CROCHET HOOK
US F/5 (3.75 mm) *or size needed to obtain correct gauge*

GAUGE
Each square = 3½"/9 cm square

OTHER SUPPLIES
Yarn needle, small amount of pink DK-weight yarn for heart (CC)

CROCHETING THE SQUARES

THE PLAIN SQUARE (MAKE 3)

- Make an adjustable ring (see page 272).

- **Rnd 1:** Ch 3 (counts as dc), 2 dc in ring, (ch 2, 3 dc) three times in ring, ch 2, join with slip st to top of ch-3, turn. *You now have four 3-dc groups and 4 ch-2 spaces.*

- **Rnd 2:** Slip st in first ch-2 space, ch 3, (2 dc, ch 2, 3 dc) in same space, *ch 1, (3 dc, ch 2, 3 dc) in next space; repeat from * around, ch 1, join with slip st to top of ch-3, turn.

- **Rnd 3:** Slip st in first ch-1 space, ch 3, 2 dc in same space, *ch 1, (3 dc, ch 2, 3 dc) in next ch-2 space, ch 1**, 3 dc in next space; repeat from * around, ending last repeat at **, join with slip st to top of ch-3, turn.

- **Rnd 4:** Slip st in first ch-1 space, ch 3, 2 dc in same space, *ch 1, (3 dc, ch 2, 3 dc) in next space**, (ch 1, 3 dc in next space) twice; repeat from * around, ending last repeat at **, ch 1, 3 dc in last space, ch 1, join with slip st to top of ch-3.

- Fasten off. Weave in ends.

THE HEART SQUARE (MAKE 1)

- With CC yarn, work Rnds 1 and 2 of plain square.

- **Rnd 3:** Slip st in ch-1 space, ch 3, 2 dc in same st, ch 1, (3 dc, ch 2, 2 dc) in next space; yo, insert hook in same space and pull up a loop, yo and pull through 2 loops, drop CC and pick up MC, yo and pull through 2 loops to complete the dc; carrying both yarns, with MC, ch 1, 3 dc in next space; with CC, ch 1, (3 dc, ch 2, 3 dc) in next space, ch 1, 3 dc in next space, changing to MC on last step of 3rd dc; with MC, ch 1, (3 dc, ch 2, 3 dc) in next space; with CC, ch 1, 3 dc in next space; with MC, ch 1, (3 dc, ch 2, 3 dc), ch 1, join with slip st to top of ch-3, turn. Cut CC.

- **Rnd 4:** With MC, repeat Rnd 4 of plain square.

- Fasten off. Weave in ends.

- With WS together and MC, working through the back loops only of each square, whipstitch (see page 276) sides of squares together to form a tube.

HEART SQUARED HAT

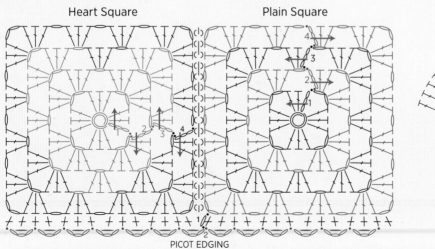

Heart Square   Plain Square

PICOT EDGING

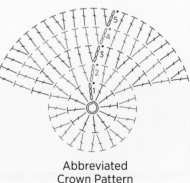

Abbreviated
Crown Pattern

CROCHETING THE CROWN

- Make an adjustable ring.
- **Rnd 1:** Ch 3, 11 dc in ring, join with slip st to top of ch-3. *You now have* 12 dc.
- **Rnd 2:** Ch 3, dc in same st, 2 dc in each dc around, join with slip st to top of ch-3. *You now have* 24 dc.
- **Rnd 3:** Ch 3, dc in same st, dc in next dc, *2 dc in next dc, dc in next dc; repeat from * around, join with slip st to top of ch-3. *You now have* 36 dc.
- **Rnd 4:** Ch 3, dc in same st, dc in next 2 dc, *2 dc in next dc, dc in next 2 dc; repeat from * around, join with slip st to top of ch-3. *You now have* 48 dc.
- **Rnd 5:** Ch 3, dc in same st, dc in next 3 dc,*2 dc in next dc, dc in next 3 dc; repeat from * around, join with slip st to top of ch-3. *You now have* 60 dc.
- Fasten off, leaving a 24"/61 cm tail to sew crown to squares.

FINISHING

ASSEMBLE THE HAT

- Working through back loops only of both pieces, whipstitch crown to upper edge of assembled squares.

ADD THE PICOT EDGING

- **Rnd 1:** With RS facing, join MC with slip st in any sc on edge of lower side of squares, ch 1, sc in each dc and ch-2 space around, skipping ch-1 spaces, join with slip st to beginning sc. *You now have* 56 sc.
- **Rnd 2:** Picot (see page 274), skip 1 sc, *slip st in next sc, picot, skip 1 sc; repeat from * around, join with slip st to first st.
- Fasten off. Weave in ends.

Crocodile Stitch Pixie Hat

DESIGNED BY *Anne-Michelle Phelan*

Make a pixie hat for all the babies in your life with this great pattern sized from newborn to four-year-old heads. The hat is worked from the top down in three sections: a crown section in double crochet, the body of the hat in crocodile stitch, and finally a rib section of half double crochet post stitches.

SIZES AND FINISHED MEASUREMENTS

To fit 0–1 (1–2, 2–4) years: 13½ (14½, 16)"/34.5 (37, 40.5) cm circumference, relaxed, and 8 (8½, 9¼)"/20.5 (21.5, 23.5 cm) cm deep

YARN

King Cole Riot DK, 70% acrylic/30% wool, 322 yds (294 m)/3.5 oz (100 g), Color 410 Ace (3)

CROCHET HOOK

US G/6 (4 mm) *or size needed to obtain correct gauge*

GAUGE

18 stitches and 10 rounds = 4"/10 cm in double crochet

OTHER SUPPLIES

Yarn needle

PATTERN ESSENTIALS

V-st (Dc, ch 1, dc) in 1 stitch or space.

CROCHETING THE CROWN

- Ch 4, slip st to first ch to form a ring.
- Rnd 1: Ch 2 (does not count as st throughout), 6 dc into ring, join with slip st to first dc. *You now have* 6 dc.
- Rnd 2: Ch 2, 2 dc in each dc around, join with slip st to first dc. *You now have* 12 dc.
- Rnd 3: Ch 2, *dc in next dc, 2 dc in next dc; repeat from * around, join with slip st to first dc. *You now have* 18 dc.
- Rnd 4: Ch 2, *dc in next 2 dc, 2 dc in next dc; repeat from * around, join with slip st to first dc. *You now have* 24 sts.
- Rnd 5: Ch 2, *dc in next 3 dc, 2 dc in next dc; repeat from * around, join with slip st to first dc. *You now have* 30 sts.
- Rnd 6: Ch 2, *dc in next 4 dc, 2 dc in next dc; repeat from * around, join with slip st to first dc. *You now have* 36 sts.
- Rnd 7: Ch 2, *dc in next 5 dc, 2 dc in next dc; repeat from * around, join with slip st to first dc. *You now have* 42 sts.
- Rnd 8: Ch 2, *dc in next 6 dc, 2 dc in next dc; repeat from * around, join with slip st to first dc. *You now have* 48 sts.
- Rnd 9: Ch 2, *dc in next 7 dc, 2 dc in next dc; repeat from * around, join with slip st to first dc. *You now have* 54 sts.

- Rnd 10: Ch 2, *dc in next 8 dc, 2 dc in next dc; repeat from * around, join with slip st to first dc. *You now have* 60 sts.

Sizes 1–2 and 2–4 year sizes only

- Rnd 11: Ch 2, *dc in next 9 dc, 2 dc in next dc; repeat from * around, join with slip st to first dc. *You now have* 66 sts.

Size 2–4 year size only

- Rnd 12: Ch 2, *dc in next 10 dc, 2 dc in next dc; repeat from * around, join with slip st to first dc. *You now have* 72 sts.
- Rnd 13: Ch 2, dc in each dc around.

CROCHETING THE CROCODILE STITCH SECTION

All sizes

- Rnd 1: Ch 4 (counts as dc, ch 1 throughout), dc in first st (counts as V-st), *skip 2 sts, V-st in next st; repeat from * around, join with slip st to 3rd chain of ch-4. *You now have* 20 (22, 24) V-sts.

- Rnd 2: Ch 3 (counts as dc throughout); working around posts of sts throughout rnd, 4 dc down the ch-3 at beginning of Rnd 1, ch 1, 5 dc up next dc to form a fan; skip next V-st, *5 dc down next dc post, ch 1, 5 dc up next dc post, skip next V-st; repeat from * around, join with slip st to top of ch-3. *You now have* 20 (22, 24) fans.

- Rnd 3: Slip st in ch-1 space of adjacent V-st in rnd below, ch 4; dc in same space, V-st in ch-1 space of next V-st, V-st between fans and ch-1 space of next V-st in rnd below, V-st in ch-1 space of next V-st; repeat from * around, join with slip st to 3rd ch of ch-4.

- **Rnd 4:** Ch 3; working around posts of sts throughout rnd, 4 dc down the dc post of rnd below, ch 1, 5 dc up the next dc; skip next V-st; *5 dc down next dc post, ch 1, 5 dc up next dc post, skip next V-st; repeat from * around, join with slip st top of ch-3.

- **Rnds 5–10:** Repeat Rnds 3 and 4 three times.

CROCHETING THE RIB

- **Set-Up Rnd:** Ch 1, sc in each dc and ch-1 space (center of V-st) around, making sure to work through sts of Rnd 9 as required, ending with sc in last dc, join with slip st to first sc. *You now have* 60 (66, 72) sc.

- **Rnd 1:** Ch 1, hdc in each sc around, join with slip st to first hdc.

- **Rnd 2:** Ch 1, *FPhdc in next st, BPhdc in next st; repeat from * around, join with slip st to first FPhdc.

- Repeat Rnd 2 one (one, two) times more.

- Fasten off. Weave in ends.

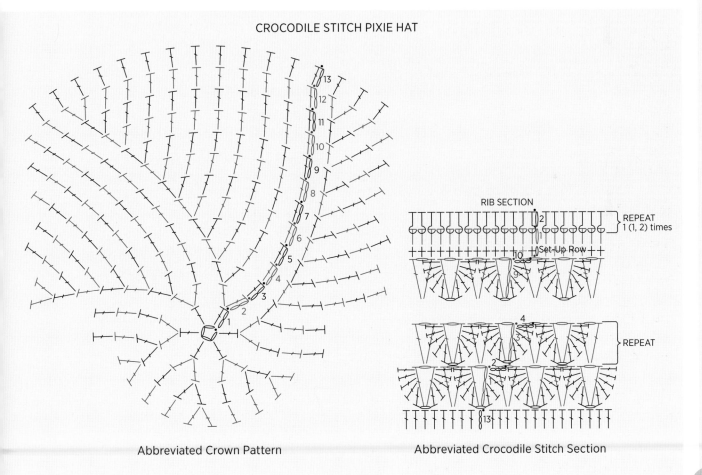

CROCODILE STITCH PIXIE HAT

Abbreviated Crown Pattern

RIB SECTION

REPEAT 1 (1, 2) times

Set-Up Row

REPEAT

Abbreviated Crocodile Stitch Section

Shine Bright, Day or Night

DESIGNED BY *Marcia Sommerkamp, Sommerkamp Designs*

Your young one will be visible day or night with a hat and armbands knitted with yarn that's hunter's orange by day and light reflective at night. The easy patterns, appropriate for beginning crocheters, include a headband for mom.

SIZES AND FINISHED MEASUREMENTS
To fit 6–12 months: 14"/35.5 cm hat circumference, 6"/15 cm hat height; 6"/15 cm wrist/armband circumference, relaxed
To fit adult woman: 17"/43 cm headband circumference, relaxed

YARN
Red Heart Reflective Yarn, 85% acrylic/15% polyester, 88 yds (80 m)/3.5 oz (100 g), Color E820 8251 Neon Orange (5)

CROCHET HOOK
US K/10½ (6.5 mm) *or size needed to obtain correct gauge*

GAUGE
10 stitches = 4"/10 cm
8 rows = 3"/7.5 cm in half double crochet of crown
22 rows = 4"/10 cm in back loop slip stitch

OTHER SUPPLIES
Yarn needle

CROCHETING THE WRISTLETS (MAKE 2)

- Work as for hat band (see below) until 15 ridges are complete. Fold band in half with RS together to join beginning and end. Working through double thickness of previous row and foundation ch, slip st in each st across to seam ends of band together. Weave in ends.

CROCHETING THE HEADBAND

- Chain 8.
- **Row 1:** Slip st in 2nd ch from hook and in each ch across, turn. *You now have 7 sts.* Work as for hat until band is 17"/43 cm or desired length. Finish as for wristlets.

CROCHETING THE HAT

THE BAND

- Chain 5.
- **Row 1:** Slip st in 2nd ch from hook and in each ch across, turn. *You now have 4 sts.*
- **Row 2:** Ch 1, BL slip st in each st across, turn.
- Repeat Row 2 until you have 31 ridges.
- Fold band in half with RS together to join beginning and end. Working through double thickness of previous row and foundation ch, slip st in each st across to seam the ends of the band together. *You now have 32 ridges.*

THE CROWN

- **Rnd 1:** Ch 1, working along side of rows, sc in top of each ridge around, join with slip st to first sc. *You now have 32 sts.*

- **Rnd 2:** Ch 1, BLsc in each st around, join with slip st to first sc.

- **Rnd 3:** Ch 2 (does not counts as hdc here and throughout), hdc in each st around, join with slip st to first hdc.

- **Rnds 4–6:** Repeat Rnd 3 three times.

- **Rnd 7:** Ch 2, (hdc2tog, hdc in next 3 sts) six times, hdc2tog, join with slip st to first hdc. *You now have 25 sts.*

- **Rnd 8:** Ch 2, hdc in first st, (hdc in next st, hdc2tog) eight times, join with slip st to first hdc. *You now have 17 sts.*

- **Rnd 9:** Ch 2, (hdc2tog, hdc in next st) five times, hdc2tog, join with slip st to first hdc. *You now have 11 sts.*

- **Rnd 10:** Ch 2, (hdc2tog) five times, hdc in last st, join with slip st to first hdc. *You now have 6 sts.*

- Cut yarn, leaving an 8"/20.5 cm tail. Thread through remaining sts, cinch tightly to close. Fasten off.

THE STAR

- Ch 4, slip st to first ch to form a ring.

- **Row 1:** Ch 1, (sc in ring, ch 3) five times, join with slip st to first sc. *You now have 5 ch-spaces.*

- **Row 2:** Ch 1, (sc, hdc, dc, hdc, sc) in each ch-space around, join with slip st to first sc. Fasten off. Using length of yarn and yarn needle, sew star to hat, using photo as a guide. Weave in ends.

SHINE BRIGHT, DAY OR NIGHT

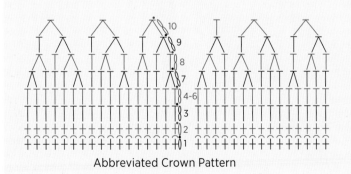

Abbreviated Crown Pattern

Star

A Winter's Night Hat

DESIGNED BY *Laura Biondi, Black Sheep Crochet*

This little hat, worked in spiral rounds, is *very* stretchy and should be able to fit a newborn to a twelve-month-old, getting baby through the whole winter. Super quick and easy to make, it's a perfect last-minute gift.

SIZE AND FINISHED MEASUREMENTS
To fit 0–12 months: 14"/35.5 cm circumference, unstretched

YARN
Crystal Palace Yarns Puffin, 100% polyester, 84 yds (78 m)/1.75 oz (50 g), Color 2129 Leaves & Sprouts (5)

CROCHET HOOK
US L/11 (8 mm) *or size needed to obtain correct gauge*

GAUGE
10 stitches and 8 rows = 4"/10 cm in half double crochet

OTHER SUPPLIES
Stitch markers, yarn needle, pompom maker or cardboard for making pompom

CROCHETING THE HAT

See chart on following page.

- Ch 3, join with slip st to form ring.

- **Rnd 1:** Ch 2 (does not count as st), 6 hdc in ring. *You now have* 6 hdc. Do not join. Pm in the first st of the rnd and move it up as you work the rnds.

- **Rnd 2:** 2 hdc in each hdc around. *You now have* 12 hdc.

- **Rnd 3:** *Hdc in next hdc, 2 hdc in next hdc; repeat from * around. *You now have* 18 hdc.

- **Rnd 4:** *Hdc in next 2 hdc, 2 hdc in next hdc; repeat from * around. *You now have* 24 hdc.

- **Rnd 5:** *Hdc in next 3 hdc, 2 hdc in next hdc; repeat from * around. *You now have* 30 hdc.
- **Rnd 6:** *Hdc in next 4 hdc, 2 hdc in next hdc; repeat from * around. *You now have* 36 hdc.
- Place a second st marker in next st and leave it in place to make it easier to count rounds for the remainder of the hat. Continue moving first st marker up each rnd as established.
- **Rnds 7–12:** Hdc in each hdc around. At the end of Rnd 12, slip st in the next st. Fasten off. Weave in ends.

MAKING THE POMPOM

- Using about 3 yds/3 m of yarn, make a pompom 2½"/6.5 cm in diameter (see page 275). Fasten the pompom securely to the top of the hat. Weave in ends.

A WINTER'S NIGHT HAT

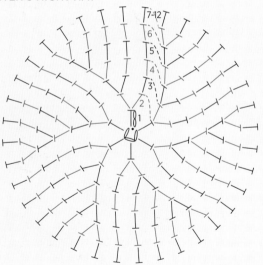

Hope Beanie

DESIGNED BY *Ashley Leither*

The Hope Beanie is all about texture. No, wait — it's all about color, too! The high-relief rib is accentuated by the multicolored yarn. And worked in a bulky weight, you'll be finished in no time.

CROCHETING THE BEANIE

- Make an adjustable ring (see page 272).

- **Rnd 1:** Ch 1, 7 sc in ring, join with slip st to first sc, pull ring closed. *You now have* 7 sts.

- **Rnd 2:** Ch 1, hdc in same st, 2 hdc in each st around, ending 1 hdc in same st as first st, join with a slip st to first hdc. *You now have* 14 sts.

- **Rnd 3:** Ch 1, hdc in same st, hdc in next st, *2 hdc in next st, hdc in next st; repeat from *, end with 1 hdc in same st as first st, join with slip st to first hdc. *You now have* 21 sts.

- **Rnd 4:** Ch 1, hdc in same st, hdc in next 2 sts, *2 hdc in next st, hdc in next 2 sts; repeat from * around, end with 1 hdc in same st as first st, join with slip st to first hdc. *You now have* 28 sts.

- **Rnd 5:** Ch 1, hdc in same st, hdc in next 3 sts, *2 hdc in next st, hdc in next 3 sts; repeat from * around, join with slip st to first hdc. *You now have* 34 sts.

- **Rnd 6:** Ch 1, dc in same st, *FPdc in next hdc, dc in next hdc; repeat from * around, join with slip st to first dc.

- **Rnd 7:** Ch 1, dc in same st, *FPdc in next FPdc, dc in next dc; repeat from * around, join with slip st to first dc.

- Repeat Rnd 7 until the beanie measures 6½"/16.5 cm tall.

- Fasten off. Weave in ends.

SIZE AND FINISHED MEASUREMENTS
To fit 6–12 months: 14"/35.5 cm circumference, relaxed

YARN
Yarn Bee First Love, 100% polyester, 143 yds (131 m)/5 oz (141 g), Color 102 Engaging 🔹

CROCHET HOOK
US N/15 (10 mm) *or size needed to obtain correct gauge*

GAUGE
Rounds 1–4 = 4"/10 cm in diameter

OTHER SUPPLIES
Yarn needle

HOPE BEANIE

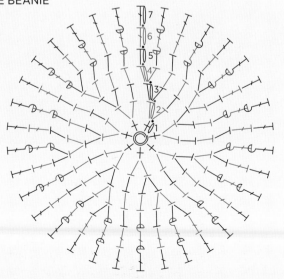

Beanie Rnds 1–7

Little Tam

DESIGNED BY *Judith Durant*

This simple little tam is worked circularly in double crochet, and the side away from you is the right, or public, side. The band at the bottom curls to the inside for a secure fit. The pattern is adapted from *Weldon's Practical Crochet* (Third Series).

SIZE AND FINISHED MEASUREMENTS
To fit toddler: 14½"/37 cm circumference, relaxed

YARN
Shelridge Farm Soft Touch DKW, 100% merino wool, 265 yds (242 m)/3.5 oz (100 g), Caribbean Waters ③

HOOK
US F/5 (3.75 mm) *or size needed to obtain correct gauge*

GAUGE
First 3 rounds = 2¼"/5.5 cm diameter
20 stitches and 12 rounds = 4"/10 cm in double crochet

OTHER SUPPLIES
Yarn needle, 8"/20.5 cm plate for blocking, pompom maker or cardboard for making pompom

PATTERN ESSENTIALS

Beg dc2tog (beginning double crochet 2 together) Ch 2, yo, insert hook into next st and pull up a loop, yo and pull through 2 loops on hook, yo and pull through all 3 loops on hook.

CROCHETING THE TAM

- Ch 5 and join with slip st to form a ring.

- **Rnd 1:** Ch 3 (counts as dc here and throughout), 11 dc in ring. *You now have* 12 dc.

- **Rnd 2:** Ch 3, dc in same st, 2 dc in each dc around. *You now have* 24 dc.

- **Rnd 3:** Ch 3, dc in same st, dc in next dc, *2 dc in next dc, dc in next dc; repeat from * around, join with slip st to top of ch-3. *You now have* 36 dc.

- **Rnd 4:** Ch 3, dc in same st, dc in next 2 dc, *2 dc in next dc, dc in next 2 dc; repeat from * around, join with slip st to top of ch-3. *You now have* 48 dc.

- **Rnd 5:** Ch 3, dc in same st, dc in next 3 dc, *2 dc in next dc, dc in next 3 dc; repeat from * around, join with slip st to top of ch-3. *You now have* 60 dc.

- **Rnd 6:** Ch 3, dc in same st, dc in next 4 dc, *2 dc in next dc, dc in next 4 dc; repeat from * around, join with slip st to top of ch-3. *You now have* 72 dc.

- **Rnd 7:** Ch 3, dc in same st, dc in next 5 dc, *2 dc in next dc, dc in next 5 dc; repeat from * around, join with slip st to top of ch-3. *You now have* 84 dc.

- **Rnd 8:** Ch 3, dc in same st, dc in next 6 dc, *2 dc in next dc, dc in next 6 dc; repeat from * around, join with slip st to top of ch-3. *You now have* 96 sts.

- **Rnd 9:** Ch 3, dc in same st, dc in next 7 dc, *2 dc in next dc, dc in next 7 dc; repeat from * around, join with slip st to top of ch-3. *You now have* 108 dc.

- **Rnd 10:** Ch 3, dc in same st, dc in next 8 dc, *2 dc in next dc, dc in next 8 dc; repeat from * around, join with slip st to top of ch-3. *You now have* 120 dc.

- **Rnd 11:** Ch 3, dc in same st, dc in next 9 dc, *2 dc in next dc, dc in next 9 dc; repeat from * around, join with slip st to top of ch-3. *You now have* 132 dc.

LITTLE TAM

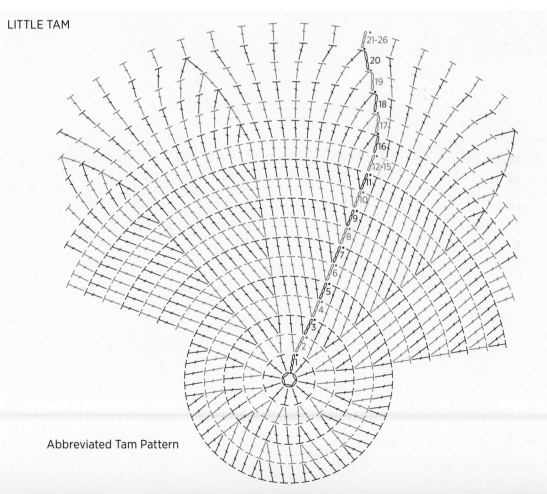

Abbreviated Tam Pattern

- **Rnds 12–15:** Ch 3, dc in each dc around, join with slip st to top of ch-3.

- **Rnd 16:** Beg dc2tog, dc in next 9 dc, *dc2tog, dc in next 9 dc; repeat from * around, join with slip st to top of ch-3. *You now have* 120 sts.

- **Rnd 17:** Beg dc2tog, dc in next 8 dc, *dc2tog, dc in next 8 dc; repeat from * around, join with slip st to top of ch-3. *You now have* 108 sts.

- **Rnd 18:** Beg dc2tog, dc in next 7 dc, *dc2tog, dc in next 7 dc; repeat from * around, join with slip st to top of ch-3. *You now have* 96 sts.

- **Rnd 19:** Beg dc2tog, dc in next 6 dc, *dc2tog, dc in next 6 dc; repeat from * around, join with slip st to top of ch-3. *You now have* 84 sts.

- **Rnd 20:** Beg dc2tog, dc in next 5 dc, *dc2tog, dc in next 5 dc; repeat from * around, join with slip st to top of ch-3. *You now have* 72 sts.

- **Rnds 21–26:** Ch 3, dc in each dc around, join with slip st to top of ch-3.

FINISHING

- Weave in ends. Block tam over an 8"/20.5 cm plate. Make a pompom 2"/5 cm in diameter (see page 275); attach to center top of tam.

Baby Duomo Cap

DESIGNED BY *Beth Graham*

This close-fitting domed cap capitalizes on comfort, warmth, and head coverage. Five spines of front post double crochet radiate down from the center on a background of back post double crochet. The cap is also reversible.

CROCHETING THE CAP

- With larger hook, begin with adjustable ring (see page 272).

- **Rnd 1:** Ch 3 (counts as dc here and throughout), dc in ring, ch 1, (2 dc, ch 1) four times in ring, join with slip st to top of ch-3. *You now have* 10 dc and 5 ch-1 spaces.

- **Rnd 2:** Slip st in next dc and in next ch-1 space, ch 3, 2 dc in same ch-1 space, BPdc in next 2 dc, (3 dc in next ch-1 space, BPdc in next 2 dc) four times, join with slip st to top of ch-3. *You now have* 25 sts.

- **Rnd 3:** Slip st in next st, (ch 3, FPdc [*corner st made*], dc) in same st, BPdc in next 4 sts, *(dc, FPdc [*corner st made*], dc) in next st, BPdc in next 4 sts; repeat from * around, join with slip st to top of ch-3. *You now have* 35 sts.

From this point forward, the center FPdc made in each corner st forms the new corner st for the next rnd.

- **Rnd 4:** Slip st in next corner st, (ch 3, FPdc, dc) in same st, BPdc in each st to next corner st, *(dc, FPdc, dc) in next corner st, BPdc in each st across to next corner st; repeat from * around, join with slip st to top of ch-3. *You now have 45 sts.*

- **Rnds 5-8:** Repeat Rnd 4, increasing in each corner in pattern. *You now have 85 sts. See chart on next page.*

- **Rnd 9:** Slip st in next st, ch 2 (does not count as st), *FPdc in next FPdc, BPdc in each st to next FPdc; repeat from * around, join with slip st to top of first FPdc.

- **Rnd 10:** Ch 2, *FPdc in next FPdc, BPdc in each st to next FPdc; repeat from * to last st, BPdc2tog in last st and beginning ch-2 of previous rnd, join with slip st to top of first FPdc.

- Repeat Rnd 10 until hat measures approximately 5"/12.5 cm from crown to edge. *Do not fasten off.*

BABY DUOMO CAP

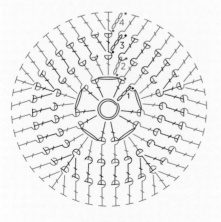

Cap Rnds 1–4

SIZE AND FINISHED MEASUREMENTS
To fit 6–24 months: 16"/40.5 cm circumference, relaxed

YARN
Koigu KPPPM, 100% merino wool, 175 yds (160 m)/1.75 oz (50 g), Color P403 **1**

CROCHET HOOK
US G/6 (4 mm) *or size needed to obtain correct gauge* and US E/4 (3.5 mm)

GAUGE
20 stitches and 16 rounds = 4"/10 cm in back post double crochet with larger hook

OTHER SUPPLIES
Yarn needle

THE RIB EDGING

- **Rnd 1 (set-up rnd):** Ch 2, *FPdc in FPdc, BPdc in next 7 sts, BPdc2tog over next 2 sts, BPdc in next 7 sts; repeat from * to last st, BPdc2tog over last st and beginning ch-2 of previous rnd, join with slip st to top of first FPdc. *You now have* 80 sts.

- **Rnd 2:** Changing to smaller hook, ch 2, *FPdc in next st, BPdc in next st; repeat from * to last st, BPdc2tog over last st and beginning ch-2 of previous rnd, join with slip st to top of first FPdc.

- **Rnd 3:** Repeat Rnd 2. For a neat finish that absorbs the beginning ch-2, join at end of final rnd with reverse slip st by inserting hook from left to right beneath first FPdc of rnd and then into top of beginning ch-2. Fasten off.

- Weave in ends. Block if desired.

BABY DUOMO CAP

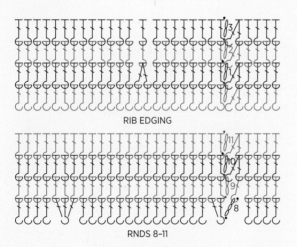

RIB EDGING

RNDS 8–11

Abbreviated Cap Pattern

Braided Headband

DESIGNED BY *Pam Daley, Pam Daley Designs*

This ribbed and braided headband is plenty stretchy, so be sure to make it a couple of inches smaller than the little head it will fit. You may use a button for decoration as shown, or choose any other embellishment that suits your fancy.

CROCHETING THE HEADBAND

- **Row 1 (WS):** Fsc 10 (see page 274), turn. *You now have* 10 sc.

- **Rows 2–5:** Ch 1, BL slip st in each st across, turn.

- **Row 6 (RS):** Ch 1, BL slip st in first 4 sts, esc in next st (counts as first fsc), fsc 9, BL slip st in remaining 5 sts, turn. *You now have* 1 loop and 9 slip sts.

- **Row 7:** Ch 1, BL slip st in first 3 sts, working in front of fsc loop from previous row, ch 4, skip next 4 sts, slip st in last 3 sts, turn. *You now have* 6 slip sts and 4 ch.

- **Rows 8 and 9:** Ch 1, BL slip st in each st across, turn. *You now have* 10 slip sts.

- Repeat Rows 6–9 until 19 loops have been completed (approximately 16"/40.5 cm, or to desired length).

Note: The headband is very stretchy; plan for at least 2"/5 cm of negative ease. Fasten off, leaving a long sewing length.

SIZE AND FINISHED MEASUREMENTS

To fit 1–4 years: 1½"/4 cm wide and 16"/40.5 cm circumference, relaxed

YARN

Red Heart Anne Geddes Baby, 80% acrylic/20% nylon, 340 yds (310 m)/3.5 oz (100 g), Color 702 Rosie ⒊

CROCHET HOOK

US G/6 (4 mm) *or size needed to obtain correct gauge*

GAUGE

23 stitches and 24 rows = 4"/10 cm in back loop slip stitch

OTHER SUPPLIES

Yarn needle, button or other embellishment of choice for decoration

BRAIDED HEADBAND

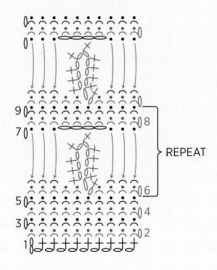

FINISHING

- Using the yarn tail and yarn needle, match the sts from the first and last rows and sew the headband together. Weave in ends.

- To make the braid, pull the 2nd loop through the first loop, then the 3rd loop through the 2nd loop; continue to the end of the headband. Sew the button at the base of the first cable loop; hook the last cable loop made over the button. (Alternatively, tack the cable loop down and sew the button over it.)

Toddler's Watch Cap

DESACKED BY *Beth Hall*

Short rows are used to create the shaping of this cozy and stretchy cap. In fact it's so stretchy, it can keep a head warm from age one to four years!

SIZE AND FINISHED MEASUREMENTS
To fit 1–4 years: 13"/33 cm circumference, stretches to 18"/45.5 cm, and 8"/20.5 cm tall

YARN
Lion Brand Vanna's Choice, 100% acrylic, 170 yds (156 m)/3.5 oz (100 g), Color 102 Aqua

CROCHET HOOK
US H/8 (5 mm) *or size needed to obtain correct gauge*

GAUGE
14 stitches and 8 rows = 4"/10 cm in back loop half double crochet

OTHER SUPPLIES
Yarn needle

CROCHETING THE CAP

- Chain 33 loosely.
- **Row 1 (RS):** Working in the back bump of each chain (see page 276), slip st in the 2nd chain from hook and in next 3 ch, sc in next 4 ch, hdc in next 12 ch, slip st in last 12 ch, turn. *You now have* 32 sts.

Note: Beginning with Row 2, work all sts in the back loop only.

- **Row 2 (short rows):** Ch 1, slip st in first 12 slip sts, turn, leaving remaining sts unworked; ch 1, slip st in next 12 sts (working back toward lower edge; these will create the cap's "ribbing"), turn; ch 1, slip st in next 12 sts, hdc in next hdc in row below and in next 11 hdc, sc in next 4 sc, slip st in next 2 sts, leaving the last 2 slip sts unworked, turn. *You now have* 30 sts.
- **Row 3:** Ch 1, slip st in next 2 sts, sc in next 4 sc, hdc in next 12 hdc, slip st in last 12 sts, turn.
- **Row 4 (short rows):** Ch 1, slip st in first 12 slip sts, turn, leaving remaining sts unworked; ch 1, slip st in next 12 sts, turn, ch 1; slip st in next 12 sts, hdc in next hdc in row below and next 11 hdc, sc in next 4 sc, slip st in next 2 sts, slip st in last 2 unworked sts in row below, turn. *You now have* 32 sts.
- **Row 5:** Ch 1, slip st in next 4 sts, sc in next 4 sc, hdc in next 12 hdc, slip st in last 12 sts, turn.
- Repeat Rows 2–5 ten times, ending with Row 5, for a total of 45 rows, or to desired length. Break yarn, leaving a long-enough tail to sew the side seam and close the top.

FINISHING

- Fold hat in half with RS together. With tail threaded onto yarn needle, catch the outside loop of the corresponding sts of the first and last rows. At top of hat, catch the top of the st every other row; gather tightly and fasten off. Weave in ends.

TODDLER'S WATCH CAP

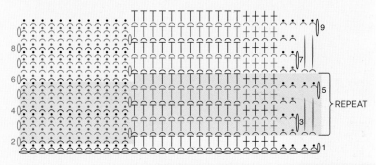

Cap Pattern

Squiggle Twins

DESIGNED BY *Janet Brani, OneLoopShy Designs*

Your daughter and her doll will be cozy and warm this winter when sporting Squiggle Twins hats. The rib stitch will stretch several inches to accommodate a variety of sizes.

SIZES AND FINISHED MEASUREMENTS
To fit doll (child): 12 (15)"/30.5 (38) cm circumference, relaxed

YARN
Skacel Yarns HiKoo Simpliworsted Marl, 55% superwash merino wool/28% acrylic/17% nylon, 140 yds (128 m)/3.5 oz (100 g), Color 652 Pretty as a Petunia (4)

CROCHET HOOK
US J/10 (6 mm) *or size needed to obtain correct gauge*

GAUGE
16 stitches and 19 rows = 4"/10 cm in slip stitch

OTHER SUPPLIES
Yarn needle

CROCHETING THE HAT

- Chain 15 (26).
- **Row 1:** Working in top loop only of each ch, slip st in 2nd ch from hook, slip st in next 10 (19) ch, turn, leaving remaining chains unworked. *You now have* 11 (20) sts.
- **Row 2:** Ch 1, FL slip st in next 11 (20) sts, turn.
- **Row 3 (RS):** Ch 1, FL slip st in next 11 (20) sts, slip st in top loop only of next 3 (5) foundation ch to complete full row, turn. *You now have* 14 (25) sts.

This completes the first short row section.

- **Row 4:** Ch 1, FL slip st in each st across, turn. *You now have* 14 (25) sts.
- **Row 5:** Ch 1, FL slip st in next 11 (20) sts, turn, leaving remaining sts unworked. *You now have* 11 (20) sts.
- **Row 6:** Ch 1, FL slip st in next 11 (20) sts, turn.
- **Row 7:** Ch 1, FL slip st 11 (20), FL slip st in next 3 (5) unworked stitches 2 rows below, turn. *You now have* 14 (25) sts.

This completes the second short row section.

- **Rows 8–55 (71):** Repeat Rows 4–7 twelve (sixteen) times.
- **Row 56 (72):** Repeat Row 4. *Do not fasten off.* There should be a total of 14 (18) short row sections.

FINISHING

- With WS together, fold hat in half and, working through both layers and matching sts, slip st in each st across, ending at the brim. *Do not fasten off.*

THE EDGING

- Ch 1, sc evenly around, working 1 sc in each horizontal bar (appearing between every other row), join with slip st to first sc. *You now have* 28 (36) sc. *Do not fasten off.*

THE SQUIGGLE

- Ch 1; working under both loops of the slip st seam, skip first st, 3 sc in next st, 3 sc (hdc) in each st across seam to within 2 sts at top of hat, skip last 2 sts of seam, slip st in top of hat. Fasten off, leaving a long sewing length.
- With yarn needle, weave yarn under 2 loops at the top of each ridge around the top of hat, bring all yarn ends and cinching

threads to the wrong side of hat and tie tightly.

Doll hat only

- Attach yarn at brim and work 2 more rows of sc at edge, decreasing a few stitches, if necessary, to fit to the chosen doll.
- Weave in ends.

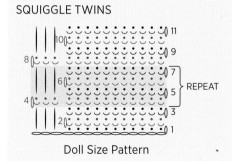

SQUIGGLE TWINS

Doll Size Pattern

Autumn Beanie

DESIGNED BY *Katherine Larson*

The stretchy brim of this cutie is crocheted in a long strip and then seamed; the openwork body and crown are worked up from the brim.

SIZE AND FINISHED MEASUREMENTS
To fit 2–4 years: 16"/40.5 cm circumference, unstretched, and 6½"/16.5 cm tall

YARN
Dream in Color Classy, 100% superwash merino wool, 250 yds (229 m)/4 oz (113 g), Color VM280 November Muse
(4)

CROCHET HOOK
US H/8 (5 mm) *or size needed to obtain correct gauge*

GAUGE
14 stitches and 8 rows = 4"/10 cm in body pattern

OTHER SUPPLIES
Yarn needle

PATTERN ESSENTIALS

V-st (Dc, ch 1, dc) in 1 stitch or space.

CROCHETING THE BRIM

- Fsc 9 (see page 274).

- **Row 1:** Ch 1, BLsc in each sc across, turn.

- **Rows 2–63:** Repeat Row 1.

- Fold ribbing in half lengthwise. Working through double thickness of the front loops of the foundation row and back loops of row just worked, slip st in each st across. *Do not fasten off.*

CROCHETING THE BODY

- **Rnd 1:** Working across side edge of ribbing, ch 3 (counts as dc here and throughout), 2 dc in same st; skip 3 rows, V-st in next row, skip 2 rows, *3 dc in next row, skip 3 rows, V-st in next row, skip 2 rows, repeat from * around, skip last row, join with slip st to top of beginning ch-3. *You now have 9 shells and 9 V-sts.*

- **Rnd 2:** Slip st in next st, ch 4 (counts as dc, ch 1 here and throughout), dc in same st, skip 2 dc, 3 dc in next ch-1 space, skip 2 dc, *V-st in next dc, skip 2 dc, 3 dc in next ch-1 space; repeat from * around, join with slip st to 3rd ch of ch-4.

- **Rnd 3:** Slip st in first ch-1 space, ch 3, 2 dc in same space, skip 2 dc, V-st in next dc, skip 2 dc, *3 dc in next ch-1 space, skip 2 dc, V-st in next dc; repeat from * around, join with slip st to top of ch-3.

- **Rnds 4–6:** Repeat Rnds 2 and 3, then repeat Rnd 2 once more.

- **Rnd 7:** Slip st in next ch-1 space, ch 3, dc in same space, skip 2 dc, *2 dc in next dc, skip 2 dc, 2 dc in next ch-1 space, skip 2 dc; repeat from * around, join with slip st to top of ch-3. *You now have* 36 dc.

- **Rnd 8:** Ch 3, dc in same space, skip 2 dc, *2 dc in next dc, skip 2 dc; repeat from * around, join with slip st to top of ch-3. *You now have* 24 dc.

- **Rnd 9:** Repeat Rnd 8. *You now have* 16 dc.

- **Rnd 10:** Ch 3, *2 dc in next dc, skip 2 dc; repeat from * around, join with slip st to top of ch-3. *You now have* 11 dc.

- **Rnd 11:** Slip st in 3rd, 5th, and 7th sts, slip st in beginning st and draw closed.

- Fasten off. Weave in ends.

AUTUMN BEANIE

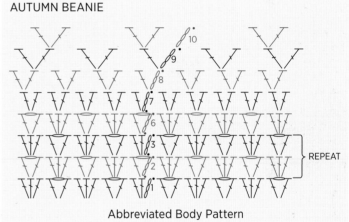

Abbreviated Body Pattern

Flower Power Beret

DESIGNED BY *Melissa Martinez*

The flower motif that forms the top of this beret is worked from the center outward, followed by rounds of double crochet, and then tapered with half double crochet followed by single crochet. The result is a roomy top with a comfortably snug brim.

SIZE AND FINISHED MEASUREMENTS
To fit 2–4 years: 16"/40.5 cm brim circumference, relaxed

YARN
Lion Brand Vanna's Choice, 100% acrylic, 170 yds (156 m)/3.5 oz (100 g), Color 173 Dusty Green (4)

CROCHET HOOK
US J/10 (6 mm) *or size needed to obtain correct gauge*

GAUGE
Rounds 1–3 = 3½"/9 cm in diameter

OTHER SUPPLIES
Yarn needle

CROCHETING THE BERET

- Ch 5, join with slip st to form a ring.

- **Rnd 1:** Ch 1, 8 sc in ring, join with slip st to first sc. *You now have* 8 sc.

- **Rnd 2:** Ch 2 (counts as dc here and throughout), 2 dc in same st, 3 dc in each sc around, join with a slip st to top of ch-2. *You now have* 24 dc.

- **Rnd 3:** Ch 2, 4 dc in same dc, skip 2 dc, *5 dc in next dc, skip 2 dc; repeat from * around, join with a slip st to top of ch-2. *You now have* eight 5-dc groups.

- **Rnd 4:** Slip st in next 2 dc, ch 3 (counts as dc), 6 dc in same dc, *skip 2 dc, sc in space between two 5-dc groups, skip 2 dc**, 7 dc in next dc; repeat from * around, ending last repeat at **, join with a slip st to top of ch-3. *You now have* 56 dc and 8 sc.

- **Rnd 5:** Slip st in next 3 dc, ch 1, sc in first dc, ch 3 (counts as dc), *2 dc in next sc, ch 3 (counts as dc), skip 3 dc**, sc in next dc, ch 3, skip 3 dc; repeat from * around, ending last repeat at **, join with slip st to first sc. *You now have* 16 dc, 8 sc, and 16 ch-3 spaces.

- **Rnd 6:** Slip st in next ch, 2 dc in same space, *dc between next 2 dc, (3 dc in next ch-3 space) twice; repeat from * around, omitting last 3 dc, join with slip st to top of ch-2. *You now have* 56 dc.

FLOWER POWER BERET

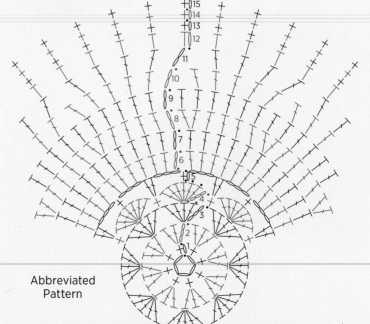

Abbreviated Pattern

- **Rnd 7:** Ch 2, dc in each dc around, join with slip st to top of ch-2.
- **Rnd 8:** Ch 2, *dc in next 4 dc, 2 dc in next dc; repeat from * around, join with slip st to top of ch-2. *You now have* 67 dc.
- **Rnd 9:** Ch 2, dc in each dc around, join with a slip st to top of ch-2.
- **Rnd 10:** Ch 2, *dc in next 5 dc, skip 1 dc; repeat from * around, join with slip st to top of ch-2. *You now have* 56 dc.
- **Rnd 11:** Ch 2, *dc in next 4 dc, skip 1 dc; repeat from * around, join with slip st to top of ch-2. *You now have* 45 dc.
- **Rnd 12:** Ch 1 (does not count as st), hdc in each dc around, join with slip st to first hdc.
- **Rnds 13–15:** Ch 1, sc in each st around, join with a slip st to first sc.
- Fasten off. Weave in ends.

Queen Anne's Lace Beanie

DESIGNED BY *Alla Koval, Alla Koval Designs*

A lacy beanie is the perfect addition to a little girl's spring and summer wardrobe. You could also make one in wool for cooler days. This beanie is crocheted in the round, beginning with the top of the crown.

CROCHETING THE CROWN

See chart on page 52.

- Begin with an adjustable ring (see page 272).
- **Rnd 1:** Ch 3 (counts as dc throughout), 11 dc in ring, join with slip st to top of ch-3. *You now have* 12 dc.
- **Rnd 2:** Ch 3, (dc in first dc, 2 dc in each dc) around, join with slip st to top of ch-3. *You now have* 24 dc.
- **Rnd 3:** Ch 3, (2 dc in next dc, dc in next dc) around, omitting last dc, join with slip st to top of ch-3. *You now have* 36 dc.
- **Rnd 4:** Ch 3, (dc in next dc, 2 dc in next dc, dc in next dc) around, omitting last dc, join with slip st to top of ch-3. *You now have* 48 dc.
- **Rnd 5:** Ch 3, (dc in next 2 dc, 2 dc in next dc, dc in next dc) around, omitting last dc, join with slip st to top of ch-3. *You now have* 60 dc.
- **Rnd 6:** Ch 3, (dc in next 3 dc, 2 dc in next dc, dc in next dc) around, omitting last dc, join with slip st to top of ch-3. *You now have* 72 dc.

SIZE AND FINISHED MEASUREMENTS
To fit toddler (child, adult): 16 (18, 20)"/40.5 (45.5, 51) cm circumference. Shown in child size

YARN
Omega Cotton Thread #5, 100% cotton, 164 yds (150 m)/1.75 oz (50 g), Color 50 White 🧵

CROCHET HOOK
US B/1 (2.25 mm) *or size needed to obtain correct gauge*

GAUGE
26 stitches and 12 rounds = 4"/10 cm in double crochet
First 3 rounds = 1¾"/4.5 cm in diameter

OTHER SUPPLIES
Yarn needle

PATTERN ESSENTIALS

Beg V-st (beginning V-stitch) Ch 5 (counts as dc and ch-2), dc in st or space indicated.

Puff st (puff stitch) Yo, insert hook into st or space and pull up a loop, (yo, insert hook into same st and pull up a loop) twice, yo and pull through all 7 loops on hook.

V-st (V-stitch) (Dc, ch 2, dc) in st or space indicated.

- **Rnd 7:** Ch 3, (dc in next 4 dc, 2 dc in next dc, dc in next dc) around, omitting last dc, join with slip st to top of ch-3. *You now have* 84 dc.

- **Rnd 8:** Ch 3, (dc in next 5 dc, 2 dc in next dc, dc in next dc) around, omitting last dc, join with slip st to top of ch-3. *You now have* 96 dc.

- **Rnd 9:** Ch 3, (dc in next 6 dc, 2 dc in next dc, dc in next dc) around, omitting last dc, join with slip st to top of ch-3. *You now have* 108 dc. *Do not fasten off.*

Sizes Medium and Large only

- **Rnd 10:** Ch 3, (dc in next 7 dc, 2 dc in next dc, dc in next dc) around, omitting last dc, join with slip st to top of ch-3. *You now have* 120 dc. *Do not fasten off.*

Size Large only

- **Rnd 11:** Ch 3, (dc in next 8 dc, 2 dc in next dc, dc in next dc) around, omitting last dc, join with slip st to top of ch-3. *You now have* 132 dc. *Do not fasten off.*

CROCHETING THE BAND

- **Rnd 1 (RS):** Ch 3, dc in each dc around. *You now have* 108 (120, 132) dc.

- **Rnd 2:** Beg V-st in first dc, *ch 2, skip next 2 dc, sc in next dc, ch 2, skip next 2 dc**, V-st in next dc; repeat from * around, ending last repeat at **, join with slip st to 3rd ch of ch-5. *You now have* 18 (20, 22) V-sts.

- **Rnd 3:** Ch 3, [(puff st, ch 2) twice, puff st, ch 1] in each V-st around, join with slip st to top of ch-3.

- **Rnd 4:** Slip st in first puff st and next ch of ch-2 space, ch 4 (counts as dc and ch-1), dc in next ch-2 space, ch 1, *dc in next ch-1 space, ch 1**, (dc in next ch-2 sp, ch 1) twice; repeat from * around, ending last repeat at **, join with slip st to 3rd ch of beg ch-4.

- **Rnd 5:** Ch 3, dc in each ch-1 space and each dc around, join with slip st to top of ch-3.

- Repeat Rnds 2–5 once (twice, twice). At end of last rnd, *do not fasten off.*

FINISHING

- **Rnd 1 (RS):** Ch 1, sc in first and each dc around, join with slip st to first sc.

- **Rnd 2:** Ch 1, (sc, ch 3, sc) in first sc, *ch 3, skip next 3 sc**, (sc, ch 3, sc) in next sc; repeat from * around, ending last repeat at **, join with slip st to first sc.

- Fasten off. Weave in ends.

- Wet or steam block.

QUEEN ANNE'S LACE BEANIE

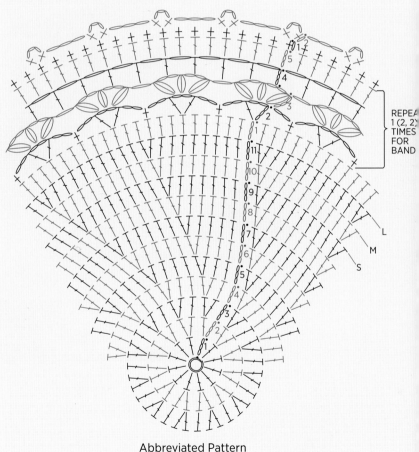

REPEAT 1 (2, 2) TIMES FOR BAND

Abbreviated Pattern

CHAPTER TWO

LITTLE
Socks
+
Bootees

Christening Bootees

DESIGNED BY *Pam Daley, Pam Daley Designs*

Back post single crochet is paired with basic stitches to create a delicate pair of bootees for special occasions. The larger size is finished with a picot edging, and ribbon ties lend an heirloom quality.

SIZES AND FINISHED MEASUREMENTS
To fit newborn (3 months): 3 (4)"/7.5 (10) cm foot length

YARN
Patons Grace, 100% mercerized cotton, 136 yds (125 m)/1.75 oz (50 g), Color 62005 Snow or 62322 Natural 🔵🔵

CROCHET HOOK
US F/5 (3.75 mm) *or size needed to obtain correct gauge*

GAUGE
20 stitches and 12 rows = 4"/10 cm in half double crochet

OTHER SUPPLIES
Yarn needle, 36"/91 cm of ¼"/6 mm ribbon for ties, Fray Check (optional)

PATTERN ESSENTIALS

Dc5tog (double crochet 5 together)
(Yo, insert hook into next st or space and pull up a loop, yo, pull through 2 loops) five times, yo and pull through all 6 loops on hook.

CROCHETING THE BOOTEE (MAKE 2)

- Chain 14 (17).

- **Rnd 1:** Dc in 4th ch from hook, dc in next 9 (12) chs, 7 dc in last ch. Working across opposite side of foundation ch, dc in next 9 (12) chs, 2 dc in last ch, join with slip st to top of ch-3. *You now have* 29 (35) dc.

- **Rnd 2:** Ch 1, sc in same st as joining, 2 sc in next 2 sts, sc in next st, hdc in next 3 (5) sts, dc in next 4 (5) sts, 2 dc in next 7 sts, dc in next 4 (5) sts, hdc in next 3 (5) sts, sc in next st, 2 sc in last 3 sts, join with slip st to first sc. *You now have* 41 (47) sts.

- **Rnd 3:** Ch 1, BPsc in each st around, join with slip st to first sc.

- **Rnd 4:** Ch 2 (counts as hdc here and throughout), hdc in each st around, join with slip st to top of ch-2.

- **Rnd 5:** Ch 2, hdc in next 12 (14) sts, (dc2tog) 7 (8) times, hdc in each st to end, join with slip st to top of ch-2. *You now have 34 (39) sts.*

- **Rnd 6:** Ch 1, sc in first 11 (13) sts, hdc in next 3 (4) sts, dc5tog, hdc in next 3 (4) sts, sc in each st to end, join with slip st to first sc. *You now have 30 (35) sts.*

- **Rnd 7:** Ch 1, sc in first 13 (14) sts, dc3tog (dc4tog), sc in each st to end, join with slip st to first st. *You now have 28 (32) sts.*

- **Rnd 8:** Ch 3 (counts as hdc and ch 1), skip next st, *hdc in next st, ch 1, skip next st; repeat from * around, join with slip st to 2nd ch of ch-3. *You now have 14 (16) ch-1 spaces.*

- **Rnd 9:** Ch 1, sc in each hdc and ch-space around, join with slip st to first sc. *You now have 28 (32) sts.*

- **Rnd 10:** Ch 1, sc in each st around, join with slip st to first sc.

- For simple edging, fasten off and weave in ends. For picot edging, continue with Rnd 11.

- **Rnd 11:** Ch 1, sc in same st, *picot, sc in next 2 sc; repeat from * around, join with slip st to first sc. Fasten off. Weave in ends.

FINISHING

- Cut two pieces of ¼"/6 mm wide ribbon, each approximately 18"/45.5 cm long. Starting and ending at center front, weave one piece of ribbon through ch-1 spaces in Rnd 8 on each slipper. Tie each ribbon in a bow in front, trim as needed.

Tip: Depending on the type of ribbon used, you may want to put a bit of Fray Check on the ends to keep them neat.

Pompom Bootees

DESIGNED BY *Kristen Stoltzfus*

These special occasion bootees are worked in a glittery bamboo and further embellished with a crocheted pompom. Chain-stitch lacings keep the bootees on the feet, where they belong.

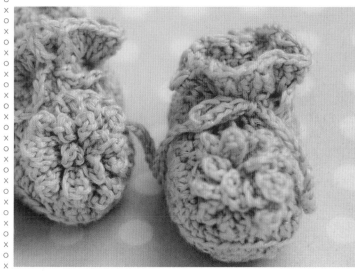

SIZE AND FINISHED MEASUREMENTS
To fit 0–3 months: 3¼"/8 cm long and 2¾"/7 cm tall when laid flat

YARN
Aunt Lydia's Crochet Thread Iced Bamboo 3, 96% viscose from bamboo/4% metallic, 100 yds (91 m), Color 3702 Pink Ice

CROCHET HOOK
US F/5 (3.75 mm) *or size needed to obtain correct gauge*

GAUGE
20 stitches and 20 rounds = 4"/10 cm in half double crochet
Rounds 1–4 = 3"/7.5 cm by 1¾"/4.5 cm

OTHER SUPPLIES
Yarn needle

PATTERN ESSENTIALS

Dc7tog (double crochet 7 together)
(Yo, insert hook into next st or space, yo and pull up a loop, yo and pull through 2 loops) 7 times, yo and pull through all 8 loops on hook.

CROCHETING THE BOOTEE (MAKE 2)

THE SOLE AND SIDES

- Chain 13.
- **Rnd 1:** 2 sc in 2nd ch from hook, sc in next 10 ch, 3 sc in last ch; working across opposite side of foundation ch, sc in next 10 ch, sc in same st as first 2 sc, join with slip st to first sc. *You now have* 26 sc.
- **Rnd 2:** Ch 1 (does not count as st throughout), 3 sc in first st, hdc in next 12 sc, 3 sc in next st, hdc in next 12 sc, join with slip st to first sc. *You now have* 24 hdc and 6 sc.
- **Rnd 3:** Slip st in next st, ch 1, 3 sc in same sc, hdc in next 14 sts, 3 sc in next st, hdc in each of next 14 sts, join with slip st to first sc. *You now have* 28 hdc and 6 sc.
- **Rnd 4:** Slip st in next st, ch 1, 3 sc in same sc, hdc in next 16 sts, 3 sc in next st, hdc in next 16 sts, join with slip st to first sc. *You now have* 32 hdc and 6 sc.
- **Rnd 5:** Ch 1, BLhdc in each st around, join with slip st to first BLhdc. *You now have* 38 hdc.
- **Rnd 6:** Ch 1, hdc in next 22 hdc, hdc3tog, hdc in next 13 hdc, join with slip st to first hdc. *You now have* 36 hdc.
- **Rnd 7:** Ch 1, hdc in next 21 hdc, hdc3tog, hdc in next 12 hdc, join with slip st to first hdc. *You now have* 34 hdc.
- **Rnd 8:** Ch 1, hdc in next 18 hdc, hdc7tog, hdc in next 9 hdc, join with slip st to first hdc. *You now have* 28 sts.
- **Rnd 9:** Ch 1, hdc in next 17 hdc, hdc3tog, hdc in next 8 hdc, join with slip st to first hdc. *You now have* 26 hdc.

THE CUFF

- **Rnd 1:** Ch 1, sc in first st, (ch 2, skip next st, sc in next st) around, join with slip st to first sc. *You now have* 13 ch-spaces.
- **Rnd 2:** Slip st in next ch-space, ch 2 (does not count as st), work 3 dc in each space around, join with slip st to first dc. *You now have* 39 dc.
- **Rnd 3:** Ch 2, (hdc in next st, slip st in next st) around, join with slip st to first hdc. Fasten off.

CROCHETING THE LACING

- Chain 70. Fasten off. Weave in ends.

CROCHETING THE POMPOM

- **Rnd 1:** Leaving a long tail for sewing, ch 2, work 6 sc in 2nd ch from hook; *do not join.*
- **Rnd 2:** 2 BLsc in each sc around, join with slip st to back loop of next sc, turn. *You now have* 12 sc.
- **Rnd 3:** Working in both loops of Rnd 2, (ch 8, slip st in next sc) around. *You now have* 11 ch-8 loops.
- **Rnd 4:** Working in front loops of Rnd 1, (ch 8, slip st in next sc) around, ch 8, slip st through center of pompom. *You now have* 7 more ch-8 loops for a total of 18 ch-8 loops.
- Fasten off.

FINISHING

- Pinch pompom into a bundle and sew at its base to secure. Sew pompom to toe of bootee. Weave lacing through chain-spaces on Rnd 1 of cuff and tie in a bow. Weave in ends.
- Repeat for the second bootee.

POMPOM BOOTEES

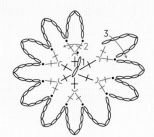

Pompom Rnds 1–3

Pompom Rnd 4

Baby Mocs

DESIGNED BY *Linne Peters*

Crocheted in dark earth tones, these bootees are all Boy. The sole and instep consist of center-start motifs, which are then joined with half double crochet. Lacings will keep the bootees on, even with baby in motion.

SIZE AND FINISHED MEASUREMENTS
To fit 6–12 months: 4"/10 cm foot length

YARN
Lion Brand Wool-Ease, 78% acrylic/19% wool/3% polyester, 162 yds (148 m)/2.5 oz (70 g), Color 232 Wood Multi (4)

CROCHET HOOK
US E/4 (3.5 mm) *or size needed to obtain correct gauge*

GAUGE
Square Motif = 1½"/38 mm by 1½"/4 cm
13 stitches and 16 rows = 4"/10 cm in single crochet

OTHER SUPPLIES
Yarn needle

CROCHETING THE MOC

THE INSTEP SQUARE (MAKE 2)

- Ch 4 and join with slip st to form a ring.
- **Rnd 1:** Ch 2 (counts as hdc throughout), 2 hdc in ring, ch 2, (3 hdc in ring, ch 2) three times, join with slip st to top of ch-2. *You now have* 12 hdc and 4 ch-2 spaces.
- **Rnd 2:** Ch 2, hdc in next 2 hdc, (2 hdc, ch 1, 2 hdc) in next space, *hdc in next 3 hdc, (2 hdc, ch 1, 2 hdc) in next space; repeat from * two more times, join with slip st to top of ch-2. *You now have* 28 hdc and 4 ch-1 spaces.
- Fasten off. Set aside.

THE SOLE (MAKE 2)

- Make two squares as for instep. After completing second square, *do not fasten off.*
- With RS together and yarn attached to one square, join sole squares along one edge with slip st. *Do not fasten off.*

THE SIDES

- **Rnd 1:** Ch 2, hdc in each st around joined squares, working 1 hdc in each junction between squares, join with slip st to top of ch-2. *You now have* 48 hdc.

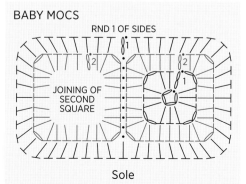

BABY MOCS

RND 1 OF SIDES

JOINING OF SECOND SQUARE

Sole

- **Rnds 2–5:** Ch 2, hdc in each hdc around, join with slip st to top of ch-2.

THE INSTEP

- With RS facing and WS of one instep square and bootee together, slip st through both layers of square and bootee to join three sides of instep to bootee. *Do not fasten off.*

THE CUFF

- **Rnd 1:** With RS facing, ch 2, hdc in each st around remaining sts of bootee, join with slip st to top of ch-2. *You now have* 30 sts.
- **Rnds 2 and 3:** Ch 2, hdc in each hdc around, join with slip st to top of ch-2. Fasten off.

FINISHING

- Weave in ends.

THE TIES

- Chain 85. Fasten off.
- Working in Rnd 1 of cuff, beginning at center front, weave ties under 3 sts, over 3 sts around. Make double knots at ends of ties and trim ends to ½"/13 mm from knot.

Little Hearts Bootees

DESIGNED BY *Sylvie Damey*

Worked from the top down, these little bootees have a drawstring that is embellished with heart motifs. The drawstrings are functional as well as decorative.

SIZES AND FINISHED MEASUREMENTS

To fit newborn (3 month, 6 month): 2¾ (3½, 4)"/7 (9, 10) cm long

YARN

Malabrigo Merino Worsted, 100% merino wool, 210 yds (192 m)/3.5 oz (100 g), Calypso (4)

CROCHET HOOKS

US H/8 (5 mm) and US I/9 (5.5 mm) for foundation *or size needed to obtain correct gauge*

GAUGE

16 stitches and 9 rows = 4"/10 cm in front loop double crochet with smaller hook

OTHER SUPPLIES

Yarn needle

CROCHETING THE BOOTEE (MAKE 2)

Note: The bootee is worked top down and in the round, starting with the ankle and ending with the sole.

- With larger hook, ch 20 (22, 24), join with slip st to form a ring.
- Switch to smaller hook for remainder of bootee.
- **Rnd 1:** Ch 3 (counts as dc here and throughout), dc in next 19 (21, 23) ch sts, join with slip st to top of ch-3. *You now have* 20 (22, 24) dc.
- **Rnd 2:** Ch 4 (counts as dc and ch 1), skip 1 st, *dc in next st, ch 1, skip 1 st; repeat from * around, join with slip st to 3rd ch of beginning ch-4.
- **Rnd 3:** Ch 3, dc in next 7 (8, 9) sts, dc2tog, dc in next st, dc2tog, dc in next 7 (8, 9) sts, join with slip st to top of beginning ch-3. *You now have* 18 (20, 22) sts.

- **Rnd 4:** Ch 3, dc in next 4 (5, 6) dc, dc2tog, dc in next 5 dc, dc2tog, dc in next 4 (5, 6), join with slip st to top of beginning ch-3. *You now have* 16 (18, 20 sts).

Size 3 months only

- **Rnd 5:** Ch 2 (counts as hdc here and throughout), hdc in next 6 sts, 2 hdc in next 2 sts, hdc in next st, 2 hdc in next 2 sts, hdc in next 6 sts, join with slip st to top of beginning ch-2. *You now have* 22 sts.

Size 6 months only

- **Rnd 5:** Ch 3, dc in next 7 sts, 2 hdc in next 2 sts, hdc in next st, 2 hdc in next 2 sts, dc in next 7 sts, join with slip st to top of ch-3. *You now have* 24 sts.

THE INSTEP

Size newborn only

- **Rnd 5:** Ch 3, dc in next 3 sts, sc in next 3 sts, skip 1 st, (3 tr, 5 dtr, 3 tr) in next st, skip 1 st, sc in next 3 sc, dc in next 3 sts, join with slip st to top of ch-3. *You now have* 24 sts.

Size 3 months only

- **Rnd 6:** Ch 3, dc in next 3 sts, sc in next 5 sts, skip 2 sts, (2 tr, 2 dtr, 3 trtr, 2 dtr, 2 tr) in next st, skip 2 sts, sc in next 5 sts, dc in last 3 sts, join with slip st to top of ch-3. *You now have* 28 sts.

Size 6 months only

- **Rnd 6:** Ch 3, dc in next 3 sts, hdc in next 6 sts, skip 2 sts, (2 tr, 2 dtr, 5 trtr, 2 dtr, 2 tr) in next st, skip 2 sts, hdc in next 6 sts, dc in last 3 sts, join with slip st to top of ch-3. *You now have* 32 sts.

THE FOOT

- **Rnd 1:** Ch 2 (counts as hdc), hdc in next 2 sts, sc in next 3 (5, 6) sts, 2 sc in next st, BLsc in next 4 (3, 4) sts, 2 BLsc in next 3 (5, 5) sts, BLsc in next 4 (3, 4) sts, 2 sc in next st, sc in next 3 (5, 6) sts, hdc in last 2 sts, join with slip st to top of ch-2. *You now have* 29 (35, 39) sts.

- **Rnd 2:** Ch 2 (3, 2), hdc (dc, hdc) in each st around, join with slip st to top of ch-2 (ch-3, ch-2).

Size 6 months only

- Ch 2, hdc in each hdc around, join with slip st to top of ch-2.

THE SOLE

Size newborn only

- **Rnd 1:** Ch 1, BLsc in same st, BLsc in next st, BLsc2tog, BLsc in next 3 sts, BLhdc in next st, BLdc in next 3 sts, (BLdc2tog) twice, BLdc in next st, (BLdc2tog) twice, BLdc in next 3 sts, BLhdc in next st, BLsc in next 3 sts, BLsc2tog, join with slip st to first st. *You now have* 22 sts.

- **Rnd 2:** Ch 2, hdc in next st, hdc2tog, hdc in next 3 sts, (hdc2tog) twice, dc in next st, (hdc2tog) twice, hdc in next 3 sts, (hdc2tog), hdc in next st, join with slip st to top of ch-2. *You now have* 16 sts.

Size 3 months only

- **Rnd 1:** Ch 2, BLhdc in next st, BLhdc2tog, BLhdc in next 8 sts, (BLhdc2tog) six times, BLhdc in next 8 sts, BLhdc2tog, BLhdc in next st, join with slip st to top of ch-2. *You now have* 27 sts.

- **Rnd 2:** Ch 3, (dc2tog) twice, dc in next 3 sts, (dc2tog) six times, dc in next 3 sts, (dc2tog) twice, join with slip st to top of ch-3. *You now have* 17 sts.

Size 6 months only

- **Rnd 1:** Ch 3, BLdc2tog, BLdc in next st, BLdc2tog, BLdc in next 8 sts, (BLdc2tog) six times, BLdc in next 8 sts, BLdc2tog, BLdc in next st, BLdc2tog, join with slip st to top of ch-3. *You now have* 29 sts.

- **Rnd 2:** Ch 2, (hdc2tog) twice, hdc in next 2 sts, dc in next 2 sts, (dc2tog) six times, dc in next 2 sts, hdc in next 2 sts, (hdc2tog) twice, join with slip st to top of ch-2. *You now have* 19 sts.

- Fasten off, leaving a long sewing length. With yarn needle and tail, sew sole closed. Weave in ends.

CROCHETING THE TIES (MAKE 2)

- Ch 4, join with slip st to form a ring.

- *Working into ring, hdc, (2 dc, sc) twice, 2 dc, hdc, slip st in ring to close heart*; ch 40 (42, 44), slip st to 4th ch from hook to form a ring; repeat from * to * for second heart. Weave in ends.

- Starting with center of bootee's side, weave tie through the eyelets in Rnd 2.

LITTLE HEARTS BOOTEES

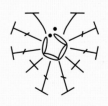

Tie Heart

Baby Crocs

DESIGNED BY *Gwen Steege*

The top edging of Crocodile Stitch on these bootees not only provides a fun finish but should also help keep them on those little feet.

SIZE AND FINISHED MEASUREMENTS
To fit an infant: 3½"/9 cm foot length and 3½"/9 cm tall

YARN
Debbie Bliss Baby Cashmerino, 55% merino wool/33% microfibre/12% cashmere, 137 yds (125 m)/1.75 oz (50 g), Color 086 Coral (2)

HOOK
US E/4 (3.5 mm) crochet hook *or size needed to obtain correct gauge*

GAUGE
Rounds 1–4 = 1¾"/4.5 cm by 3¼"/8 cm
20 stitches = 4"/10 cm in single crochet

OTHER SUPPLIES
Yarn needle

CROCHETING THE BOOTEES (MAKE 2)

- Chain 10.

- **Rnd 1:** Sc in 2nd ch from hook, sc in next 7 ch, 5 sc in last ch (toe); working on opposite side of foundation ch, sc in next 7 ch, 2 sc in last ch (heel), join with slip st to first sc. *You now have* 22 sc.

- **Rnd 2:** Ch 2 (counts as hdc here and throughout), hdc in same st, hdc in next 7 sc, 2 hdc in next 5 sc, hdc in next 7 sc, 2 hdc last 2 sts, join with slip st to top of ch-2. *You now have* 30 hdc.

- **Rnd 3:** Ch 2, hdc in same st, hdc next 11 sts, 2 hdc in each of next 5 sts, hdc in next 11 sts, 2 hdc in each of last 2 sts, join with slip st to top of ch-2. *You now have* 38 sc.

- **Rnd 4:** Ch 2, hdc in next 14 hdc, 2 hdc in next 5 hdc, hdc in next 16 hdc, 2 hdc in next 2 hdc. *You now have* 45 hdc.

- **Rnd 5:** Ch 1, BLsc in same st, BLsc in each st around, join with slip st to first BLsc, join with slip st to first BLsc.

- **Rnd 6:** Ch 1, sc in each sc around, join with slip st to first sc.

- **Rnd 7:** Ch 2, hdc in next 15 sts, hdc2tog six times, hdc in next 15 sts, hdc2tog, join with slip st to top of ch-2. *You now have* 38 hdc.

- **Rnd 8:** Ch 1, sc in same st, sc in next 15 sts, sc2tog three times, sc in next 16 sts, join with slip st to first sc. *You now have* 35 sts.

- **Rnd 9:** Ch 1, sc2tog twice, sc in each st to last 4 sts, sc2tog twice, join with slip st to first sc. *You now have* 31 sts.

- **Rnd 10:** Ch 2, hdc in each sc around, join with slip st to top of ch-2.

- **Rnd 11:** Ch 1, sc in first 9 sc, sc2tog seven times, sc in last 8 sc, join with slip st to first sc. *You now have* 24 sts.

- **Rnds 12 and 13:** Ch 1, sc in each st around, join with slip st to first sc.

- **Rnd 14:** Ch 1, 2 sc in first st, sc in next 3 sc, *2 sc in next sc, sc in next 3 sc; repeat from * around. *You now have* 30 sts.

- Work Rnds 1–6 of Crocodile Stitch.

- Fasten off. Weave in ends.

PATTERN ESSENTIALS

Crocodile Stitch (multiple of 5 stitches)

Instructions are given for right-handed crocheters with left-handed instructions in brackets.

Rnd 1: Ch 4 (counts as dc, ch 1), skip 1 sc, dc in next 2 sc, *ch 1, skip 1 sc, dc in next sc, ch 1, skip 1 sc, dc in next 2 sc; repeat from * around to last st, ch 1, skip 1 sc, join with slip st to 3rd ch of ch-4.

Rnd 2: *Holding piece with first st to be worked rotated to the 3 o'clock [9 o'clock] position and working from right to left [left to right], 5 dc around post of next dc; ch 1, rotate piece 180° to the 9 o'clock [3 o'clock] position, 5 dc around post of next dc, slip st in next dc; repeat from * around, ending with slip st in same place as Rnd 1 joining slip st.

Rnd 3: Ch 3 (counts as dc here and throughout), dc in same st, *ch 1, dc in next space between 2 dc at center of Crocodile Stitch, ch 1**, 2 dc in next slip st; repeat from * around, ending last repeat at **, join with slip st to top of ch-3.

Rnd 4: Working around posts as for Rnd 2, ch 1, 5 dc around starting ch of row below, ch 1, 5 dc around post of next dc, slip st in next dc, *5 dc around next dc, ch 1, 5 dc around next dc, slip st in next dc; repeat from * around.

Rnd 5: Slip st in next space, slip st between 2 dc at center of Crocodile Stitch, ch 4 (counts as dc, ch 1), 2 dc in next slip st, *ch 1, dc in next space between 2 dc at center of Crocodile Stitch, ch 1, 2 dc in next slip st, ch 1; repeat from * around, join with slip st to top of ch-3.

Rnd 6: Repeat Rnd 2.

BABY CROCS

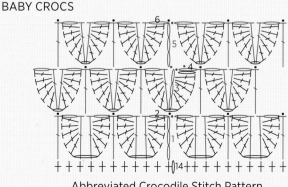

Abbreviated Crocodile Stitch Pattern

Monster Bootees

DESIGNED BY *Justyna Kacprzak, Cute and Kaboodle*

Simple moccasins with monster faces will keep your little one entertained. Make several pairs and use your imagination to create as many different faces as you like!

SIZE AND FINISHED MEASUREMENTS
To fit 0–6 months: 3¼"/8 cm foot length

YARN
Arelan Kotek, 100% acrylic, 330 yds (300 m)/3.5 oz (100 g), Brown **2**

CROCHET HOOKS
US G/6 (4 mm), *or size needed to obtain correct gauge*; 3 mm and 2 mm steel hooks

GAUGE
18 stitches and 16 rows = 4"/10 cm in half double crochet with larger hook

OTHER SUPPLIES
Stitch marker, scraps of white and black yarn for features, sewing needle and coordinating thread, yarn needle, two ⅜"/10 mm buttons

CROCHETING THE BOOTEE (MAKE 2)

THE TOE

- With larger hook, ch 10.

- **Rnd 1:** Hdc in 2nd ch from hook, hdc in next 7 ch, 3 hdc in last ch; working on the opposite side of foundation ch, hdc in next 7 ch, 2 hdc in last ch. *You now have* 20 hdc. Do not join. Pm in the first st of the rnd and move it up as you work the rnds.

- **Rnd 2:** (Hdc in next 9 hdc, 2 hdc in next hdc) twice. *You now have* 22 hdc.

- **Rnd 3:** Hdc in next 3 hdc, 2 hdc in next hdc, hdc in next hdc, 2 hdc in next hdc, hdc in last 16 hdc. *You now have* 24 hdc.

- **Rnds 4–7:** Hdc in each hdc around.

- **Row 8:** Hdc in next 5 hdc, turn, leaving remaining sts unworked.

- **Row 9:** Ch 1 (does not count as hdc), hdc in next 16 hdc, turn, leaving the remaining sts unworked. *You now have* 16 hdc.

- **Rows 10–14:** Ch 1, hdc in next 16 hdc, turn.

- **Row 15:** Ch 1, slip st in next 4 sts, hdc in next 8 sts, turn, leaving the remaining sts unworked. *You now have* 8 hdc.

- **Rows 16 and 17:** Ch 1, hdc in next 8 hdc, turn.

- **Rnd 18:** Ch 1, sc in next 8 sts; skip row-end sts of Rows 18, 17, 16, and 15; skip next 4 sts in Row 14, work 8 sc evenly spaced across row ends of Rows 13 through 8; sc in each of the next 8 unworked sts from Row 7; work 8 sc evenly spaced across the row ends of Rows 8, 9, 10, 11, 12, and 13; skip next 4 sts in Row 14, skip next 4 row-end sts; join with slip st to first sc in Rnd 18. *You now have* 32 sc. Fasten off.

THE ANKLE AND STRAP

Left Bootee

- With RS facing, join yarn to 27th sc of Rnd 18.

- **Row 1:** Ch 2 (counts as hdc here and throughout), hdc in next 4 sts, hdc2tog, hdc in next 6 sts, hdc2tog, hdc in next 5 sts, turn. *You now have* 18 hdc.

- **Row 2:** Ch 2, hdc in each hdc across, ch 13, turn.

- **Row 3:** Dc in 3rd ch from the hook, ch 1, skip 1 ch (*buttonhole made*), dc in next 9 ch, hdc in next 18 hdc. Fasten off.

Right Bootee

- With WS facing, join yarn to 14th sc of Row 17.

- Work Rows 1–3 as for left bootee.

CROCHETING THE FEATURES

THE TEETH (MAKE 4)

- With medium hook and white yarn, ch 4.

- **Row 1:** Sc in 2nd ch from hook, sc in next 2 sc, turn. *You now have* 3 sts.

- **Rows 2 and 3:** Ch 1, sc in each sc across, turn.

- Fasten off, leaving a tail for sewing.

THE EYES (MAKE 4)

- With medium hook and white yarn, ch 2.

- **Rnd 1:** 6 sc in 2nd ch from hook, join with slip st to first sc. *You now have* 6 sc.

- **Rnd 2:** Ch 1, 2 sc in each sc around, join with slip st to first sc. *You now have* 12 sts.

- Fasten off, leaving a tail for sewing.

THE PUPILS (MAKE 4)

- With smallest hook and black yarn, ch 2.

- **Rnd 1:** 5 sc in 2nd ch from hook, join with slip st to first sc.

- Fasten off, leaving a tail for sewing.

ASSEMBLING THE BOOTEES

- Sew pupils to centers of eyes. Using photo as a guide, sew the eyes and teeth onto each bootee. Sew the openings on the heels closed. Sew buttons on outside corner of bootee top.

Baby Mukluks

DESIGNED BY *Claudia Barbo*

These seamless bootees start in the center of the sole and are worked in the round to the instep. The instep is then worked back and forth, and the cuff is joined and worked in the round using front and back post double crochet.

SIZE AND FINISHED MEASUREMENTS
To fit 0–3 months: 3¼"/8 cm foot length

....

YARN
Debbie Bliss Baby Cashmerino, 55% merino wool/33% microfiber/12% cashmere, 137 yds (125 m)/1.75 oz (50 g), Color 203 Teal ②

CROCHET HOOK
US E/4 (3.5 mm) *or size needed to obtain correct gauge*

....

GAUGE
20 stitches and 6 rows = 4"/10 cm in single crochet

OTHER SUPPLIES
Stitch markers, yarn needle

CROCHETING THE BOOTEE (MAKE 2)

THE SOLE

- Chain 14.

- **Rnd 1:** 2 sc in 2nd ch from hook, sc in next 10 ch, 2 sc in next 2 ch, pm in last sc for toe; working along opposite side of foundation ch, 2 sc in next ch, sc in next 10 ch, 2 sc in next ch, 2 sc in turning ch, pm in last sc for heel. Do not join; pm in the first st of the rnd and move markers up as you work the rnds. *You now have* 32 sc.

- **Rnd 2:** Sc in each sc around.

- **Rnd 3:** 2 sc in first sc, sc in next 12 sc, 2 sc in next 3 sc (move marker up to first of last 2 sc), 2 sc in next 2 sc, sc in next 12 sc, 2 sc in next sc, sc in next sc. *You now have* 39 sc.

- **Rnd 4:** Repeat Rnd 2.

THE SIDES

- **Rnd 1:** Ch 2 (does not count as st), BLhdc in each sc around.

- **Rnds 2 and 3:** Hdc in each hdc around.

THE INSTEP

- **Row 1:** Sc in each hdc to center toe marker, remove marker, sc in next 2 hdc, sc2tog, turn, leaving remaining sts unworked.

- **Row 2:** Ch 1, skip first sc, sc in next 4 sc, sc2tog, turn.
- **Row 3:** Ch 1, skip first sc, sc in next 4 sc, sc2tog in next ch and next sc in Row 1, turn.
- **Row 4:** Ch 1, skip first sc, sc in next 4 sc, sc2tog in next ch and next hdc in Row 3 of sides, turn.
- **Rows 5–14:** Repeat Rows 3 and 4 five times.
- **Row 15:** Repeat Row 3 (18 sts left unworked on sides). Do not turn at end of last row.
- **Row 16:** Sc in next 9 hdc to center back of heel, join with slip st to next sc (first sc of instep Row 1).

THE CUFF

- **Rnd 1:** Ch 1, sc in next 8 sc, 2 sc in next sc, sc in each st around, join with slip st to first sc. *You now have* 24 sc.
- **Rnd 2:** Ch 2 (counts as dc), dc in each sc around, join with slip st to top of ch-2.
- **Rnd 3:** Ch 2, *FPdc in next dc, BPdc in next dc; repeat from * around, join with slip st to top of ch-2.
- Repeat Rnd 3 four times or to desired length.

THE EDGING

- **Rnd 1:** Ch 1, sc in each hdc around, join with slip st to first sc.
- **Rnd 2:** Ch 1, work reverse sc in each sc around, join with slip st to first st.
- Cut yarn. Weave in ends.

Bumpy Bootees

DESIGNED BY *Edie Eckman*

These highly textured bootees look especially enticing in delicious sorbet-colored shades. Worked in a combination of treble and single crochet, a chain woven through just above the heel helps keep the bootees on baby's feet.

SIZE AND FINISHED MEASUREMENTS

To fit 0–3 months: approximately 4½"/11.5 cm circumference and 3½"/9 cm foot length

YARN

Plymouth Yarn Sesia Bimbo, 100% cotton, 195 yds (178 m)/1.75 oz (50 g), Color 1252 ①

CROCHET HOOK

Size E/4 (3.5 mm) *or size needed to obtain correct gauge*

GAUGE

10 stitches and 10 rounds = 2"/5 cm in pattern stitch

OTHER SUPPLIES

Yarn needle

PATTERN ESSENTIALS

Pattern Stitch (multiple of 2 stitches)

Rnd 1: Ch 1, sc in same st, tr in next st, *sc in next st, tr in next st; repeat from * around, join with slip st to first sc.

Rnd 2: Ch 1, sc in same st and in each st around, join with slip st to first sc.

Repeat Rnds 1 and 2 for pattern.

CROCHETING THE BOOTEE (MAKE 2)

THE TOE AND FOOT

- Ch 4, join with slip st to form ring.
- **Rnd 1:** Ch 3 (counts as dc), 11 dc in ring, join with slip st to top of ch-3. *You now have* 12 dc.
- **Rnd 2:** Ch 1, (sc, tr) in first st, *sc in next dc, tr in next dc**, (sc, tr) in next dc; repeat from * around, ending last repeat at **, join with slip st to first sc. *You now have* 16 sts.
- **Rnd 3:** Ch 1, sc in each st around, join with slip st to first sc.
- **Rnd 4:** Ch 1, (sc, tr) in first sc, *sc in next sc, tr in next sc, (sc, tr) in next sc; repeat from * around, join with slip st to first sc. *You now have* 22 sts.

- **Rnd 5:** Repeat Rnd 3.
- **Rnds 6–13:** Work in established pattern st.

THE HEEL

- **Row 1 (RS):** Ch 1, sc in next 8 sc, turn, leaving remaining sts unworked.
- **Row 2:** Ch 1, sc in next 5 sc, turn, leaving remaining sts unworked.
- **Row 3:** Ch 1, sc in next 5 sc, sc in next sc 3 rows below, turn. *You now have 6 sts.*
- **Row 4:** Ch 1, sc in next 6 sc, sc in next sc 3 rows below, turn. *You now have 7 sts.*
- **Row 5:** Ch 1, sc in next 7 sc, sc in next sc 3 rows below, turn. *You now have 8 sts.*
- **Row 6:** Ch 1, sc in next 8 sc, sc in next sc 3 rows below, turn. *You now have 9 sts.*
- **Row 7:** Ch 1, sc in next 9 sc, sc in next sc 3 rows below, turn. *You now have 10 sts.*
- **Row 8:** Ch 1, sc in next 10 sc, sc in next sc 3 rows below, turn. *You now have 11 sts.*

THE LEG

Work now progresses in rnds.

- **Rnd 1 (RS):** Ch 1, (sc in next st, tr in next st) around, ending with a slip st through next sc and top of first sc of rnd to join. *You now have 22 sts.*
- **Rnd 2:** Ch 1, sc in each st around.
- **Rnds 3–12:** Work even in pattern st.
- Fasten off.

CROCHETING THE TIES (MAKE 2)

- Chain 86. Fasten off.
- Beginning at front of leg, weave tie underneath treble crochet bumps on Rnd 3 of leg.
- Weave in ends.

BUMPY BOOTEES

REPEAT RNDS 6–7 FOR PATTERN

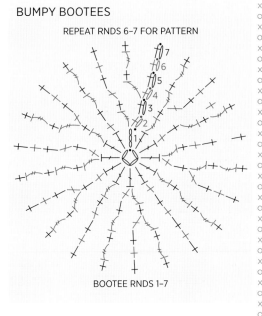

BOOTEE RNDS 1–7

Teeny Tiny Socks

DESIGNED BY *Brenda K. B. Anderson*

This pair is constructed from the toe up and features a simple, smooth, and stretchy stitch pattern. A post-stitch ribbed cuff and an afterthought heel finish these little bitty socks. One pair uses less than 25 grams of sock yarn.

SIZE AND FINISHED MEASUREMENTS

To fit 3–6 months: 4"/10 cm foot length, 3"/7.5 cm height, and 4¾"/12 cm cuff circumference

YARN

Lorna's Laces Shepherd Sock, 80% superwash merino wool/20% nylon, 430 yds (393 m)/3.5 oz (100 g), Powder Blue (1)

CROCHET HOOK

US C/2 (2.75 mm) *or size needed to obtain correct gauge*

GAUGE

22 stitches and 20 rounds = 4"/10 cm in extended single crochet

OTHER SUPPLIES

Stitch markers (one of a contrasting color), yarn needle

CROCHETING THE SOCK (MAKE 2)

- Chain 7.

- **Set-Up Row:** Working into back bump of each ch (see page 276), esc in 2nd ch from hook and in each ch across. *You now have* 6 esc.

- **Rnd 1:** Working on opposite sides of the foundation ch, 2 esc in same ch, esc in next 4 ch, 2 esc in next ch; continuing on Set-Up Row sts, working in a spiral, 2 esc in first esc, esc in next 4 sts, 2 esc in next st, do not join. *You now have* 16 sts. Pm in the first st of the rnd and move it up as you work the rnds.

- **Rnd 2:** (2 esc in next st, esc in next 6 sts, 2 esc in next st) twice. *You now have* 20 sts.

- **Rnd 3:** (2 esc in next st, esc in next 8 sts, 2 esc in next st) twice, esc in next st (marked st) to shift beginning of rnd; move marker to following st to indicate new beginning of rnd. *You now have* 24 sts.

- **Rnds 4–9:** Esc in each st around.

- **Rnd 10:** (2 esc in next st, esc in next 10 sts, 2 esc in next st) twice. *You now have* 28 sts.

- **Rnd 11:** Esc in each st around.

- **Rnd 12:** (2 esc in next st, esc in next 12 sts, 2 esc in next st) twice. *You now have* 32 sts.

- **Rnd 13:** Esc in next 16 sts, loosely ch 16, skip next 16 sts for heel opening; place a contrasting stitch marker in the first skipped st of this rnd. Before continuing, make sure that chain is not twisted.

- **Rnds 14–16:** Esc in each st around.

- **Rnd 17:** (Esc2tog, esc in next 12 sts, esc2tog) twice. *You now have* 28 sts.

- **Rnd 18:** Esc in each st around.

- **Rnd 19–23:** (Esc in next st, FPdc in next st) 14 times. ***Note:*** Be careful when you are making your esc sts as it's easy to accidentally skip a st after working a post st. It helps to count your sts after Rnd 19 to make sure you are placing your esc sts correctly.

- **Rnd 24:** (Esc in next st, FPdc in next st) 13 times, sc in next st, slip st in last st. Fasten off.

THE HEEL

- Hold the sock so that the ribbed cuff is pointing away from you and the toe is pointing toward your lap. The heel opening should be facing out, ready to be worked into across the under-the-foot edge of the heel opening.

- **Rnd 1:** Insert hook into the corner of the heel opening just to the right of the marked st and pull up a loop, ch 1 (does not count as st), esc in same space, esc in marked st and in remaining 15 skipped sts across heel opening, 2 esc in corner of heel opening; working across opposite edge of heel opening in chain sts, esc into each of next 16 ch, esc in same corner of the heel opening as the first st of rnd. *Do not join. You now have* 36 sts. Pm in the first st of the rnd and move it up as you work the rnds.

- **Rnd 2:** (Esc2tog, esc in next 14 sts, esc2tog) twice. *You now have 32 sts.*

- **Rnd 3:** (Esc2tog, esc in next 12 sts, esc2tog) twice. *You now have 28 sts.*

- **Rnd 4:** (Esc2tog, esc in next 10 sts, esc2tog) twice. *You now have 24 sts.*

- **Rnd 5:** (Esc2tog, esc in next 8 sts, esc2tog) twice. *You now have 20 sts.*

- **Rnd 6:** (Esc2tog, esc in next 6 sts, esc2tog) twice. *You now have 16 sts.*

- Fasten off, leaving a long tail.

FINISHING

- Fold the small opening in the heel flat to make a horizontal seam. Use yarn needle to whipstitch (see page 276) the heel opening closed. Weave in ends. Block if desired.

Sunshine Boot Toppers

DESIGNED BY *Janet Brani, OneLoopShy Designs*

Rays of sunshine fall from the cuff of these warming boot toppers. Changing from half double crochet to single crochet creates the taper at the ankle, and all stitches are worked into the back loop only for a nice stretchy rib.

SIZE AND FINISHED MEASUREMENTS

To fit toddler/child: 7"/18 cm long, excluding edging, and 6"/15 cm leg circumference, relaxed

YARN

Skacel Yarns HiKoo Simplicity, 55% superwash merino wool/28% acrylic/17% nylon, 117 yds (107 m)/1.75 oz (50 g), Color 004 Goldfish

CROCHET HOOK

US F/5 (4 mm) *or size needed to obtain correct gauge*

GAUGE

17 stitches and 12 rows = 4"/10 cm in back loop only half double crochet rib

OTHER SUPPLIES

Yarn needle

CROCHETING THE TOPPERS (MAKE 2)

- **Row 1 (foundation row):** Fsc 5 (see page 274), fhdc 25 (see page 274) working first hdc in base of previous fsc, turn. *You now have 30 sts.*

- **Row 2:** Ch 2 (does not count as st), BLhdc in next 25 sts, BLsc in next 5 sts, turn. Mark this row as RS.

- **Row 3:** Ch 1, BLsc in next 5 sts, BLhdc in next 25 sts, turn.

- **Rows 4–17:** Repeat Rows 2 and 3 seven more times.

- **Row 18:** Repeat Row 2.

WORK THE SEAM

- Fold the sock lengthwise with WS together and slip st ends together, working under 1 loop of each side. *Do not fasten off.*

ADD THE EDGING

- Turn sock inside out so WS are facing; working around the top edge, *ch 8, sc in 4th ch from hook, ch 1, skip 1 ch, hdc in next ch, ch 1, skip 1 ch, dc in next ch, slip st in top of ridge 2 rows over; repeat from * around for nine "rays."

- Fasten off. Weave in ends.

SUNSHINE BOOT TOPPERS

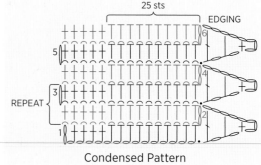

Condensed Pattern

Mommy & Me Leg Warmers

DESIGNED BY *Annelies Baes*

These cozy warmers start with the upper band, which is worked in rows and then seamed to form a cuff. The body is then crocheted onto the cuff and worked in rounds. The bottom band is crocheted separately in rows, seamed, and attached to the leg warmer.

SIZES AND FINISHED MEASUREMENTS

To fit baby (mommy): 5½ (13½)"/14 (34.5 cm) long and 5½ (9)"/14 (23) cm cuff circumference

YARN

Baby: Scheepjeswol Donna, 50% merino wool/50% acrylic, 122 yds (112 m)/1.75 oz (50 g), Color 692 Lila 〈3〉

Mommy: Malabrigo Arroyo, 100% superwash merino wool, 335 yds (306 m)/3.5 oz (100 g), Color 134 Regatta Blue 〈3〉

CROCHET HOOKS

3 mm *or sizes needed to obtain correct gauge*

GAUGE

23 stitches and 28 rows = 4"/10 cm in back loop single crochet with smaller hook

23 stitches and 11 rows = 4"/10 cm in leg pattern with larger hook

OTHER SUPPLIES

Yarn needle

PATTERN ESSENTIALS

Shell (Sc, ch 3, dc) in 1 stitch or space.

MOMMY & ME LEG WARMERS

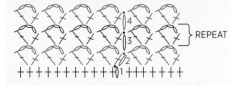

Abbreviated Pattern

CROCHETING THE UPPER CUFF

- With smaller hook, ch 7 (11).
- **Row 1:** Sc in 2nd ch from hook, sc in each ch across. *You now have* 6 (10) sts.
- **Row 2:** Ch 1 (does not count as st), BLsc in each sc across, turn.
- **Rows 3–30 (3–58):** Repeat Row 2. Cut yarn, leaving a 12"/30.5 cm tail for seaming. Fasten off.
- Fold the ribbing in half with RS together to join beginning to end. Working through a double thickness of the front loops of the foundation row and back loops of row just worked, slip st in each st across. *Do not fasten off.*

CROCHETING THE LEG

- With RS facing and seam to inside, change to larger hook.

Baby size only

- **Rnd 1 (RS):** Ch 1, sc in every row around top edge of cuff, join with slip st to first sc. *You now have* 30 sc.

Mommy size only

- **Rnd 1:** Ch 1; working in row-end sts, sc in first st, 2 sc in next st, sc in next 27 sts, 2 sc in next st, sc in last 28 sts, join with slip st to first sc. *You now have* 60 sc.

Both sizes

- **Rnd 2 (WS):** Ch 1, shell in first sc, skip next 2 sc, *shell in next sc, skip next 2 sc; repeat from * around, join with slip st to first sc, turn. *You now have* 10 (20) shells.
- **Rnd 3:** Ch 1, shell in each ch-3 space around, join with slip st to first sc, turn.
- **Rnds 4–11 (4–29):** Rep Rnd 3 eight (twenty-six) times. *Do not turn.*
- **Last Rnd (RS):** Ch 1, 3 sc in each ch-3 space around, join with slip st to first sc. Cut yarn, leaving a 24"/61 cm tail for sewing. Fasten off.

CROCHETING THE LOWER CUFF

- Follow instructions for upper cuff. Hold the lower cuff and bottom of leg with RS together; use the tail attached to the leg to slip st pieces together. Weave in ends.
- Repeat for second leg warmer.

CHAPTER THREE

LITTLE
Tops
+
Dresses

Dad & Me Necktie Shirts

DESIGNED BY *Dana Bincer, Yarnovations.com*

It's baby's Business Casual Friday every day with T-shirts embellished with crocheted neckties. The ties are worked in two pieces and joined, then sewn to a T-shirt and Onesie.

SIZES AND FINISHED MEASUREMENTS
To fit baby (dad): 2½ (4)"/6.5 (10) cm wide and 7 (18)"/18 (45.5) cm long

YARN
Bernat Handcrafter Crochet Thread 5, 100% acrylic, 371 yds (339 m)/3 oz (85 g), Color 31116 Loyal Blue **❶**

CROCHET HOOKS
US size 6 steel (1.8 mm) for baby tie, US size 00 steel (3.5 mm) for dad tie *or sizes needed to obtain correct gauge*

GAUGE
32 stitches and 28 rows = 4"/10 cm in pattern stitch with smaller hook and single strand of yarn
27 stitches and 23 rows = 4"/10 cm in pattern stitch with larger hook and yarn doubled

OTHER SUPPLIES
Yarn needle, sewing needle and coordinating thread, T-shirt, Onesie

PATTERN ESSENTIALS

Pattern Stitch (worked over an odd number of stitches)

Row 1: Ch 1, (sc in next dc, dc in next sc) across to last st, sc in last st, turn.

Row 2: Ch 1, (dc in next sc, sc in next dc) across to last st, dc in last st, turn.

Repeat Rows 1 and 2 for pattern.

CROCHETING THE TIES

Note: Yarn is used single throughout for baby tie, doubled for dad's.

- Chain 3.
- **Row 1:** (Dc, sc, dc) in 3rd ch from hook, turn. *You now have 3 sts.*
- **Row 2 (increase row):** Ch 1, (dc, sc) in first st, dc in next st, (sc, dc) in last st, turn. *You now have 5 sts.*
- **Row 3 (increase row):** Ch 1, (dc, sc) in first st, dc in next st, sc in next st, dc in next st, (sc, dc) in last st, turn. *You now have 7 sts.*
- Continue in pattern, increasing 1 st at each end of every row until you have 19 (25) sts.
- **Row 10 (13) (decrease row):** Ch 1, dc2tog, (sc in next st, dc in next st) to last 3 sts, sc in next st, dc2tog, turn. *You now have 17 (23) sts.*

DAD & ME NECKTIE SHIRTS

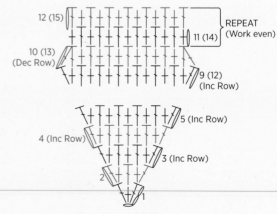

Condensed Pattern

- [Work even in pattern for 6 (10) rows, decrease 1 st at each end of next row] four (seven) times. *You now have* 9 sts. Work even in pattern for 6 more rows.
- Fasten off, leaving a long sewing length.

THE KNOT

- Chain 10.
- **Row 1 (RS):** Sc in 2nd ch from hook, (dc in next st, sc in next st) three times, dc in next st, slip st in next st, turn. *You now have* 9 sts.
- **Row 2:** Ch 1, skip slip st, slip st in next st, (dc in next st, sc in next st) three times, dc in next st, turn. *You now have* 8 sts.
- **Row 3:** Ch 1, (sc in next st, dc in next st) three times, slip st in next st, skip remaining st, turn. *You now have* 7 sts.
- **Row 4:** Ch 1, skip slip st, (sc in next st, dc in next st) three times, turn. *You now have* 6 sts.
- **Row 5:** Ch 1, (sc in next st, dc in next st) three times, turn.
- **Rows 6–8:** Repeat Row 5 three times.
- **Row 9:** Ch 1, (sc in next st, dc in next st) twice, sc in next st, (dc, sc) in last st, turn. *You now have* 7 sts.
- **Row 10:** Ch 1, (dc in next st, sc in next st) three times, dc in next st, turn.
- **Row 11:** Ch 1, (sc in next st, dc in next st) three times (sc, dc) in last st, turn. *You now have* 8 sts. *Do not fasten off.*

ASSEMBLING

- Center last row of necktie to flat sides of Rows 1–11 (the concave side is the top to be sewn closest to tee's collar). Using yarn needle and tail from tie, sew together with whipstitch (see page 276) across. Weave in end.
- Picking up dropped loop at end of knot piece, slip st around the tie, working 1 slip st at the end of each row and 1 slip st in each sc or dc; join with slip st to first st. Fasten off. Weave in ends.
- Block and sew to Onesie or T-shirt.

The Back's Where It's At Bolero

DESIGNED BY *Sylvie Damey*

This baby bolero jacket is worked from the top down in front loop double crochet. An open square is left in the center back to hold a motif that's worked separately and sewn in.

CROCHETING THE BACK MOTIF

- Ch 4, join with slip st to form a ring.
- **Rnd 1:** Ch 3 (counts as dc throughout), 11 dc in ring, join with slip st to top of ch-2. *You now have* 12 dc.
- **Rnd 2:** Ch 4 (counts as dc and ch 1), *dc in next st, ch 1; repeat from * around, join with slip st to 3rd ch of ch-4. *You now have* 24 sts.

THE BACK'S WHERE IT'S AT BOLERO

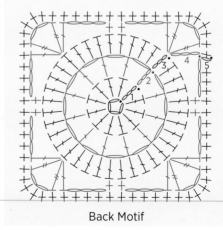

Back Motif

- **Rnd 3:** Ch 3, 2 dc in next space, *dc in next dc, 2 dc in next space; repeat from * around, join with slip st to top of ch-3. *You now have 36 dc.*

- **Rnd 4:** Ch 3, (tr, ch 2, tr, dc) in same st, *ch 3, skip 3 dc, sc in next 2 dc, ch 3, skip 3 dc**, (dc, tr, ch 2, tr, dc) in next st; repeat from * around, ending last repeat at **; join with slip st to top of ch-3.

- **Rnd 5:** Ch 1, sc in same st and next tr, *4 sc in next space, (sc in next 2 sts, 3 sc in next space) twice**, sc in next 2 sts; repeat from * around, ending last repeat at **, join with slip st to first sc. Fasten off, leaving a long tail for sewing.

CROCHETING THE JACKET

- Chain 62.

- **Row 1 (RS):** Dc in 4th ch from hook, *2 dc in next ch, dc in next 2 ch; repeat from * to last ch, 2 dc in last ch, turn. *You now have* 80 sts.

SIZE AND FINISHED MEASUREMENTS

To fit 0–3 months: 16"/40.5 cm chest circumference

YARN

Brown Sheep Company Cotton Fleece, 80% cotton/20% merino wool, 215 yds (197 m)/3.5 oz (100 g), Color CW900 Perry's Primrose (3)

CROCHET HOOK

US H/8 (5 mm) *or size needed to obtain correct gauge*

GAUGE

18 stitches and 9 rows = 4"/10 cm in front loop double crochet

OTHER SUPPLIES

Straight pins, yarn needle

- **Row 2:** Ch 3 (counts as dc throughout), FLdc in each st across, turn.
- **Row 3:** Repeat Row 2.
- **Row 4 (increase row):** Ch 3, *2 FLdc in next st, FLdc in next 3 sts; repeat from *, ending with 2 FLdc in next st, FLdc in each of last 2 sts, turn. *You now have* 100 sts.
- **Rows 5 and 6:** Ch 3, FLdc in each st across, turn.

THE BACK OPENING

You'll work on one side only to leave an open gap in the center of back for motif insert.

- **Row 7 (increase row, RS):** Working only over the first 42 sts, ch 3, (FLdc in next 2 sts, 2 FLdc in next st) 13 times, FLdc in last 2 sts. *You now have* 55 sts.
- **Row 8:** Ch 3, FLdc in next 54 sts, turn.
- **Row 9:** Ch 3, FLdc in next 18 sts, skip 25 sts for sleeve opening, FLdc in next 11 sts, turn. *You now have* 30 sts for body.
- **Rows 10–12:** Ch 3, FLdc in next 29 sts, turn.
- **Fasten off.**

THE SECOND SECTION

- With RS facing, skip 16 sts after first crocheted section, join yarn in next st and work over last 42 sts of back as follows.
- **Row 7 (increase row, RS):** Ch 3, (FLdc in next 2 sts, 2 FLdc in next st) 13 times, FLdc in last 2 sts. *You now have* 55 sts.
- **Row 8:** Ch 3, FLdc in next 54 sts, turn.
- **Row 9:** Ch 3, FLdc in next 10 sts, skip 25 sts for sleeve opening, FLdc in next 19 sts, turn. *You now have* 30 sts for body.
- **Rows 10–12:** Ch 3, FLdc in next 29 sts, turn.
- **Fasten off.**

THE LOWER BODY

- With RS facing, join yarn to outside edge of first crocheted section.
- **Row 13:** Ch 3, FLdc in next 29 sts, ch 14, FLdc in next 30 sts, turn. *You now have 60 sts and 1 ch-space.*
- **Row 14:** Ch 3, FLdc in next 29 sts, work 16 dc in the ch-14 space, FLdc in next 30 sts, turn. *You now have 76 sts.*
- **Rows 15–17:** Ch 3, FLdc in each st across, turn.

THE EDGING

- With RS facing, join yarn to bottom corner of right front, ch 1, work 1 rnd in reverse sc around all edges of body, working 1 st in each st, 2 sts along each end of FLdc rows, and 2 sts in each corner, join with slip st to first st. Fasten off.

CROCHETING THE SLEEVES

- With RS facing, join yarn between 2 FLdc sts at center of underarm.
- **Rnd 1:** Ch 3, 2 dc around post of first underarm dc, FLdc in next 25 sleeve sts, 2 dc around post of last underarm dc, join with slip st to top of ch-3, turn. *You now have 30 sts.*
- **Rnds 2–9:** Ch 3, FLdc in next 29 sts, join with slip st to top of ch-3, turn. *Do not turn at end of last rnd.*
- With RS facing, ch 1, reverse sc in each st around, join with slip st to first st. Fasten off.
- Repeat sleeve in other armhole opening.

MAKING THE TIES (MAKE 4)

- Using the photo as a guide, mark the location of each tie along top edge of cardigan, placing first pair of ties low enough to be comfortable around baby's neck. For each tie, cut 2 lengths of yarn 12"/30.5 cm long. Hold both pieces together and thread them through edge of cardigan (just in from the reverse sc edging), using hook if necessary to pull them through. Twist the lengths together, accentuating initial twist of yarn. Fold in half and tie an overhand knot to join the ends. Trim ends.

FINISHING

- Working on RS of cardigan, place motif inside back opening, with RS of motif facing out. Pin in place. Using tail from motif, sew motif to cardigan, inserting needle only in top loop of each st around motif for an invisible join.
- Weave in ends. Block if desired.

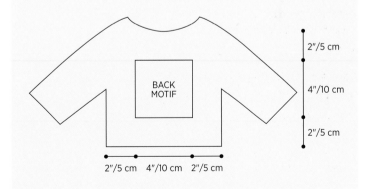

THE BACK'S WHERE IT'S AT BOLERO

BACK MOTIF

2"/5 cm
4"/10 cm
2"/5 cm

2"/5 cm   4"/10 cm   2"/5 cm

Tiny Tango Vest

DESIGNED BY *Kristen Stoltzfus*

It only takes one to tango in this adorable ruffled vest. With five layers of ruffles, the vest front is open to make tummy-time comfy.

SIZES AND FINISHED MEASUREMENTS
To fit 0–3 (6 months): 15 (18)"/38 (45.5) cm chest circumference
Note: The fronts don't meet. There is a 2"/5 cm gap in front.

YARN
Red Heart Anne Geddes Baby DK weight, 80% acrylic/20% nylon, 340 yds (310 m)/3.5oz (100g), Color #764 Taffy (3)

CROCHET HOOK
US H/8 (5 mm) *or size needed to obtain correct gauge*

GAUGE
18 stitches and 12 rows = 4"/10 cm in body pattern
18 stitches and 10 rows = 4"/10 cm in double crochet

OTHER SUPPLIES
Yarn needle

CROCHETING THE BACK

- Chain 35 (43).
- **Row 1:** Dc in 3rd ch from hook and in each ch across, turn. *You now have* 33 (41) dc.
- **Row 2:** Ch 1, sc in first dc, *ch 1, skip 1 dc, sc in next dc; repeat from * across, turn. *You now have* 16 (20) ch-spaces.
- **Row 3:** Ch 2 (does not count as st here and throughout), dc in first sc and in next space, 2 dc in each space across, dc in last sc, turn. *You now have* 33 (41) dc.
- **Rows 4–17 (21):** Repeat Rows 2 and 3 seven (nine) times.

THE RUFFLE BASE SECTION

- **Row 1 (WS):** Ch 2, dc in first 2 dc, (BPdc in next dc, dc in next 3 dc) seven (nine) times, BPdc in next dc, dc in each of last 2 dc, turn. *You now have* 8 (10) BPdc, 23 (31) dc.
- **Row 2:** Ch 1, work 1 FPdc in each BPdc and 1 dc in each dc across, turn.
- **Row 3:** Ch 2, work 1 BPdc in each FPdc and 1 dc in each dc across, turn.
- **Rows 4 and 5 (4–9):** Repeat Rows 2 and 3 one (three) times. Fasten off.

TINY TANGO VEST

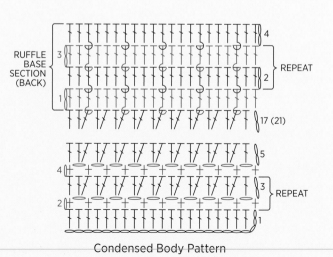

Condensed Body Pattern

CROCHETING THE RIGHT FRONT

- With RS facing, working in opposite loops of foundation ch, join yarn with slip st in first ch.
- **Row 1:** Ch 2, dc in first 11 (15) ch sts, turn, leaving remaining sts unworked. *You now have* 11 (15) dc.
- **Rows 2–17 (21):** Repeat Rows 2–17 (21) of back.

THE RUFFLE BASE SECTION

- **Row 1 (WS):** Ch 2, dc in first dc, (BPdc in next dc, dc in next 3 dc) two (three) times, BPdc in next dc, dc in last dc, turn. *You now have* 3 (4) BPdc, 8 (11) dc.

- **Rows 2–5 (9):** Repeat Rows 2–5 (9) of back Ruffle Base Section. Fasten off.

CROCHETING THE LEFT FRONT

- With right front at right and working on opposite side of foundation ch, skip next 11 ch sts and join yarn with slip st to next ch.
- **Row 1:** Ch 2, dc in same ch, dc in each ch across, turn. *You now have* 11 (15) dc.
- **Rows 2–17 (21):** Repeat Rows 2–17 (21) of back.

THE RUFFLE BASE SECTION

- **Rows 1–5 (9):** Repeat Rows 1–5 (9) of right front. Fasten off.
- Sew side seams, leaving 3½ (4)"/9 (10) cm unjoined at top for armhole.

CROCHETING THE RUFFLES

- **Row 1:** Working on surface of sts, with RS facing and hem away from you, join yarn with slip st in first post st of ruffle base Row 1; [(ch 5, slip st) in next post st of Row 1] across right front, back, and left front, turn. *You now have* 13 (17) ch-5 loops.

- **Row 2:** Ch 1, [(dc, tr) five times, dc] in each loop across, ch 1, slip st in last slip st. Fasten off.

Size 0–3 months only

- Repeat Rows 1 and 2 of ruffle on post sts of Rows 3 and 5 for three ruffle rows total.

Size 6 months only

- Repeat Rows 1 and 2 of ruffle on post sts of Rows 3, 5, 7, and 9 for five ruffle rows total.

CROCHETING THE EDGINGS

- Join yarn with slip st in underarm seam, ch 1, sc evenly around armhole, join with slip st to first sc. Fasten off. Repeat for other side.

- With RS of front facing, join yarn in side of dc at right-hand corner, ch 1, (hdc, dc) in side of dc; working in sides of rows, work 1 dc in each sc and 2 dc in each dc to shoulder "seam"; (sc in opposite side of foundation ch) 11 times; working in sides of rows, work 1 dc in each sc and 2 dc in each dc to side of last dc, (dc, hdc, slip st) in side of last dc. Fasten off.

- Weave in ends. Block.

TINY TANGO VEST

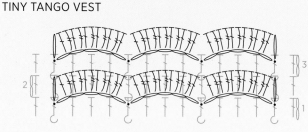

Condensed Ruffles Pattern

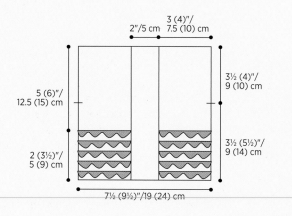

3 (4)"/
7.5 (10) cm

2"/5 cm

3½ (4)"/
9 (10) cm

5 (6)"/
12.5 (15) cm

3½ (5½)"/
9 (14) cm

2 (3½)"/
5 (9) cm

7½ (9½)"/19 (24) cm

Summer Kisses Cardigan

DESIGNED BY *Thomasina Cummings, Thomasina Cummings Designs*

This cardigan with cap sleeves in newborn size is worked from the top down without seams, so it's a really quick project to work. The short sleeves are ideal for summer, but they could just as easily be worn over a long-sleeved top in cooler weather. The finished item can be left plain or trimmed with lace, ribbon, or your choice of embellishment, making it an ideal unisex baby shower gift.

SIZE AND FINISHED MEASUREMENTS
To fit newborn: 14"/35.5 cm chest circumference

YARN
Cascade Ultra Pima, 100% pima cotton, 220 yds (201 m)/3.5 oz (100 g), Color 3720 Sage ⑤

CROCHET HOOK
US G/6 (4 mm) *or size needed to obtain correct gauge*

GAUGE
16 stitches and 12 rows = 4"/10 cm in double crochet

OTHER SUPPLIES
Yarn needle, three ⅝"/16 mm buttons, sewing needle and coordinating thread, decorative trim (optional)

PATTERN ESSENTIALS

X-st (X-stitch) Worked over 2 sts or spaces and counts as 2 sts. Skip next st or space, dc in next st or space; working in front of previous dc, dc in skipped st or space.

CROCHETING THE CARDIGAN

THE YOKE

Note: Except where noted, yoke sts and the first row of the body are worked *between* the sts of the previous row. When instructed to work in "spaces," begin in the space between sts that immediately follows the post st, and then work into subsequent spaces between sts.

- Chain 47.
- **Row 1 (RS):** Dc in 4th ch from hook and in each ch across, turn. *You now have 45 sts.*

- **Row 2 (WS):** Sc in first dc, ch 2 (this combination counts as 1 dc throughout), dc in next dc, *BPdc in next dc; dc in next 5 spaces; repeat from * to last 3 dc, BPdc in next dc, dc in next 2 dc, turn. *You now have* 53 sts.

- **Row 3:** Sc in first dc, ch 2, dc in next dc, *FPdc in next st, dc in next 6 spaces; repeat from * to last 3 dc, FPdc in next st, dc in next 2 dc, turn. *You now have* 61 sts.

- **Row 4:** Sc in first dc, ch 2, dc in next dc, *BPdc in next st, dc in next 7 spaces; repeat from * to last 3 dc, BPdc in next st, dc in next 2 dc, turn. *You now have* 69 sts.

- **Row 5:** Sc in first dc, ch 2, dc in next dc, *FPdc in next st, dc in next 8 spaces; repeat from * to last 3 dc, FPdc in next st, dc in next 2 dc, turn. *You now have* 77 sts.

You now have a curved piece with eight sections, each separated by post sts. At each end of the piece are 2 dc that will later form the button bands.

- **Rows 6–10:** Continue increasing in this manner, keeping the post sts lined up, until you have 13 sts per section and 117 sts total.

THE BODY

- **Row 1 (RS):** Sc in first dc, ch 2, dc in next dc, FPdc in next st, (X-st worked over next 2 spaces) seven times, *yo, insert hook from front to back to front around the post of next post st, skip next 27 sts for sleeve, insert hook from front to back to front around the post of next post st, yo, draw yarn through sts, (yo, draw yarn through 2 loops on hook) twice to complete FPdc (*sleeves made and tucked inside*), (X-st worked

over next 2 spaces) seven times, FPdc in next st**, (X-st worked over next 2 spaces) seven times; repeat from * to ** to complete second sleeve and remaining section of body, dc in last 2 dc, turn. *You now have* 65 sts.

Note: The sleeves are currently tucked inside the body. You may find it easier to move them from inside to outside to work the next row. Keep FPdc and X sts lined up throughout body of cardigan.

- **Row 2:** Sc in first st, ch 2, dc in next dc, BPdc in next st, ([X-st worked over next 2 sts] seven times, BPdc in next st) four times, dc in next 2 dc, turn. *You now have* 65 sts.

- **Row 3:** Sc in first st, ch 2, dc in next dc, FPdc in next st, ([X-st worked over next 2 sts] seven times, FPdc in next st) four times, dc in next 2 dc, turn.

- **Rows 4–9:** Repeat Rows 2 and 3 three times.

- **Row 10:** Repeat Row 2.

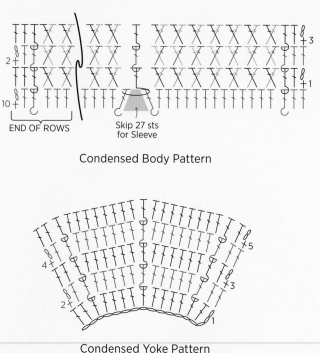

SUMMER KISSES CARDIGAN

END OF ROWS — Skip 27 sts for Sleeve

Condensed Body Pattern

Condensed Yoke Pattern

FINISHING

THE BOTTOM EDGING

- **Row 1 (RS):** Ch 1, sc in each st across, turn. *You now have* 65 sts.
- **Row 2:** Ch 1, sc in each sc across. Fasten off.

THE SLEEVE EDGING

- Join yarn to inside edge of sleeve opening.
- **Rnd 1 (RS):** Ch 1, sc in each st around, join with slip st to first sc, turn. *You now have* 27 sts.
- **Rnd 2:** Repeat Rnd 1.
- Fasten off. Repeat for second sleeve.
- Weave in ends.
- Buttons should be sized to fit snugly through spaces between double crochet on front. Sew buttons securely to the yoke, evenly spaced and aligned with double crochet openings.

SUMMER KISSES CARDIGAN

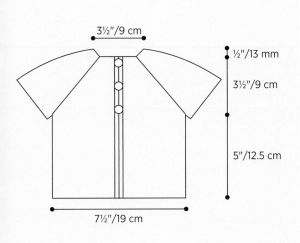

3½"/9 cm

½"/13 mm

3½"/9 cm

5"/12.5 cm

7½"/19 cm

Reversible Sweater

DESIGNED BY *René E. Wells, Granny an Me Designs*

Baby will look smart and keep warm in this wool-blend cardigan. It is worked from the top down in double crochet — sometime in the front loop, sometimes in the back, and sometimes both — and the front bands are worked in single crochet. You could also add buttons, using between-stitch spaces for buttonholes.

SIZE AND FINISHED
MEASUREMENTS
To fit newborn–6 months: 19"/48.5 cm
chest circumference

YARN
Opal Dancing Sock 6-fach, 75% virgin
wool/25% nylon, 459 yds (420 m)/5.3
oz (150 g), Color 7366 **1**

CROCHET HOOK
US F/5 (3.75 mm) *or size needed to
obtain correct gauge*

GAUGE
23 stitches and 11 rows = 4"/10 cm in
double crochet

OTHER SUPPLIES
Yarn needle

PATTERN ESSENTIALS

Make corner (2 dc, ch 2, 2 dc) in 1 stitch.

CROCHETING THE YOKE

- Fdc 50 (see page 273), turn.

Note: Work into the front or back loop
when indicated. The last st of each row is
worked into both loops.

- **Set-Up Row:** Work into both loops as
follows.

  - **Front:** Ch 3 (counts as dc), dc in next
  7 sts, make corner in next st;

  - **Sleeve:** Dc in next 8 sts, make corner
  in next st;

  - **Back:** Dc in next 14 sts, make corner
  in next st;

  - **Sleeve:** Dc in next 8 sts, make corner
  in next st;

  - **Front:** Dc in last 8 sts, turn. *You now
  have* 62 dc and 4 corner spaces.

- **Row 1:** Ch 3 (counts as dc here and throughout), (BLdc in each
st to corner, make corner in ch-2 space) four times, BLdc in
each st to end, turn. *You now have* 78 dc.

- **Row 2:** Ch 3, (FLdc in each st to corner, make corner in ch-2
space) four times, FLdc in each st to end, turn. *You now have*
94 dc.

- **Row 3–8:** Repeat Rows 1 and 2 three times. *You now have*
190 dc.

THE LOWER BODY

- Fold sweater along shoulders so fronts are on top of back
with sleeves outward.

- Join fronts to back and separate sleeves as follows.

- **Row 9:** Ch 3, BLdc in each st to corner, 2 dc in corner space,
skip next 44 dc, 2 dc in next corner space on back (front is
joined to back), BLdc in each st along back, 2 dc in back corner space, skip next 44 dc, 2 dc in next front corner space,
BLdc in each st to end, turn. *You now have* 110 dc.

- **Row 10:** Ch 3: FLdc in each st across, turn.

- **Row 11:** Ch 3, BLdc in each st across, turn.

- **Rows 12–23:** Continue in established pattern. Fasten off.

CROCHETING THE SLEEVES

- Join yarn with slip st at underarm at back side corner.

- **Row 1:** Ch 3, BLdc in each st across, turn. *You now have* 42 sts.

REVERSIBLE SWEATER

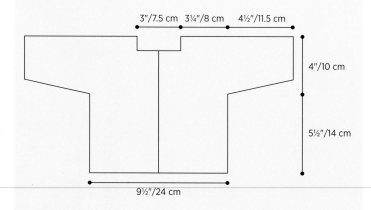

Pretty in Pink

DESIGNED BY *Anastasia Popova*

This lovely little dress is worked from the top down. The buttoned front piece makes dressing easier, and the buttons add charm. The hem is finished with a ruffled edging.

- **Row 2:** Ch 3, working in front loop only, dc2tog, work in pattern to last 2 sts, dc2tog, turn. *You now have* 40 sts.

- **Rows 3–12:** Repeat Rows 1 and 2. *You now have* 30 sts.

- Fasten off, leaving a long tail for sewing.

CROCHETING THE FRONT BANDS (MAKE 2)

- **Row 1:** Join yarn with slip st at lower front edge, sc evenly up edge to neck, turn.

- **Rows 2–4:** Ch 1, sc in each sc across, turn.

- Fasten off.

FINISHING

- Weave in ends invisibly so sweater can be worn with either side as the right side.

SIZES AND FINISHED MEASUREMENTS

To fit newborn (3 months): 15 (18)"/38 (45.5) cm chest circumference and 11 (11½)"/28 (29) cm length

YARN

Martha Stewart Crafts Extra Soft Wool Blend, 65% acrylic/35% wool, 164 yds (150 m)/3.5 oz (100 g), Color 503 Gerbera Daisy (4)

CROCHET HOOK

US 7 (4.5mm) *or size needed to obtain correct gauge*

GAUGE

15 stitches and 8 rows = 4"/10 cm in double crochet
2 pattern repeats and 7 rows = 4"/10 cm in skirt pattern

OTHER SUPPLIES

Yarn needle, four ½"/13 mm buttons, sewing needle and coordinating thread

PATTERN ESSENTIALS

Shell (2 dc, ch 1, 2 dc) in 1 stitch or space.

V-st (Dc, ch 1, dc) in 1 stitch or space.

CROCHETING THE FRONT YOKE

- Chain 14 (18).

- **Row 1:** 2 dc in 4th ch from hook, dc in each ch to last 2 ch, 2 dc in next ch, dc in next ch, turn. *You now have* 14 (18) dc.

- **Row 2:** Ch 2 (counts as dc here and throughout), 2 dc in next dc, dc in each st across to last 2 dc, 2 dc in next dc, dc in top of turning ch, turn. *You now have* 16 (20) sts.

- **Rows 3 and 4 (3–5):** Repeat Row 2. *You now have* 20 (26) sts.

- **Next Row:** Work 1 row of sc evenly across both sides and top of the front piece, placing approximately 2 sc in each row end. Fasten off.

CROCHETING THE MAIN YOKE

- Chain 23 (27).

- **Row 1:** 2 dc in 4th ch from hook, 2 dc in next ch, dc in next 1 (2) ch, 2 dc in next 3 ch, dc in next 7 (9) ch, 2 dc in next 3 ch, dc in next 1 (2) ch, 2 dc in next 2 ch, dc in next ch, turn. *You now have* 31 (35) sts.

- **Row 2:** Ch 2 (counts as dc here and throughout), 2 dc in next 2 dc, dc in next 4 (5) dc, 2 dc in next 3 dc, dc in next 11 (13) dc, 2 dc in next 3 dc, dc in next 4 (5) dc, 2 dc in next 2 dc, dc in top of turning chain, turn. *You now have* 41 (45) sts.

- **Row 3:** Ch 2, 2 dc in next 2 dc, dc in next 7 (8) dc, 2 dc in next 3 dc, dc in next 15 (17) dc, 2 dc in next 3 dc, dc in next 7 (8) dc, 2 dc in next 2 dc, dc in last st, turn. *You now have* 51 (55) sts.

- **Row 4:** Ch 2, 2 dc in next 2 dc, dc in next 10 (11) dc, 2 dc in next 3 dc, dc in next 19 (21) dc, 2 dc in next 3 dc, dc in next 10 (11) dc, 2 dc in next 2 dc, dc in last st, turn. *You now have* 61 (65) sts.

3-month size only

- **Row 5:** Ch 2, 2 dc in next 2 dc, dc in next 14 dc, 2 dc in next 3 dc, dc in next 25 dc, 2 dc in next 3 dc, dc in next 14 dc, 2 dc in next 2 dc, dc in last st. Do not turn. *You now have* 75 sts.

THE EDGING

Newborn size only

- **Row 1:** Working in row-end sts across side, ch 1, (2 sc in next row-end st, ch 2, skip next row) twice; working across opposite side of foundation ch, sc in next 21 ch; working in row-end sts across side, (ch 2, skip next row, 2 sc in next row-end st) twice, turn. *You now have* 29 sc and 4 ch-2 buttonholes.

3-month size only

- **Row 1:** Working in row-end sts across side, ch 1, (2 sc in next row-end st, ch 2, skip next row) twice, 2 sc in next row-end st; working across opposite side of foundation ch, sc in next 25 ch; working in row-end sts across side, ch 1, 2 sc in next row-end st, (ch 2, skip next row, 2 sc in next row-end st) twice, turn. *You now have* 37 sc and 4 ch-2 buttonholes.

Both sizes

- **Row 2:** Ch 1, sc in each st across. Do not fasten off.

CONNECT THE YOKE

- With WS of front yoke and main yoke facing, overlap sides of main yoke over 2 sts on each side of front yoke, leaving the center 16 (22) sts of the front yoke uncovered. Pin in place.

- **Rnd 1:** Ch 2, working through double thickness of main yoke and front yoke, 2 dc in same st of main yoke and in first st of front, dc in same st of main yoke and in next st of front; working through single thickness of main yoke, dc in next 2 dc, ch 3, skip next 14 (18) sts of main yoke, dc in next 27 (33) sts, ch 3, skip next 14 (18) sts of yoke, dc in next 2 sts of yoke; working through double thickness of main yoke and front yoke together, 2 dc in next st of main yoke and next st of front yoke, dc in same st of main yoke and in next st of front yoke, dc in next 16 (22) sts of front yoke, join with slip st to top of beginning ch-2. *You now have* 60 (72) sts.

Sewing Buttons

We highly recommend sewing buttons onto baby clothes with a sewing needle and thread. Repeat the thread path many times to be sure the button will not come off, even if baby uses it for teething. If your buttons have large holes, you can sew first with thread, then cover the thread with yarn.

CROCHETING THE SKIRT

- **Set-Up Rnd:** Ch 3 (counts as dc, ch 1 here and throughout), 2 dc in same st, skip next 2 sts, V-st in next st, (skip next 2 sts, shell in next st, skip next 2 sts, V-st in next st) to last 2 sts, skip next 2 sts, dc in base of ch-3, join with slip st in ch-3 space (*first shell completed*). *You now have* 10 (12) shells and 10 (12) V-sts.

- **Rnds 1–11:** Ch 3, 2 dc in first space, V-st in next space, (shell in next space, V-st in next space) around, dc in first space (*first shell completed*), join with slip st in ch-3 space.

- **Rnds 12 and 13:** Ch 3, 2 dc in first sp, shell in each space around, ending dc in first space (*first shell completed*), join with slip st in ch-3 space. *You now have* 20 (24) shells.

- **Rnd 14:** Ch 3, (dc in next st or space, ch 1) around, join with slip st in ch-3 space. *You now have* 200 (240) sts.

- **Rnd 15:** Ch 1, sc in each st and ch-1 space around, join with slip st to first sc.

- Fasten off.

FINISHING

- Weave in ends. Block. Sew buttons on front yoke opposite buttonholes.

PRETTY IN PINK

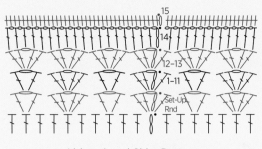

Abbreviated Skirt Pattern

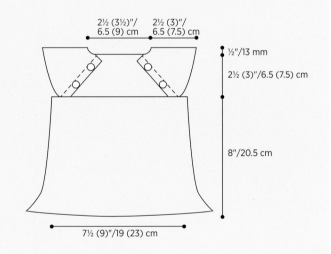

In the Woods Vest

DESIGNED BY *Justyna Kacprzak, Cute and Kaboodle*

This warm little side-to-side vest can be boyish, girlish, or neutral, depending on the color. Shopping for buttons will be fun.

SIZE AND FINISHED MEASUREMENTS
To fit 0–3 months: 16"/40.5 cm chest circumference

YARN
Himalaya El Örgü İplikleri Everyday, 100% acrylic, 273 yds (250 m)/3.5 oz (100 g), Color 70022 Brown

CROCHET HOOK
US 7 (4.5 mm) *or size needed to obtain correct gauge*

GAUGE
18 stitches and 12 rows = 4"/10 cm in back loop half double crochet

OTHER SUPPLIES
Yarn needle, eight ⅝"/16 mm buttons, sewing needle and coordinating thread

PATTERN ESSENTIALS

X-st (X-stitch) Worked over 2 sts or spaces and counts as 2 sts. Skip 1 st, hdc in next st, hdc in skipped st.

CROCHETING THE VEST

- Chain 41.
- **Row 1 (WS):** Hdc in 2nd ch from hook, (X-st over next 2 sts) seven times, hdc in next 25 ch, turn. *You now have 40 sts.*
- **Row 2:** Ch 1 (does not count as st throughout), BLhdc in next 25 hdc, (X-st over next 2 sts) seven times, hdc in last st, turn.
- **Row 3:** Ch 1, hdc in first st, (X-st over next 2 sts) seven times, hdc in next 25 hdc, turn.

- **Rows 4 and 5:** Repeat Rows 2 and 3.

- **Row 6:** Ch 1, BLhdc in next 25 hdc, (X-st over next 2 sts) three times, hdc in next st, turn. *You now have* 32 sts.

- **Row 7:** Ch 1, hdc in first st, (X-st over next 2 sts) three times, hdc in next 25 hdc, turn.

- **Rows 8–15:** Repeat Rows 6 and 7 four times.

- **Row 16:** Ch 1, BLhdc in next 25 sts, (X-st over next 2 sts) three times, hdc in next st, ch 9, turn.

- **Row 17:** Hdc in 2nd ch from hook, (X-st over next 2 sts) seven times, hdc in next 25 sts, turn. *You now have* 40 sts.

- **Rows 18–21:** Repeat Rows 6 and 7 twice.

- **Row 22:** Ch 1, hdc in first st, (X-st over next 2 sts) 12 times, hdc in next st, turn. *You now have* 26 sts.

- **Row 23:** Ch 1, sc in next 26 sts, turn.

- **Rows 24 and 25:** Repeat Rows 22 and 23.

- **Row 26:** Ch 1, hdc in first st, (X-st over next 2 sts) 12 times, hdc in next st, ch 19, turn.

- **Row 27:** Hdc in 2nd ch from hook, (X-st over next 2 sts) nine times, hdc in next 25 sts, turn. *You now have* 44 sts.

- **Row 28:** Ch 1, BLhdc in next 25 hdc, (X-st over next 2 sts) eight times, hdc in next st, skip 1 st, hdc in next st, turn.

- **Row 29:** Ch 1, hdc in first st, (X-st over next 2 sts) nine times, hdc in next 25 hdc, turn.

- **Row 30:** Ch 1, BLhdc in next 25 hdc, 8 X-sts in next 16 sts, hdc in next st, skip 1 st, hdc in next st, turn.

- **Row 31:** Ch 1, hdc in first st, (X-st over next 2 sts) nine times, hdc in next 25 hdc, turn.

- **Row 32:** Ch 1, BLhdc in next 25 hdc, (X-st over next 2 sts) six times, hdc in next st, turn. *You now have* 38 sts.

- **Row 33:** Ch 1, hdc in first st, (X-st over next 2 sts) six times, hdc in next 25 sts, turn.

- **Rows 34–41:** Repeat Rows 32 and 33 four times.

- **Row 42:** Ch 1, BLhdc in next 25 hdc, (X-st over next 2 sts) six times, hdc in next st, ch 7, turn.

- **Row 43:** Hdc in 2nd ch from hook, (X-st over next 2 sts) nine times, hdc in next 25 hdc. *You now have* 44 sts.

- **Row 44:** Ch 1, BLhdc in next 25 hdc, (X-st over next 2 sts) eight times, hdc in next st, skip 1 st, hdc in next st, turn.

- **Row 45:** Ch 1, hdc in next st, (X-st over next 2 sts) nine times, hdc in next 25 sts, turn.

- **Row 46:** Ch 1, BLhdc in next 25 hdc, (X-st over next 2 sts) eight times, hdc in next st, skip 1 st, hdc in next st, turn.

- **Row 47:** Ch 1, BLhdc in next st, (X-st over next 2 sts) nine times, hdc in next 25 hdc, turn.

- **Row 48:** Ch 1, BLsc in next 25 sts, turn.

THE LOWER EDGING

- **Row 1 (RS):** Ch 1, hdc in next 25 sts, turn.

- **Row 2:** Ch 1, hdc in next 24 sts, 3 hdc in last sc; working along the bottom edge, work 71 sc evenly spaced across to next corner, 3 sc in corner; working on the opposite side of the foundation ch, sc in each of the next 24 ch, turn. *You now have* 125 sts.

- **Row 3:** Ch 1, hdc in next st, FPhdc in next st, BPhdc in next st, *ch 1, skip 1 st, (BPhdc in next st, FPhdc in next st) twice, BPhdc in next st, repeat from * three more times, FPhdc in next st, BPhdc in next st, (hdc, FPhdc, hdc) in next hdc, (BPhdc in next st, FPhdc in next st) 36 times, BPhdc in next st, (hdc, FPhdc, hdc) in next hdc, (BPhdc in next st, FPhdc in next st) 12 times, hdc in next st, turn. *You now have* 129 sts.

- **Row 4:** Ch 1, sc in first st, (BPsc in next st, FPsc in next st) to last st of Row 3, sc in the last st of Row 3; do not turn. Do not fasten off.

THE UPPER EDGING

- Work evenly in sc across top edge of vest as follows: work 6 sc across side edge of button band and buttonhole band, 16 sts along each vertical armhole/strap edge, 6 sc along each vertical neck edge, 7 sc on tops of each front strap, 15 sc along front and back necks, 6 sc at underarm.

- Fasten off. Weave in ends. Sew buttons opposite buttonholes: two buttons on each front shoulder strap and four buttons on button band.

Handsome Boy's Vest

DESIGNED BY *Annalee Rose*

This simple but sophisticated vest has a band of half double crochet at the bottom and decorative vertical stripes of front-post double crochet. It is worked in two pieces and seamed.

IN THE WOODS VEST

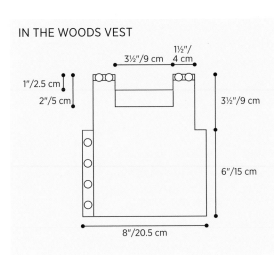

....
SIZE AND FINISHED MEASUREMENTS
To fit 3–6 months: 18"/45.5 cm chest circumference

....
YARN
Berroco Ultra Alpaca Fine, 50% Peruvian wool/30%
nylon/20% superfine alpaca, 433 yds (400 m)/3.5 oz (100 g),
Color 1281 Redwood Mix (**1**)

....
CROCHET HOOKS
US D/3 (3.25 mm) and US E/4 (3.5 mm) *or size needed to
obtain correct gauge*

....
GAUGE
21 stitches and 20 rows = 4"/10 cm in half double crochet with
larger hook

....
OTHER SUPPLIES
Yarn needle, stitch marker

CROCHETING THE FRONT

- With smaller hook, ch 49.

- **Row 1:** Sc in 2nd ch from hook and in each ch across, turn.
  You now have 48 sts. Mark this as a RS row.

- **Row 2 (WS):** Ch 1, sc in each sc across, turn.

- **Rows 3–7:** Repeat Row 2 five times, ending with a RS row.

- Switch to larger hook.

- **Row 8 (WS):** Ch 2 (does not count as st throughout), hdc in
  each sc across, turn.

- **Row 9:** Ch 2, hdc in next 10 hdc, FPdc in next 3 sts 2 rows
  below, hdc in next 22 hdc, FPdc in next 3 sts 2 rows below,
  hdc in next 10 hdc, turn.

- **Row 10:** Ch 2, hdc in each st across, turn.

- Repeat Rows 9 and 10 until piece measures 7"/18 cm from
  beginning, ending on a WS row.

THE ARMHOLE SHAPING

- **Next Row (RS):** Slip st in first 4 sts, ch 2, hdc in first 6 hdc,
  FPdc in next 3 sts 2 rows below, hdc in next 22 hdc, FPdc
  in next 3 sts 2 rows below, hdc in next 6 hdc, turn, leaving
  remaining sts unworked. *You now have* 40 sts.

- Repeat Rows 2 and 3 until piece measures 1½"/4 cm from beginning of
  armhole shaping, ending with a WS
  row. *Do not fasten off.*

THE LEFT SHOULDER

- Continue working in pattern over the
  first 11 sts until piece measures 11"/28
  cm from the bottom edge, ending on a
  RS row. Fasten off.

THE RIGHT SHOULDER

- With RS facing, skip 18 sts from left
  shoulder, join yarn with slip st in next
  st, ch 2, hdc in same st; work in pattern
  across remaining 10 sts. *You now have*
  11 sts. Continue in pattern until piece
  measures the same as left shoulder,
  ending with a RS row. Fasten off.

CROCHETING THE BACK

- Work same as front through armhole
  shaping.

- Work even until piece measures
  11½"/29 cm, or 3 rows less than front.

- **Last Row:** Ch 2, hdc in next 11 hdc, slip
  st in next 18 sts, ch 2, hdc in last 11 hdc.
  Fasten off.

- With RS together, sew front to back at
  shoulder and side seams, leaving neck
  and armholes open.

FINISHING

ARMHOLE EDGINGS

- With RS facing and smaller hook,
  attach yarn at underarm seam.

- **Rnd 1:** Ch 1, sc evenly around armhole,
  do not join. Pm in the first st of the rnd
  and move it up as you work the rnds.

- **Rnd 2:** Sc in each sc around, placing sc2tog at each of the two underarm corners.

- **Rnd 3:** Repeat Rnd 2, slip st to next sc. Fasten off.

- Repeat for other armhole.

NECKBAND

- With RS facing and smaller hook, attach yarn to center of back neck, ch 1, sc evenly around neckline, placing sc2tog at each of the four inside corners, join with slip st to first sc. Fasten off.

- Weave in ends. Block.

HANDSOME BOY'S VEST

Kimono Shell Sweater

DESIGNED BY *Laura Hontz*

With or without the shell edging, this darling kimono will suit any baby — boy or girl. Snaps are used for closures.

SIZE AND FINISHED MEASUREMENTS
To fit 3–6 months, 18½"/47 cm chest circumference

YARN
Sirdar Crofter DK, 60% acrylic/25% cotton/15% wool, 184 yds (170 m)/1.75 oz (50 g), Color 0033 Hepburn **(3)**

CROCHET HOOK
US G/6 (4 mm) *or size needed to obtain correct gauge*

GAUGE
16 stitches and 12 rows = 4"/10 cm in half double crochet

OTHER SUPPLIES
Yarn needle, sewing needle and coordinating thread, two snaps

PATTERN ESSENTIALS

Fhdc (foundation half double crochet) *Yo, insert hook into ch at base of previous st, yo and pull up loop, yo and draw through 1 loop (chain made), yo and pull through 3 loops (half double crochet made). Repeat from * for desired length. **Note:** This method is for adding stitches onto existing crochet work.

CROCHETING THE SWEATER

THE BACK

- Chain 39.

- **Set-Up Row (WS):** Hdc in 3rd ch from hook, hdc in each ch across, turn. *You now have* 37 hdc.

- **Rows 1–10:** Ch 2 (does not count as hdc here and throughout), hdc in each hdc across, turn.

- **Row 11 (RS):** Ch 2, hdc in each hdc across; ch 25, turn.

THE SLEEVES

- **Row 12 (WS):** Hdc in 3rd ch from hook and in next 22 ch, hdc in each hdc across back, fhdc 23 at end of row, turn. *You now have* 83 hdc.

- **Rows 13–20:** Ch 2, hdc in each hdc across, turn.

THE RIGHT FRONT

- **Row 1 (RS):** Ch 2, hdc in next 35 sts, turn, leaving remaining sts unworked. *You now have* 35 hdc.

- **Row 2:** Ch 2, hdc in each hdc across, turn.

- **Row 3:** Ch 2, hdc in each st to last st, 2 hdc in last st, turn. *You now have* 36 hdc.

- **Rows 4–7:** Repeat Rows 2 and 3 twice. *You now have* 38 hdc.

- **Row 8:** Ch 2, hdc in next 16 hdc, turn, leaving remaining sleeve sts unworked. *You now have* 16 hdc.

- **Row 9:** Repeat Row 3. *You now have* 17 hdc.

- **Rows 10–19:** Repeat Rows 2 and 3 five times. *You now have* 22 hdc.

- **Row 20:** Repeat Row 2.

- Fasten off.

THE LEFT FRONT

- With RS facing, skip 13 back neck sts, join yarn with slip st in next st.

- **Rows 1 and 2:** Ch 2, hdc in each hdc across, turn. *You now have* 35 hdc.

- **Row 3 (RS):** Ch 2, 2 hdc in first st, hdc in each st across, turn. *You now have* 36 hdc.

- **Row 4:** Ch 2, hdc in each hdc across, turn.

- **Rows 5 and 6:** Repeat Rows 3 and 4. *You now have* 37 hdc.

- **Row 7:** Repeat Row 3. *You now have* 38 hdc. Fasten off.

- **Row 8:** Skip first 23 sts, join yarn in next st, ch 2, hdc in same st, hdc in each st across, turn. *You now have* 15 hdc.

- **Row 9:** Ch 2, 2 hdc in first st, hdc in each st across, turn. *You now have* 16 hdc.

- **Row 10:** Ch 2, hdc in each hdc across, turn.

- **Row 11:** Ch 2, 2 hdc in first dc, hdc in each hdc across, turn. *You now have* 17 hdc.

- **Rows 12–19:** Repeat Rows 10 and 11 four times.

- **Row 20:** Repeat Row 10. Fasten off.

- Fold sweater in half at shoulders. Sew sleeve and side seams.

CROCHETING THE SHELL EDGING

- With RS facing, join yarn to lower right front edge at right underarm seam. Ch 1, counting each row end as st, *skip next st, 5 dc in next st, skip next st, slip st in next st; repeat from * across row, up right front of sweater, around neck edge, down left side of sweater, and across bottom of left side front, slip st in last st. Fasten off.

FINISHING

- Fold right front over left front. With sewing needle and thread, sew one snap near lower edge of sweater and another at bottom of the V.

KIMONO SHELL SWEATER

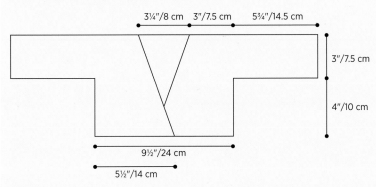

3¼"/8 cm 3"/7.5 cm 5¾"/14.5 cm

3"/7.5 cm

4"/10 cm

9½"/24 cm

5½"/14 cm

Prism Pinafore

DESIGNED BY *Edie Eckman*

Colorful variegated yarn creates cheerful stripes in this seamless baby dress. The skirt is worked first in side-to-side rows, then joined. Work the bodice from the skirt up to the neck, and add three cute buttons to finish it off.

....

SIZE AND FINISHED MEASUREMENTS
To fit 3–6 months: 17"/43 cm chest circumference and 12"/30.5 cm length

....

YARN
Wisdom Yarns Poems Socks, 75% superwash wool, 25% nylon, 459 yds (420 m)/3.5 oz (100 g), Color 960 Cotton Candy **①**

....

CROCHET HOOKS
US H/8 (5 mm) and US 7 (4.5 mm) *or size needed to obtain correct gauge*

....

GAUGE
18 stitches and 10 rows = 4"/10 cm in back loop double crochet with smaller hook

....

OTHER SUPPLIES
Stitch markers, yarn needle, sewing needle and coordinating thread, three ½"/13 mm buttons

PATTERN ESSENTIALS
....

Button loop (Sc, ch 3, slip st) in same st.

CROCHETING THE SKIRT

- With larger hook, ch 38.

- **Row 1 (WS):** With smaller hook and working in back bumps of chain (see page 276), dc in 3rd ch from hook and in each ch across, turn. *You now have* 36 dc.

- **Row 2:** Ch 3 (counts as dc here and throughout), BLdc in next 17 sts, BLhdc in next 14 sts, BLsc in next 5 sts, turn.

- **Row 3:** Ch 3, BLdc in each st across, turn.

- Repeat Rows 2 and 3 twenty-six times, then work Row 2 once more.
- Fold skirt with RS together.
- **Joining Row:** Ch 1 and, working through double thickness in both loops of foundation ch and both loops of last row, sc in each st across.
- *You now have* 56 rows (28 ridges).

CROCHETING THE BODICE

- Turn skirt right side out and arrange seam at center back. Place marker at center front on top edge.
- **Rnd 1 (RS):** Working along side edge of skirt rows/ridges, join yarn by working standing hdc at center front, hdc in side of next row, ch 1, (hdc in next 2 rows, ch 1) around, join with slip st to top of first hdc. *You now have* 56 hdc and 28 ch-spaces.
- **Rnd 2:** Ch 3, dc in each hdc and ch-1 space around, join with slip st to top of ch-3. *You now have* 84 sts.

THE ARMHOLES

- **Row 1 (RS):** Ch 3, dc in next 18 dc, ch 23 loosely, skip next 4 dc, dc in next 38 dc, ch 23 loosely, skip next 4 dc, dc in last 19 sts; *do not join*, turn. *You now have* 76 sts and 2 ch-23 loops.

Note: On Row 2, work into back bumps of ch sts.

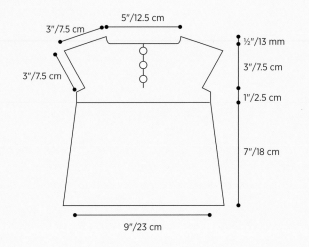

PRISM PINAFORE

5"/12.5 cm
3"/7.5 cm
3"/7.5 cm
½"/13 mm
3"/7.5 cm
1"/2.5 cm
7"/18 cm
9"/23 cm

- **Row 2 (WS):** Ch 2 (counts as dc here and throughout), dc in next 16 dc, *dc3tog over next 2 dc and next ch, pm in st just made, dc in next 21 ch, dc3tog over next ch and next 2 dc, pm in st just made*, dc in next 34 dc, repeat from * to * once, dc in last 17 dc, turn. *You now have* 114 sts.
- **Rows 3–6:** Ch 2, *dc in each dc to 1 st before marked st, dc3tog over next 3 sts, moving marker to new st; repeat from * three times, dc in each dc to end, turn. *You will have* 82 sts at the end of Row 6.
- **Row 7:** Ch 2, *dc in each dc to 1 st before marked st, dc4tog over next 4 sts, moving marker to new st, dc in each st to 2 sts before marked st, dc4tog over next 4 sts, moving marker to new st; repeat from * once more, dc in each st to end, turn. *You now have* 70 sts.
- **Row 8:** Removing markers as you come to them, ch 1, *sc in each dc to marked st, (sc2tog) five times; repeat from * once, sc in each dc to end, turn. *You now have* 60 sts.

CROCHETING THE EDGING

- **Rnd 1 (RS):** Ch 1, sc in each sc across, placing 3 sc in corner of left front neck; work 11 sc evenly down left edge of front placket; working a total of 11 sc up right edge of front placket, work (2 sc, button loop) three times, work 2 sc, ending with 2 sc in same place as first sc, join with slip st to first sc.
- **Rnd 2:** Ch 1, sc in each sc across neck edge to top left neck. Fasten off.
- Weave in ends. Sew buttons to left front placket opposite button loops.

Vintage Bluebell Sacque

DESIGNED BY *Michele DuNaier, MAD Cap Fancies*

Crocheted from the top down, this jacket is worked with basic crochet stitches along with shell and fan combinations. The ribbons are both decorative and utile — they keep the jacket closed in a baby-safe fashion.

SIZE AND FINISHED MEASUREMENTS
To fit 6–12 months: 21"/53.5 cm chest circumference

YARN
Lion Brand Baby Soft, 60% acrylic/40% nylon, 459 yds (420 m)/5 oz (142 g), Color 106 Pastel Blue **(3)**

CROCHET HOOKS
US I/9 (5.5 mm) *or size needed to obtain correct gauge* and US H/8 (5 mm)

GAUGE
16 stitches = 4"/10 cm in double crochet with larger hook
3 shells and 7 rows = 3"/7.5 cm in body pattern

OTHER SUPPLIES
Stitch markers, yarn needle, 2½ yds/2.3 m of ¼"/6 mm satin ribbon, two purchased satin flowers (optional), sewing needle and coordinating thread for attaching the optional flowers

PATTERN ESSENTIALS

Fan [(Dc, ch 1) four times, dc] in 1 stitch or space.
Shell (Hdc, dc, ch 1, dc, hdc) in 1 stitch or space.

CROCHETING THE SACQUE

THE YOKE

- Using larger hook, ch 56.

- **Row 1 (WS):** Sc in 2nd ch from hook, *2 sc in next ch, sc in next 2 ch; repeat from * across, turn. *You now have* 73 sc.

- **Row 2:** Ch 3 (counts as dc here and throughout), pm to indicate RS; dc in each sc across, turn.

- **Row 3:** Ch 1, *sc in next 3 dc, 2 sc in next dc; repeat from * to last st, sc in turning ch, turn. *You now have* 91 sc.

- **Row 4:** Repeat Row 2.

- **Row 5:** Ch 1, sc in first dc, *2 sc in next sc, sc in next 4 dc; repeat from * across, turn. *You now have* 109 sc.

- **Row 6:** Ch 4, skip first 3 sc, slip st in next sc, (ch 4, skip 2 sc, slip st in next sc) 35 times, turn. *You now have* 36 ch-spaces.

- **Row 7:** Ch 4, slip st in first ch-space, (ch 4, slip st in next ch-space) to last ch-space, (ch 4, slip st) twice in last ch-space, turn. *You now have* 37 ch-spaces.

- **Row 8:** Ch 1, slip st in first ch-space, (ch 2, dc, ch 1, dc, hdc) in first ch-space (counts as first shell), shell in each ch-space across, turn. *You now have* 37 shells.

- Pm in shells 6, 14, 24, and 32; leave markers in place through sleeve section.

- **Row 9:** Ch 2, shell in each of next 5 ch-1 spaces, shell in ch-1 space of first marked shell, ch 7, skip 7 shells for armhole, shell in ch-1 space of 2nd marked shell, shell in each of next 9 ch-1 spaces, shell in ch-1 space of 3rd marked shell, ch 7, skip 7 shells for armhole, shell in ch-1 space of 4th marked shell, shell in each of next 5 ch-1 spaces, hdc in turning ch, turn. *You now have 23 shells and 2 ch-7 spaces.*

THE BODY

- Expand shells by adding a ch-space between them as follows.
- **Row 1:** Ch 3, (shell, ch 1) in each ch-1 space to next ch-7 space, *skip first ch, (shell in next ch, ch 1, skip 1 ch) three times**, (shell, ch 1) in each ch-1 space to next ch-7 space, repeat from * to ** once, (shell, ch 1) in each of next 5 ch-1 spaces, shell in ch-1 space of last shell, dc in turning ch, turn. *You now have 29 shells.*

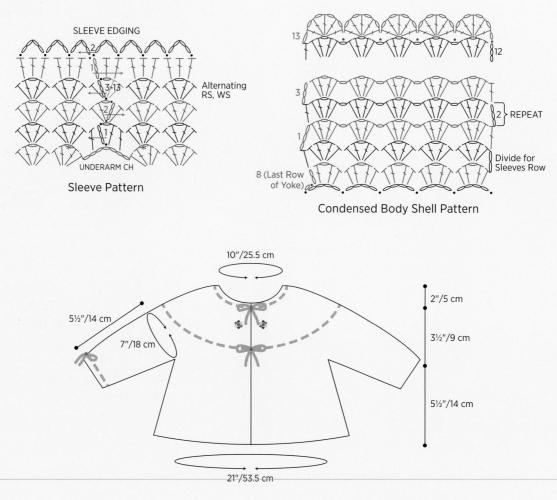

VINTAGE BLUEBELL SACQUE

SLEEVE EDGING

Alternating RS, WS

UNDERARM CH

Sleeve Pattern

REPEAT

Divide for Sleeves Row

8 (Last Row of Yoke)

Condensed Body Shell Pattern

10"/25.5 cm

5½"/14 cm

7"/18 cm

2"/5 cm

3½"/9 cm

5½"/14 cm

21"/53.5 cm

- **Row 2:** Ch 3, (shell in ch-1 space of shell, ch 1, skip next ch-1 space) across to last shell, shell in ch-1 space of last shell, dc in turning ch, turn.

- **Rows 3–12:** Repeat Row 2. *You now have 14 rows of shells, counting the 2 rows done in yoke section.*

- **Row 13:** Ch 1, fan in ch-1 space of first shell, (slip st in ch-1 space between shells, fan in ch-1 space of next shell) across row, ch 1, slip st in turning chain, turn. *You now have 29 fans. Do not fasten off.*

THE BODY EDGING

- Change to smaller hook.

- **Row 1:** With yarn still attached at lower right-hand corner, pivot to work in the sides of rows up right side of front; work 30 sc evenly spaced up right side of front, (sc, ch 2, 2 dc) in right corner of neck; working in unused loops of starting chain, (ch 1, dc2tog over 2 ch) 27 times around neck, ch 1, (2 dc, ch 2, sc) in left corner of neck; work 30 sc evenly spaced down left side of front, ending in left corner at end of body Row 12, turn.

- **Row 2:** Ch 4, skip 1 sc, slip st in next sc, (ch 4, skip 1 sc, slip st in next sc) up left front to left neck corner, ch 4, skip 1 dc, slip st in next dc, (skip next ch-space, slip st in next dc, ch 4) across neck to right neck corner, slip st in neck corner, ch 4 around corner, skip 1 sc, slip st in next sc, (ch 4, skip 1 sc, slip st in next sc) down right front, ending at start of body edging Row 1. Fasten off.

CROCHETING THE SLEEVES (MAKE 2)

You should still have two markers under each armhole.

- **Row 1 (WS):** With larger hook, join yarn with slip st under armhole at center ch of the ch-7, ch 3, skip 1 ch, dc in next ch, shell in ch-1 space of next marked shell, (shell in ch-1 space of next 7 shells around armhole, shell in ch-1 space of other marked shell, skip next ch, dc in next ch, dc in same ch as beginning slip st, ch 1, join with slip st to 3rd ch of beginning ch-3, turn. *You now have 9 shells and 4 dc.*

- **Row 2:** Ch 1, (Slip st, ch 3, hdc) in first ch-1 space (*half shell made*), shell in ch-1 space of next 9 shells around armhole, (hdc, dc) in same place as beginning half shell, ch 1, join with a slip st to top of beginning ch-3 to complete the shell, turn. *You now have 10 shells.*

- **Row 3–13:** Repeat Row 2.

THE SLEEVE EDGING

- Change to smaller hook.

- **Row 1 (RS):** Ch 3, dc in next ch-1 space, (dc in next dc, skip 2 hdc, dc in next dc, dc in next ch-space) around, ending dc in next dc, skip 2 hdc, join with slip st to top of ch-3, turn. *You now have 30 dc.*

- **Row 2:** (Ch 4, skip 1 dc, slip st in next dc) around to last 2 sts, ch 4, skip 1 dc, slip st in first slip st. *You now have 15 ch-spaces.*

- Fasten off.

FINISHING

- Remove markers. Weave in ends. Block.

- Weave ribbon through body edging Row 1 (at neck only), Row 6 of the yoke, and Row 1 of the sleeve edging (on both sleeves), and tie into a bow.

- With sewing needle and thread, tack ribbon down in several places to prevent baby from pulling it out.

- Sew rosettes on yoke as pictured, if desired.

Pinwheel Vest

DESIGNED BY *Lorna Miser, Lorna Miser Designs*

This clever design uses a full circle motif for the back and two half circles for the front. Tied with a simple ribbon bow, this vest will become a favorite.

SIZE AND FINISHED MEASUREMENTS
To fit 6–18 months: 20"/51 cm chest circumference and 10"/25.5 cm length

YARN
Cascade Yarns Pinwheel, 100% acrylic, 440 yds (400 m)/7 oz (200 g), Color 16 Grapes (4)

CROCHET HOOK
US I/9 (5.5 mm) *or size needed to obtain correct gauge*

GAUGE
First 3 rounds of back = 3½"/9 cm in diameter

OTHER SUPPLIES
Stitch markers, yarn needle, 1 yd (1 m) of ⅜"/9.5 mm satin ribbon

CROCHETING THE VEST

THE BACK

- Ch 4, join with slip st to form a ring.
- **Rnd 1:** Ch 3 (counts as dc here and throughout), 12 dc in ring, join with slip st to top of ch-3. *You now have 13 sts.*
- **Rnd 2:** Ch 4 (counts as dc and ch 1), *dc in next st, ch 1; repeat from * around, join with slip st to 3rd ch of beginning ch-4.

- **Rnd 3:** Ch 6 (counts as dc and ch 3), *dc in next st, ch 3; repeat from * around, join with slip st to 3rd ch of beginning ch-6.
- **Rnd 4:** Slip st in next ch-1 space, ch 3, 2 dc in same space, ch 2, *3 dc in next space, ch 2; repeat from * around, join with slip st to top of beginning ch-3.
- **Rnd 5:** Slip st in next dc, ch 6, dc in next space, ch 3, *skip 1 dc, dc in next dc, ch 3, dc in next space, ch 3; repeat from * around, join with slip st to 3rd ch of beginning ch-6. *You now have 26 sts and 26 spaces.*
- **Rnd 6:** Ch 3, 2 dc in next space, *dc in next st, 2 dc in next space; repeat from * around, join with slip st to top of beginning ch-3. *You now have 78 sts.*

- **Rnd 7:** Ch 5 (counts as dc and ch 2), skip 1 dc, *dc in next dc, skip 1 dc, ch 2; repeat from * around, join with slip st to 3rd ch of beginning ch-5.

- **Rnd 8:** Slip st in next space, ch 3, dc in same space, ch 1, (2 dc, ch 1) in each space around, join with slip st to top of beginning ch-3.

- **Rnd 9:** Slip st in next space, ch 3, 2 dc in same space, 3 dc in each space around, join with slip st to top of beginning ch-3. *You now have* 117 sts.

- **Rnd 10 (squaring rnd):** Ch 1, sc in first 3 sts, *hdc in next 3 sts, dc in next 3 sts, tr in next 3 sts, dtr in next 3 sts, ch 5, dtr in next 3 sts, ch 5, dtr in next 3 sts, tr in next 3 sts, dc in next 3 sts, hdc in next 3 sts**, sc in next 6 sts; repeat from * around, ending last repeat at **. (This final side becomes the neck edge of the back.)

- **Rnd 11:** Ch 3, dc in each st around, working (3 dc, ch 3, 3 dc) in each ch-5 corner space, join with slip st to top of beginning ch-3. Pm in 11th dc to right of top left-hand corner and to left of top-right-hand corner spaces.

PINWHEEL VEST

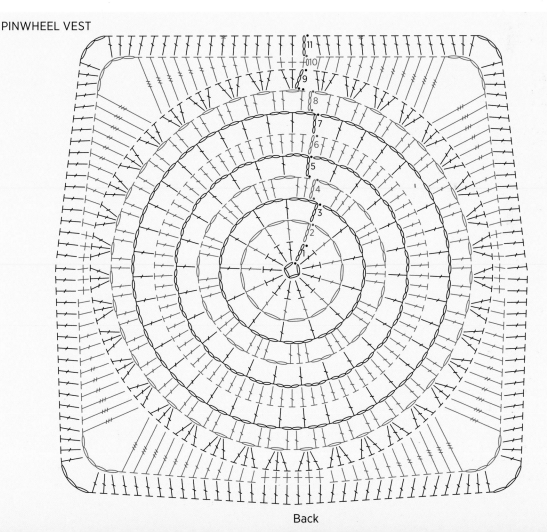

Back

THE RIGHT FRONT

- Ch 4, join with slip st to form a ring.

- **Row 1 (RS):** Ch 3 (counts as dc here and throughout), 6 dc in ring, turn. *You now have* 7 sts.

- **Row 2:** Ch 4 (counts as dc and ch 1), *dc in next st, ch 1; repeat from * to last st, dc in top of turning chain, turn. *You now have* 6 ch-1 spaces.

- **Row 3:** Ch 6 (counts as dc and ch 3), *dc in next st, ch 3; repeat from * to last st, dc in 3rd ch of turning ch, turn. *You now have* 6 ch-3 spaces.

- **Row 4:** Ch 5 (counts as dc and ch 2), *3 dc in next space, ch 2; repeat from *

to last st, dc in 3rd ch of turning ch, turn. *You now have* 20 dc and 7 ch-2 spaces.

- **Row 5:** Ch 3, dc in next space, *ch 3, skip 1 dc, dc in next dc, ch 3, dc in next space; repeat from * to last st, dc in top of turning ch, turn. *You now have* 12 ch-3 spaces.

- **Row 6:** Ch 3, dc in next dc, *2 dc in next space, dc in next dc; repeat from * across, ending with last dc in top of turning ch, turn. *You now have* 39 sts.

- **Row 7:** Ch 5 (counts as dc and ch 2), skip 1 dc, *dc in next dc, skip 1 dc, ch 2; repeat from * to last st, dc in top of turning ch, turn. *You now have* 20 dc and 19 ch-2 spaces.

- **Row 8:** Ch 4 (counts as dc and ch 1), (2 dc, ch 1) in each space across to last st, dc in top of turning ch, turn. *You now have* 40 dc and 20 ch-1 spaces.

- **Row 9:** Ch 3, skip first space, 3 dc in each space to across last space, skip last space, dc in 3rd ch of turning ch, turn. *You now have* 56 sts.

- **Row 10 (squaring for shoulder):** Ch 1, *sc in next 3 sts, hdc in next 3 sts, dc in next 3 sts, tr in next 3 sts, ch 1, 3 sc around the post of last tr made, sc in each st across, turn.

- **Row 11:** Ch 3, dc in next 43 sts, skip next sc, slip st in next sc worked in side of tr, slip st in next sc. *Do not fasten off.*

Join the Shoulder

- Holding right front and back with RS together and working through both layers, starting in row-end sc on right front and marked dc in top edge of back, slip st shoulder sts together. *Do not fasten off.*

Join the Right Side Edge

- With RS facing, work 40 slip sts evenly spaced across left side edge of right front.

- With RS of right front and back together and working through double thickness, slip st in each of next 20 sts. *Do not fasten off.*

Shape the Right Armhole

- Turn body RS out.

- Ch 3, dc in each st around armhole, join with slip st to top of beginning ch-3. *You now have* 40 sts. Fasten off.

PINWHEEL VEST

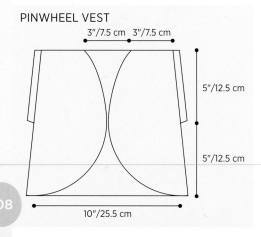

3"/7.5 cm 3"/7.5 cm

5"/12.5 cm

5"/12.5 cm

10"/25.5 cm

THE LEFT FRONT

- Work same as right front through Row 9.

- Row 10 (squaring for shoulder, WS): Ch 1, sc in each st across to last 11 sts, ch 3 (counts as tr), tr in next 2 sts, dc in next 3 sts, hdc in next 3 sts, sc in next 3 sts, turn.

Join the Shoulder

- Row 11: Holding left front and back with RS together and working through both layers, ch 1, slip st in each of next 12 sts to marker on back left shoulder; working through single layer of left front only, sc in next ch-3 space, dc in

each st across to beginning of Row 10 (bottom corner). *Do not fasten off.*

Join the Left Side Edge

- Work 40 slip sts evenly spaced across right side edge of left front. Fasten off.

- With RS of left front and back together, join yarn with slip st at bottom edge and working through double thickness, slip st in each of next 19 sts. *Do not fasten off.*

Shape the Left Armhole

- Work as for right armhole.

FINISHING

- Weave in ends. Cut ribbon in half and tie one end of each half to each side at the center front.

PINWHEEL VEST

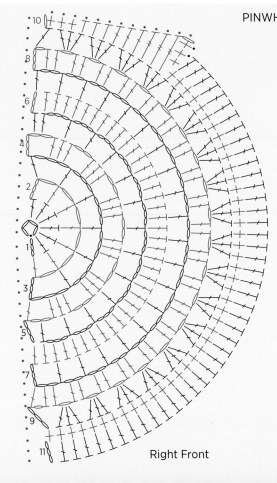

Right Front

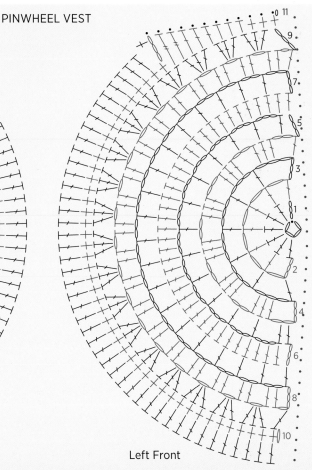

Left Front

Boy's Cardigan

DESIGNED BY *Annelies Baes*

This trendy little cardigan is worked in separate pieces and seamed. The entire cardigan is worked in a crocheted version of Moss Stitch. Make a girl's version with a simple change of color and buttons.

SIZE AND FINISHED MEASUREMENTS
To fit 6–12 months: 22"/56 cm chest circumference

YARN
Schoppel-Wolle Admiral Stärke 6, 75% virgin wool/25% nylon, 437 yds (400 m)/5.3 oz (150 g), Color 6601 Marsgrün

CROCHET HOOK
US E/4 (3.5 mm) *or size needed to obtain correct gauge*

GAUGE
18 stitches and 17 rows = 4"/10 cm in Moss Stitch

OTHER SUPPLIES
Stitch markers or contrasting thread, yarn needle, four ⅞"/22 mm buttons, sewing needle and coordinating thread

CROCHETING THE CARDIGAN

THE BACK

- Chain 51.
- **Row 1 (RS):** Work Row 1 of Moss Stitch. *You now have* 50 sts.
- **Rows 2–28:** Work Row 2 of Moss Stitch.
- Fasten off.

Shape the Armhole

- **Row 29 (RS):** Skip 6 sts, slip st to join yarn in next st, ch 2, work in pattern across to last 6 sts, turn, leaving remaining sts unworked. *You now have* 38 sts.
- **Rows 30–47:** Work Row 2 of Moss Stitch.
- Fasten off.

THE LEFT FRONT

- Chain 27.
- **Row 1 (RS):** Work Row 1 of Moss Stitch. *You now have* 26 sts.
- **Rows 2–28:** Work Row 2 of Moss Stitch.
- Fasten off.

Shape the Armhole and Neck

- **Row 29 (RS):** Skip 6 sts, slip st in next st, ch 2, work in pattern across to last st, turn, leaving last st unworked. *You now have* 19 sts.
- **Row 30:** Ch 1, work in pattern across, turn.
- **Row 31:** Ch 2, work in pattern to last st, turn, leaving last st unworked. *You now have* 18 sts.
- **Row 32:** Ch 2, work in pattern to end of row, turn.
- **Row 33:** Ch 2, work in pattern to last 2 sts, sc in next sc, turn, leaving last st unworked. *You now have* 17 sts.
- **Rows 34–45:** Repeat Rows 30–33 three times. *You will have* 11 sts at the end of Row 45.
- **Rows 46 and 47:** Repeat Rows 30 and 31. *You will have* 10 sts at the end of Row 47. Fasten off.

PATTERN ESSENTIALS

Moss Stitch (worked over an even number of sts)

Row 1: Sc in 3rd ch from hook (beginning ch-2 counts as dc), *dc in next ch, sc in next ch; repeat from * across, turn.

Row 2: Ch 2 (counts as dc throughout), sc in next dc, *dc in next sc, sc in next dc; repeat from * across, turn.

Repeat Row 2 for pattern, working 1 sc in each dc and 1 dc in each sc.

BOY'S CARDIGAN

Condensed Moss Stitch Pattern in Rows

THE RIGHT FRONT

- **Rows 1–27:** Work as for left front. Do not fasten off at end of last row.

Shape the Armhole and Neck

- **Row 28 (WS):** Ch 2, work in pattern to last 2 sts, sc in next sc, turn, leaving last st unworked. *You now have* 25 sts.
- **Row 29:** Ch 1, work in pattern to last 6 sts, turn, leaving last 6 sts unworked. *You now have* 19 sts.
- **Rows 30-44:** Work as for left front Rows 31–45. *You now have* 11 sts.
- **Row 45:** Ch 1, work in pattern to end of row, turn.
- **Row 46:** Ch 2, work in pattern to last st, skip last st, turn. *You now have* 10 sts.
- **Row 47:** Ch 1, work in pattern to end of row, turn.

THE SLEEVES (MAKE 2)

- Ch 36, join with slip st to first ch to form a ring.

- **Rnd 1:** Ch 1, sc in first ch, dc in next ch, *sc in next ch, dc in next ch; repeat from * around, join with slip st to first sc, turn. *You now have* 36 sts.

- **Rnd 2:** Ch 2 (counts as dc here and throughout), sc in next dc, *dc in next sc, sc in next dc; repeat from * around, join with slip st to top of ch-2, turn.

- **Rnd 3:** Ch 1, sc in first st, dc in next sc, *sc in next dc, dc in next sc; repeat from * around, join with slip st to first sc, turn.

- **Rnd 4:** Repeat Rnd 2.

- **Rnd 5 (increase rnd):** Ch 2, sc in first dc, *dc in next sc, sc in next dc; repeat from * to last st, (dc, sc) in last sc, join with slip st to top of ch-2, turn. *You now have* 38 sts.

- **Rnd 6:** Repeat Rnd 3.

- **Rnds 7 and 8:** Repeat Rnds 2 and 3.

- **Rnd 9 (increase rnd):** Ch 1, (sc, dc) in first st, *sc in next dc, dc in next sc; repeat from * to last st, (sc, dc) in last dc, join with slip st to first sc, turn. *You now have* 40 sts.

- **Rnd 10:** Ch 2, *sc in next dc, dc in next sc; repeat from * to end of rnd, join with slip st to top of ch-2, turn.

- **Rnd 11 (increase rnd):** Repeat Rnd 5. *You now have* 42 sts.

Begin working back and forth in rows.

- **Row 12:** Ch 2 (counts as 1 dc), sc in same st, *dc in next sc, sc in next dc; repeat from * to last st, (dc, sc) in last st, *do not join*, turn. *You now have* 44 sts.

- **Row 13:** Ch 2, sc in next dc, *dc in next sc, sc in next dc; repeat from * across, turn.

- **Rnd 14:** Repeat Rnd 13. Fasten off, leaving a 24"/61 cm tail for sewing.

ASSEMBLING THE PIECES

- Place left front and back together with RS together. Join side and shoulder seams with slip st. Repeat for right front.

- Mark center of sleeves with stitch marker or colored thread. Place one sleeve into armhole with RS together, aligning unjoined rnds of sleeve with body underarm shaping (6 skipped sts on front and back) and sleeve center with shoulder seam; join seams with slip st. Repeat for second sleeve.

- Working across foundation ch edge of sleeve, work 1 rnd of slip st, join with slip st. Fasten off.

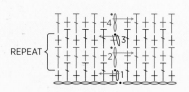

REPEAT

Abbreviated Moss Stitch Pattern
in Rnds for Sleeves

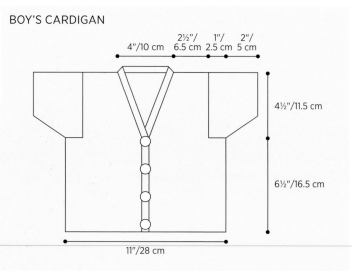

BOY'S CARDIGAN

4"/10 cm   2½"/ 6.5 cm   1"/ 2.5 cm   2"/ 5 cm

4½"/11.5 cm

6½"/16.5 cm

11"/28 cm

CROCHETING THE FRONT BANDS

- **Row 1:** With RS facing, join yarn with slip st to bottom of right front, ch 1; sc evenly around right front, neck, and left front, placing 1 sc in each row or st, turn.

- **Row 2:** Ch 1, BLsc in first sc, FLsc in next sc, *BLsc in next sc, FLsc in next sc; repeat from * across, turn. **Note:** It does not make a difference if you end with BLsc or FLsc; you always start with BLsc.

- **Row 3:** Repeat Row 2, beginning with BLsc, turn.

If you are making this cardigan for a boy, make the buttonholes on the left front, if you are making this cardigan for a girl, make them on the right front; instructions written below are for a boy's cardigan.

- **Row 4 (buttonhole row):** Ch 1, BLsc in first sc, FLsc in next sc, *ch 2, skip 2 sc, (BLsc in next sc, FLsc in next sc) three times; repeat from * three more times; work remainder of row in pattern: (BLsc, FLsc) across, turn.

- **Row 5:** Repeat Row 2, working pattern sts in buttonhole ch-spaces. At the end of the row, turn work 90° to work along bottom edge.

- **Last Row:** Ch 1, slip st in each st along lower edge. Fasten off.

FINISHING

- Weave in ends. Block cardigan and allow to dry. Sew on buttons opposite buttonholes.

Rosetta Cardigan

DESIGNED BY *Annelies Baes*

Rosetta Cardigan is presented in three sizes so you can keep your little girl in fashion from six months to two years of age. Raglan sleeves and eyelet-and-lace trimmings make it fancy enough for solid yarn, too. It is worked without seams, from the top down.

SIZES AND FINISHED MEASUREMENTS

To fit 0–6 (6–12, 12–24) months: 20 (22½, 26½)"/51 (57, 67.5) cm chest circumference. Sample shown is size 6–12 months.

YARN

Schoppel Wolle Zauberball Stärke 6, 75% virgin wool/25% nylon, 437 yds (400 m)/5.3 oz (150 g), Color 2079 By the Flower ③

CROCHET HOOK

US E/4 (3.5 mm) *or size needed to obtain correct gauge*

GAUGE

20 stitches and 16 rows = 4"/10 cm in half double crochets

OTHER SUPPLIES

Yarn needle, stitch markers, four ⅝"/16 mm buttons, sewing needle and coordinating thread

PATTERN ESSENTIALS

HdcV-st (half double crochet V-stitch) (Hdc, ch 1, hdc) in 1 stitch or space.

CROCHETING THE CARDIGAN

THE YOKE

- Chain 44 (48, 50).

- **Row 1 (RS):** HdcV-st in 3rd ch from hook, hdc in next 7 (8, 8) ch, hdcV-st in next ch, hdc in next 24 (26, 28) ch, hdcV-st in next ch, hdc in next 7 (8, 8) ch, hdcV-st in last ch, turn. *You now have 46 (50, 52) hdc and 4 ch-spaces.*

- **Row 2:** Ch 2 (does not count as st here and throughout), 2 hdc in first hdc, hdcV-st in next ch-space, hdc in next 9 (10, 10) hdc, hdcV-st in next ch-space, hdc in next 26 (28, 30) hdc, hdcV-st in next ch-space, hdc in next 9 (10, 10) hdc, hdcV-st in next ch-space, 2 hdc in last hdc, turn. *You now have 56 (60, 62) hdc and 4 ch-spaces.*

Note: From now on, work hdcV-st in every ch-space and 1 hdc in every hdc unless otherwise indicated.

- **Rows 3–13 (15, 18):** Ch 2, 2 hdc in first hdc, *hdc in each hdc across to next ch space, hdcV-st in next space; repeat from * three times, hdc in each hdc across to last hdc, 2 hdc in last hdc, turn. *You now have 166 (190, 222) hdc and 4 ch-spaces.*

Separate the Sleeves

Note: Discontinue increasing sts at the beginning and end of rows for the V-neck. Sleeves will be separated, and you will continue working on the both fronts and back.

Size 0–6 months only

- **Row 14 (WS):** Ch 2, hdc in next 25 hdc for right front, *yo, insert hook into next ch-space and pull up a loop, skip next 33 sleeve sts, yo, insert hook into next ch-space and pull up a loop, yo and pull through all 5 loops on hook (*hdc2tog made*)**; hdc2tog, hdc in next 46 hdc, hdc2tog; repeat from * to ** once, hdc in last 25 hdc for left front, turn. *You now have 100 hdc.*

- **Row 15:** Ch 2, hdc in each hdc across, turn.

- **Rows 16–29:** Repeat Row 15. At end of Row 29, do not fasten off; do not turn.

Size 6–12 months only

- **Row 16 (WS):** Ch 2, hdc in next 29 hdc for right front, *yo, insert hook in next ch-space and pull up a loop, skip next 38 sleeve sts, yo, insert hook in next ch-space and pull up a loop, yo and pull through all 5 loops on hook (*hdc2tog made*)**; hdc2tog, hdc in next 52 hdc, hdc2tog; repeat from * to ** once; hdc in last 29 hdc for left front, turn. *You now have 114 hdc.*

- **Row 17:** Ch 2, hdc in each hdc across, turn.

- **Rows 18–33:** Repeat Row 17. At end of Row 33, *do not fasten off; do not turn.*

Size 12–24 months only

- **Row 19 (RS):** Ch 2, hdc in next 35 hdc for left front, *yo, insert hook in next ch-space and pull up a loop, skip 44 next sleeve sts, yo, insert hook in next ch-space and pull up a loop, yo and pull through all 5 loops on hook**; hdc2tog, hdc in next 60 hdc, hdc2tog; repeat from * to ** once, hdc in last 35 hdc for right front, turn. *You now have* 134 hdc.

- **Row 20:** Ch 2, hdc in each hdc across, turn.

- **Rows 21–41:** Repeat Row 20. At end of Row 41, *do not fasten off; do not turn.*

CROCHETING THE EDGINGS

THE FRONT AND NECK EDGING

All sizes

- With RS facing, turn 90° to work across right front edging.

- **Row 1 (WS):** Ch 2, 2 hdc in front edging just made; along bottom edge work (2 hdc in next hdc) 98 times, hdc in last 2 hdc; 2 hdc in front edging, turn. *You now have* 201 hdc.

- **Row 2 (eyelet row, WS):** Ch 2, hdc in first st, ch 2, skip next st, *hdc in next st, ch 2, skip 1 hdc; repeat from * across right front edge, back neck edge, and down left front edge, ending hdc in last st. Do not fasten off; do not turn.

THE BOTTOM EDGING

- Turn garment to work across bottom edge.

Size 0–6 months only

- **Row 1 (WS):** Ch 2, 2 hdc in front edging just made; along bottom edge work (2 hdc in next hdc) 98 times, hdc in last 2 hdc; 2 hdc in front edging, turn. *You now have* 201 hdc.

Size 6–12 months only

- **Row 1 (WS):** Ch 2, hdc in front edging just made; along bottom edge hdc in next 5 sts, (2 hdc in next hdc) 104 times, hdc in last 5 sts; 2 hdc in front edging, turn. *You now have* 221 hdc.

Size 12–24 months only

- **Row 1 (WS):** Ch 2, hdc in front edging just made; along bottom edge work (2 hdc in next hdc) 134 times; 2 hdc in front edging, turn. *You now have* 271 hdc.

All sizes

- **Row 2:** Ch 2, (dc, ch 1, dc) in first hdc, *dc in next 3 sts, dc2tog over next 3 sts (skipping center st), dc in next 3 sts, (dc, ch 1, dc) in next st; repeat from * to end of row, turn.

- **Row 3:** Ch 2, (dc, ch 1, dc) in first ch-space, *ch 1, skip 1 dc, dc in next dc, ch 1, skip 1 dc, dc2tog over next 3 sts (skipping center st), ch 1, skip 1 dc, dc in next dc, ch 1, skip 1 dc, (dc, ch 1, dc) in next ch-space; repeat from * across, turn.

- **Row 4:** Ch 2, (dc, ch 1, dc) in first ch-space, *dc in next (dc, ch-space, dc), dc2tog over next 3 sts (skipping center st), dc in next (dc, ch-space, dc), (dc, ch 1, dc) in next ch-space; repeat from * across, turn.

- **Row 5:** Repeat Row 3.

- **Row 6:** Ch 1, sc in first dc, (sc, ch 2, sc) in first ch-space, *sc in next (dc, ch-space, dc), skip 1 ch, sc in next st, skip 1 ch, sc in next (dc, ch-space, dc), (sc, ch 2, sc) in next ch-space; repeat from * across, sc in last dc; turn 90° to work final edging row across fronts and neck.

- **Last Row:** Sc evenly across right front edge, back neck edge, and left front edge, working in each hdc and each ch st, join with slip st to first sc of row 6. Fasten off.

ROSETTA CARDIGAN

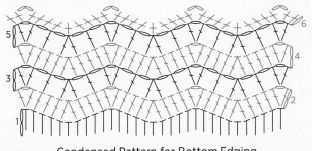

Condensed Pattern for Bottom Edging

CROCHETING THE SLEEVES

Size 0–6 months only

- **Rnd 1:** With WS facing, join yarn with slip st at underarm, ch 2, hdc in first st, 3 hdc around the leg of hdc2tog, hdc in next 33 hdc, 3 hdc around the leg of hdc2tog, join with slip st to first hdc, turn. *You now have* 40 hdc.

Size 6–12 months only

- **Rnd 1:** With WS facing, join yarn with slip st at underarm, ch 2, hdc around the leg of hdc2tog, hdc in next 38 hdc, hdc around the leg of hdc2tog, join with slip st to first hdc, turn. *You now have* 40 hdc.

Size 12–24 months only

- **Rnd 1:** With RS facing, join yarn with slip st at underarm, ch 2, hdc in first st, 3 hdc around the leg of hdc2tog, hdc in next 45 hdc, 2 hdc around the leg of hdc2tog, join with slip st to first hdc, turn. *You now have* 50 hdc.

All sizes

- **Rnd 2:** Ch 2, hdc in each hdc around, join with slip st to first hdc, turn. *You now have* 40 (40, 50) hdc.

- **Rnd(s) 3 (3 and 4, 3–8):** Repeat Rnd 2.

- **Rnd 4 (5, 9):** Ch 3 (counts as dc), *dc in next 3 sts, dc2tog over next 3 sts, dc in next 3 sts**, (dc, ch 1, dc) in next st; repeat from * three (three, four) times; ending last repeat at **, (dc, ch 1) in first st; join with slip st to top of ch-3, turn.

- **Rnd 5 (6, 10):** Slip st in next ch-1 space, ch 3, *ch 1, skip 1 dc, dc in next dc, ch 1, skip 1 dc, dc2tog over next 3 sts, ch 1, skip 1 dc, dc in next dc, ch 1, skip 1 dc, **(dc, ch 1, dc) in next ch-space; repeat from * around, ending last repeat at **, dc in next beginning ch-1 space, ch 1, join with slip st to top of ch-3, turn. *Do not fasten off.*

Size 0–6 months only: Proceed to sleeve Edging Rnd.

Sizes 6–12 (12–24) months only

- **Rnd 7 (11):** Ch 1, slip st in ch-space, ch 3, *dc in next (dc, space, dc), dc2tog over next 3 sts, dc in next (dc, space, dc)**, (dc, ch 1, dc) in next space; repeat from * around, ending last repeat at **, (dc, ch 1) in beginning ch-1 space, join with slip st to top of ch-3, turn.

- **Rnd 8 (12):** Slip st in next ch-1 space, ch 3, *ch 1, skip 1 dc, dc in next dc, ch 1, skip 1 dc, dc2tog over next 3 sts, ch 1, skip 1 dc, dc in next dc, ch 1, skip 1 dc, **(dc, ch 1, dc) in next ch-space; repeat from * around, ending last repeat at **, dc in next beginning ch-1 space, ch 1, join with slip st to top of ch-3, turn. *Do not fasten off.*

All sizes

- **Edging Rnd:** Ch 1, *(sc, ch 2, sc) in next space, sc in next (dc, space, dc), skip 1 ch, sc in next st, skip 1 ch, sc in next (dc, space, dc); rep from * around, join with slip st to first sc. Fasten off.

- Repeat for second sleeve.

FINISHING

- Weave in ends. On right front edge, pm at bottom of V-neck and at bottom of body section, then place two markers evenly spaced between them. Sew one button at each marker. Use eyelet row openings as buttonholes.

- Block cardigan and allow to dry.

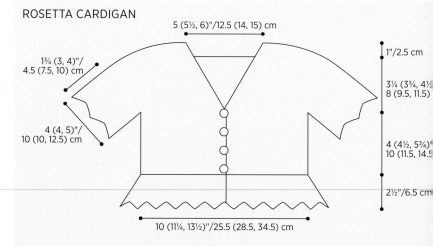

ROSETTA CARDIGAN

5 (5½, 6)"/12.5 (14, 15) cm

1¾ (3, 4)"/4.5 (7.5, 10) cm

1"/2.5 cm

3¼ (3¾, 4½)"/8 (9.5, 11.5)

4 (4, 5)"/10 (10, 12.5) cm

4 (4½, 5¾")/10 (11.5, 14.5)

2½"/6.5 cm

10 (11¼, 13½)"/25.5 (28.5, 34.5) cm

Unforgettable Vest

DESCRIBED BY *Nirmal Kaur Khalsa, Nirmal's Designs*

Changing hook sizes creates a subtle and clever rib shaping at the bottom of this vest. Crocheted in one piece with only a single short seam makes finishing easy. You won't forget how much fun this was to make!

PATTERN ESSENTIALS

Seed Stitch (for gauge swatch only) (multiple of 2+1, add 1 for loose chain)

Chain a multiple of 2 sts.

Row 1: Sc in 2nd ch from hook, (ch 1, skip 1 ch, sc in next ch) across, turn.

Row 2: Ch 1, sc in first sc, (sc, ch 1) in each ch-1 space across to last ch-1 space, sc in last ch-1 space, sc in last sc, turn.

Row 3: Ch 1, sc in first sc, (ch 1, sc) in each ch-1 space across to last 2 sts, ch 1, sc in last sc, turn.

Repeat Rows 2 and 3 for pattern.

SIZE AND FINISHED MEASUREMENTS

To fit 6–12 months: 21"/53.5 cm chest circumference and 9½"/24 cm length

YARN

Red Heart Boutique Unforgettable, 100% acrylic, 280 yds (256 m)/3.5 oz (100 g), Color 3955 Winery (4)

CROCHET HOOKS

US I/9 (5.5 mm) *or size needed to obtain correct gauge* and US H/8 (5 mm)

GAUGE

18 stitches and 19 rows = 4"/10 cm in Seed Stitch with larger hook

OTHER SUPPLIES

Yarn needle

CROCHETING THE VEST

- With larger hook, ch 41, slip st in first ch to form armhole opening, ch 23 for side of vest.

- **Row 1 (RS):** With smaller hook, sc in 2nd ch from hook and in next 6 ch sts; with larger hook, (ch 1, skip 1 ch, sc in next ch) across side, around armhole opening and across other side of foundation ch to last 7 sts; with smaller hook, sc in last 7 sts, turn. *You now have* 87 sts.

- **Row 2:** With smaller hook, ch 1, sc in first sc, BLsc in next 6 sc; with larger hook, sc in next ch-space, (ch 1, sc) in each ch-1 space across to last 7 sts; with smaller hook, BLsc in last 7 sts, turn.

- **Row 3:** With smaller hook, ch 1, sc in first sc, BLsc in next 6 sts; with larger hook, (ch 1, sc) in each ch-1 space to last 8 sts, ch 1, skip 1 sc; with smaller hook, BLsc in last 7 sts, turn.

- **Rows 4–24:** Repeat Rows 2 and 3, ending with Row 3 of pattern.

DIVIDE FOR NECK OPENING

- **Row 1:** Work in pattern Row 3 for 20 sts, ch 35, skip 35 sts for neck opening; being careful not to twist ch, sc in next ch-space, continue in pattern across remaining sts, turn.

- **Row 2:** Work in pattern Row 2 across, working in back bump of each ch across neck opening chain, continue in pattern Row 2 across remaining sts, turn.

- **Rows 3–24:** Work even in established pattern.

- **Next Row (connecting row):** With WS of front and back together, fold vest in half vertically, bringing other ribbed edge behind next sts to be worked; working through double thickness of both pieces, sc through back loop of front sc and both loops of back sc for first 7 sts. Fasten off, leaving an 18"/45.5 cm sewing length.

FINISHING

- With yarn needle and length of yarn, and working through back loops, seam the next 16 sts of sides together. Weave in ends.

UNFORGETTABLE VEST

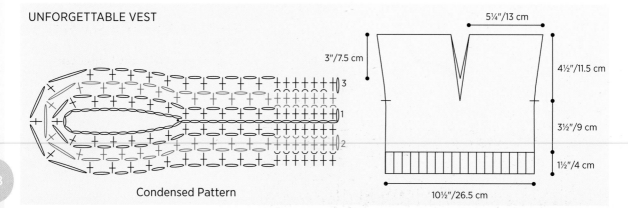

Condensed Pattern

5¼"/13 cm

3"/7.5 cm

4½"/11.5 cm

3½"/9 cm

1½"/4 cm

10½"/26.5 cm

Six-Button Vest

DESIGNED BY *Brenda K. B. Anderson*

This unusual vest is made flat, in sideways-turned rows, in one piece. It is perfect for squirmy babies, since you just pop it on over the head and then button the sides. The only sewing required is attaching the buttons.

SIZE AND FINISHED MEASUREMENTS
To fit 6 months: 20"/51 cm chest circumference and 9½"/24 cm length

YARN
Berroco Vintage DK, 50% acrylic/40% wool/10% nylon, 288 yds (263 m)/3.5 oz (100 g), Color 2194 Breezeway ❸

CROCHET HOOK
US G/6 (4 mm) *or size needed to obtain correct gauge*

GAUGE
20½ stitches and 20 rows = 4"/10 cm in stitch pattern

OTHER SUPPLIES
Stitch markers, yarn needle, six ⅞"/22 mm buttons, sewing needle and coordinating thread

PATTERN ESSENTIALS

Scfl (single crochet in the frontmost loop) Insert hook from bottom to top under the horizontal bar lying just below the top 2 loops of the hdc, yo and pull up a loop, yo and pull through 2 loops.

Stitch Pattern (any multiple, add 1 for turning chain)

Row 1: Hdc in 2nd ch from hook and in each ch across, turn.

Row 2: Ch 1, scfl in each st across, turn.

Row 3: Ch 1, hdc in each st across, turn.

Repeat Rows 2 and 3 for pattern.

119

CROCHETING THE VEST

SECTION 1 (LEFT UNDERARM)

Note: Vest begins at wearer's left side (see diagram on page 122).

- Chain 31.
- **Row 1 (WS):** Sc in back bump (see page 276) of 2nd ch from hook and in each ch across, turn. *You now have 30 sc.*
- **Row 2 (RS):** Ch 1 (does not count as st here and throughout), BLsc in next 8 sts, hdc in next 22 sts, turn.
- **Row 3:** Ch 1, scfl in next 22 sts, BLsc in next 8 sts, turn.
- **Rows 4–11:** Repeat Rows 2 and 3 four more times.
- **Row 12:** Ch 1, BLsc in next 8 sts, hdc in next 21 sts, 2 hdc in the last st, turn. *You now have 31 sts.*
- **Row 13:** Ch 1, scfl in next 23 sts, BLsc in next 8 sts, turn.
- **Row 14:** Ch 1, BLsc in next 8 sts, hdc in next 22 sts, 2 hdc in the last st, turn. *You now have 32 sts.*
- **Row 15:** Ch 1, scfl in next 24 sts, BLsc in next 8 sts, turn.
- **Row 16:** Ch 1, BLsc in next 8 sts, hdc in next 23 sts, 2 hdc in the last st, ch 60 (to create the left shoulder and left front), turn. *Do not fasten off.*

SECTION 2 (LEFT FRONT AND BACK)

- **Row 17:** Sc in 2nd ch from hook and in next 58 chs, scfl in next 25 sts, BLsc in next 8 sts, turn. *You now have 92 sts.*
- **Row 18:** Ch 1, BLsc in next 8 sts, hdc in next 76 sts, BLsc in next 8 sts, turn.
- **Row 19:** Ch 1, BLsc in next 8 sts, scfl in next 76 sts, BLsc in next 8 sts, turn.
- **Row 20:** Ch 1, BLsc in next 8 sts, hdc in next 37 sts, 2 hdc in next 2 sts (to help shape top of shoulder), hdc in next 18 sts, ch 2, skip next 2 sts (for buttonhole), hdc in next 8 sts, ch 2, skip next 2 sts (for buttonhole), hdc in next 7 sts, sc in both loops of next st, ch 2, skip next 2 sts (for buttonhole), sc in both loops of next st, BLsc in last 4 sts, turn. *You now have 94 sts and three buttonholes made.*
- **Row 21:** Ch 1, BLsc in next 5 sts, 2 sc in ch-2 space, BLsc in next st, scfl in next 7 sts, 2 sc in next ch-2 space, scfl in next 8 sts, 2 sc in next ch-2 space, scfl in next 60 sts, BLsc in next 8 sts, turn.
- **Row 22:** Ch 1, BLsc in next 8 sts, hdc in next 78 sts, BLsc in next 8 sts, turn.
- **Row 23:** Ch 1, BLsc in next 8 sts, scfl in next 78 sts, BLsc in next 8 sts, turn.
- **Row 24:** Ch 1, BLsc in next 8 sts, hdc in next 38 sts, 2 hdc in next st, pm in 2nd of these hdc sts (place marker A — see diagram), 2 hdc in next st, hdc in next 7 sts, pm in the last st made, hdc in next 31 sts, BLsc in next 8 sts, turn. *You now have 96 sts. Do not fasten off.*

SECTION 3 (FRONT)

- **Row 25:** Ch 1, BLsc in next 8 sts, scfl in next 32 sts (ending with marked st; remove marker), turn, leaving remaining back sts unworked. *You now have 40 sts.*
- **Row 26:** Ch 1, BL slip st in next 3 sts, hdc in next 29 sts, BLsc in next 8 sts, turn.
- **Row 27:** Ch 1, BLsc in next 8 sts, scfl in next 27 sts, turn, leaving remaining sts unworked. *You now have 35 sts.*
- **Row 28:** Ch 1, BL slip st in next 3 sts, hdc in next 24 sts, BLsc in next 8 sts, turn.
- **Row 29:** Ch 1, BLsc in next 8 sts, scfl in next 24 sts, turn, leaving remaining sts unworked. *You now have 32 sts.*
- **Row 30:** Ch 1, hdc in next 24 sts, BLsc in next 8 sts, turn.
- **Rows 31–40:** Repeat Rows 29 and 30 five more times.
- **Row 41:** Ch 1, BLsc in next 8 sts, scfl in next 24 sts, ch 4, turn.
- **Row 42:** Hdc in 2nd ch from hook and in next 2 chs, hdc in next 24 sts, BLsc in next 8 sts, turn. *You now have 35 sts.*

- **Row 43:** Ch 1, BLsc in next 8 sts, scfl in next 26 sts, ch 7, turn.

- **Row 44:** Hdc in 2nd ch from hook and in next 5 ch-sts, hdc in next 26 sts, BLsc in next 8 sts, turn. *You now have* 40 sts.

- Fasten off. Place stitch marker in the last stitch made (place marker B — see diagram).

SECTION 4 (BACK)

- **Row 1:** With WS facing, join yarn in marked st (marker A), ch 1, scfl in same st and in next 39 sts, BLsc in next 8 sts, turn. *You now have* 48 sts.

- **Row 2 (RS):** Ch 1, BLsc in next 8 sts, hdc in next 40 sts, turn.

- **Row 3:** Ch 1, scfl in next 40 sts, BLsc in next 8 sts, turn.

- **Rows 4–19:** Repeat Rows 2 and 3 eight more times.

- **Row 20:** Repeat Row 2.

- Fasten off. Place marker C in last st made (see diagram).

SECTION 5 (RIGHT FRONT AND BACK)

- **Row 1:** With WS facing, join yarn in back loop of marked st at bottom front (marker B), ch 1, BLsc in same st and in next 7 sts, scfl in next 32 sts, ch 8, beginning with marked st at back shoulder (marker C), scfl in next 40 sts, BLsc in next 8 sts, turn. *You now have* 96 sts.

- **Row 2:** Ch 1, BLsc in next 8 sts, hdc in next 38 sts, hdc2tog across next 2 sts, hdc2tog across the following 2 ch-sts, hdc in next 6 chs, hdc in next 32 sts, BLsc in next 8 sts, turn. *You now have* 94 sts.

- **Row 3:** Ch 1, BLsc in next 8 sts, scfl in next 78 sts, BLsc in next 8 sts, turn.

- **Row 4:** Ch 1, BLsc in next 8 sts, hdc in next 78 sts, BLsc in next 8 sts, turn.

- **Row 5:** Repeat Row 3.

- **Row 6:** Ch 1, BLsc in next 8 sts, hdc in next 37 sts, hdc2tog twice, hdc in next 37 sts, BLsc in next 8 sts, turn. *You now have* 92 sts.

- **Row 7:** Ch 1, BLsc in next 4 sts, sc in both loops of next st, ch 2, skip next 2 sts (for buttonhole), sc in both loops of next st, scfl in next 7 sts, ch 2, skip next 2 sts (for buttonhole), scfl in next 8 sts, ch 2, skip next 2 sts (for buttonhole), scfl in next 57 sts, BLsc in next 8 sts, turn. *You now have* 92 sts and three buttonholes made.

- **Row 8:** Ch 1, BLsc in next 8 sts, hdc in next 57 sts, 2 hdc in next ch-2 space, hdc in next 8 sts, 2 hdc in next ch-2 space, hdc in next 7 sts, BLsc in next st, 2 sc in next ch-2 space, BLsc in next 5 sts, turn.

- **Row 9:** Ch 1, BLsc in next 8 sts, scfl in next 76 sts, BLsc in next 8 sts, turn. *You now have* 92 sts.

- **Row 10:** Ch 1, BLsc in next 8 sts, hdc in next 25 sts, pm in last of these 25 sts (place marker D — see diagram), hdc in next 51 sts, BLsc in next 8 sts.

- Fasten off.

Note: There is 1 extra row across the right shoulder compared to the left shoulder. This is to make the front edges of the vest near the buttonholes look the same from one side to the other. The small difference in width of the shoulders can be evened out in blocking and will not be noticeable.

SECTION 6 (RIGHT UNDERARM)

- **Row 1:** With WS facing, beginning with marked st at back right side (marker D), pull up loop from back bar of marked st, ch 1, scfl in same st and in next 24 sts, BLsc in next 8 sts, turn. *You now have* 33 sts.

- **Row 2:** Ch 1, BLsc in next 8 sts, hdc in next 23 sts, hdc2tog, turn. *You now have* 32 sts.

- **Row 3:** Ch 1, scfl in next 24 sts, BLsc in next 8 sts, turn.

- **Row 4:** Ch 1, BLsc in next 8 sts, hdc in next 22 sts, hdc2tog, turn. *You now have* 31 sts.

- **Row 5:** Ch 1, scfl in next 23 sts, BLsc in next 8 sts, turn.

- **Row 6:** Ch 1, BLsc in next 8 sts, hdc in next 21 sts, hdc2tog, turn. *You now have* 30 sts.

- **Row 7:** Ch 1, scfl in next 22 sts, BLsc in next 8 sts, turn.

- **Row 8:** Ch 1, BLsc in next 8 sts, hdc in next 22 sts, turn.

- **Rows 9–16:** Repeat Rows 7 and 8 four more times. *Do not fasten off.*

CROCHETING THE EDGINGS

- Rotate piece 90°; work 14 sc evenly spaced along row ends of underarm to marker D, slip st in each st along front edge, ending at bottom of right front. Fasten off.

- Beginning at bottom corner of left front, with RS facing, join yarn by pulling up a loop, ch 1, slip st in each st along left front edge ending at underarm edge; work 14 sc evenly spaced across row-end sts along underarm edge. Fasten off.

THE NECK EDGING

Note: Make sure that the neck edging does not constrict the neck opening too much. The neck should be able to stretch to accommodate at least a 17"/43 cm head (or the size of the recipient's head, if you know the measurement). Check this as you work. If the neck is getting too tight, use a larger hook or add more stitches in the first round.

- **Rnd 1:** With RS facing, join yarn by pulling up a loop at right-hand corner of back neck (or left-hand corner, if you crochet left-handed), ch 1, work 20 sc evenly spaced across back neck, 16 sc along side of neck, 10 sc across front neck, 16 sc along other side edge of neck; do not join. Pm in the first st of the rnd and move it up as you work the rnds. *You now have* 62 sc.

- **Rnds 2–4:** BLsc in each sc around; *do not join.* At the end of Rnd 4, join with slip st to next st. Fasten off.

FINISHING

- Weave in ends. Block to dimensions. Because of the shoulder shaping, you may find it easier to block this vest while it is folded at the shoulders.

- Sew buttons to the underarm sections to correspond with buttonholes, placing buttons on the last hdc ridge from either edge.

SIX-BUTTON VEST

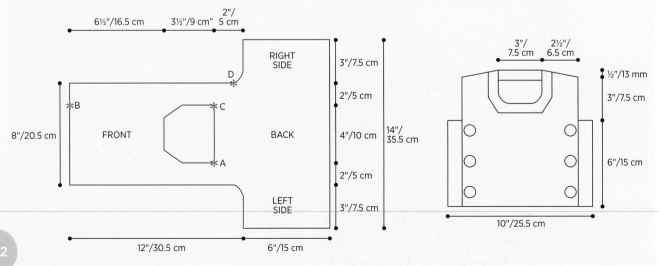

Floral Lace Cardigan

DESIGNED BY *Vicky Chan*

This sweet-looking cardigan is worked seamlessly from the top down. Juxtaposing the simple stripes of the body, the lovely floral lace lends beautiful details to the yoke and hem.

SIZE AND FINISHED MEASUREMENTS

To fit 18–24 months: 22"/56 cm chest circumference and 12"/30.5 cm length

YARN

King Cole Bamboo Cotton 4 ply, 52% cotton/48% bamboo, 405 yds (371 m)/3.5 oz (100 g), Color 1019 Cream (1)

CROCHET HOOKS

US C/2 (2.75 mm) and US D/3 (3.25 mm) *or size needed to obtain correct gauge*

GAUGE

22 stitches and 12 rows = 4"/10 cm in double crochet with larger hook, blocked

OTHER SUPPLIES

Stitch markers, yarn needle, three 14 mm buttons, sewing needle, coordinating thread

CROCHETING THE CARDIGAN

THE YOKE

See chart on following page.

- Chain 74.
- **Row 1 (WS):** Sc in 2nd ch from hook, *ch 1, skip 1 ch, sc in next ch; repeat from * across, turn. *You now have* 37 sc and 36 ch-1 spaces.
- **Row 2 (RS):** Ch 3 (counts as dc here and throughout), dc in first sc, 3 dc in each sc across to last sc, 2 dc in last sc, turn. *You now have* 109 dc.
- **Row 3:** Ch 3, dc in next dc, *ch 1, skip next dc, dc in next dc; repeat from * to last st, dc in last st, turn. *You now have* 53 ch-1 spaces.

Note: Rows 4–6 together form a band of 18 flowers.

- **Row 4:** Ch 1, sc in first dc, *ch 3, skip next dc, 3-dc cluster in next dc, ch 3, skip next ch-1 space, sc in next ch-1 space; repeat from * across, placing final sc in last dc, turn. *You now have 18 clusters.*

- **Row 5:** Ch 1, sc in first sc, *(slip st, ch 3, sc) in next ch-3 sp, ch 2, (sc, ch 3, slip st) in next ch-3 space; repeat from * to last st, sc in last st, turn.

- **Row 6:** Ch 4 (counts as dc, ch 1 here and throughout), (2-dc cluster, ch 3, 2-dc cluster) in next ch-2 space, *ch 3, (2-dc cluster, ch 3, 2-dc cluster) in next ch-2 space; repeat from * across, ending ch 1, dc in last sc, turn. *You now have 35 ch-3 spaces.*

- **Row 7:** Ch 4, *dc in next cluster, ch 1, dc in next ch-3 space, ch 1; repeat from * to last 2-dc cluster, dc in next cluster, ch 1, skip next ch, dc in top of ch-3 turning ch; turn. *You now have 73 dc and 72 ch-1 spaces.*

- **Row 8:** Ch 3, dc in each ch-1 space and dc across, turn. *You now have 145 dc.*

- **Row 9:** Ch 4, skip next dc, dc in next dc, *ch 1, skip 1 dc, dc in next dc; repeat from * across, turn. *You now have 73 dc and 72 ch-1 spaces.*

- **Row 10:** Ch 3, 2 dc in next ch-1 space, dc in next dc and ch-1 space, 2 dc in next dc, *dc in next 7 sts, 2 dc in next dc; repeat from * across until 2 spaces remain; dc in next ch-1 space, dc in next dc, 2 dc in last ch-1 space, dc in 3rd ch of ch-4 turning ch, turn. *You now have 165 dc.*

- **Rows 11–14:** Ch 3, dc in each dc across, turn.

- **Row 15:** Ch 4, skip next dc, dc in next dc, (ch 1, skip 1 dc, dc in next dc) 10 times, ch 1, dc in same dc, ch 11 for right underarm, skip next 37 dc for right armhole, dc in next dc, ch 1, dc in same dc, (ch 1, skip 1 dc, dc in next dc) 22 times, ch 1, dc in same dc, ch 11 for left underarm, skip next 37 dc for left armhole, dc in next dc, ch 1, dc in same dc, (ch 1, skip 1 dc, dc in next dc) 10 times, ch 1, dc in top of ch-3 at end of row, turn. *You now have 25 sts for each front, 37 sts for each armhole, and 49 sts for back.*

THE BODY

- **Row 16:** Ch 3, dc in each ch-1 space and dc across left front; dc in first 6 ch of left underarm, pm in dc just made, dc in next 5 ch; dc in each dc and ch-1 space across back; dc in first 6 ch of right underarm, pm in dc just made, dc in next 5 ch; dc in each dc and ch-1 space across right front, ending 2 dc in space formed by ch-4, turn. *You now have 121 dc.*

FLORAL LACE CARDIGAN

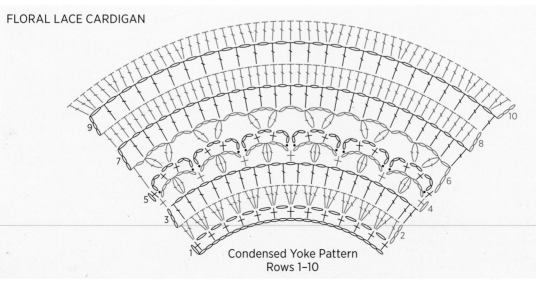

Condensed Yoke Pattern
Rows 1–10

Note: On the following rows, move markers up to corresponding st in each row to keep track of side increases.

- **Row 17:** Repeat Row 9. *You now have 61 dc and 60 ch-1 spaces.*

- **Row 18 (increase row):** Ch 3, (dc in each dc and ch-1 space to 1 st before marker, 2 dc in next st, dc in marked st, 2 dc in next st) twice, dc in each dc and ch-1 space, ending 2 dc in space formed by ch-4, turn. *You now have 125 dc.*

- **Row 19:** Ch 3, dc in each dc across, turn.

- **Row 20 (increase row):** Ch 3, (dc in each dc to 1 st before marker, 2 dc in next st, dc in marked st, 2 dc in next st) twice, dc in each dc across, turn. *You now have 129 dc.*

- **Rows 21 and 22:** Repeat Rows 19 and 20. *You now have 133 dc.*

- **Row 23:** Repeat Row 9.

- **Row 24:** Repeat Row 18. *You now have 137 dc.*

- **Rows 25 and 26:** Repeat Rows 23 and 24. *You now have 141 dc.*

- **Rows 27 and 28:** Repeat Rows 19 and 20. *You now have 145 dc.*

- **Rows 29 and 30:** Ch 3, dc in each dc across, turn.

- **Row 31–34:** Repeat Rows 3–6. *You now have 24 flowers.*

- **Row 35:** Ch 3, dc in same st, (dc, ch 1, dc) in each ch-3 space across, 2 dc in top of ch-3, turn. *You now have 145 sts.*

- **Row 36:** Ch 3, dc in each ch-1 space and dc across. Fasten off.

FINISHING

THE BUTTON BAND

- With RS facing and smaller hook, join yarn with slip st to left front at neck edge.

- **Row 1 (RS):** Ch 1, work 2 sc in each dc and ch-3 sp, and 1 sc in each sc across right front edge, turn. *You now have 67 sc.*

- **Rows 2–4:** Ch 1, sc in each sc across, turn.

- Fasten off.

THE BUTTONHOLE BAND

- With RS facing and smaller hook, join yarn with slip st to right front at lower edge.

- **Rows 1 and 2:** Repeat Rows 1 and 2 of button band.

- **Row 3 (RS):** Ch 1, sc in next 43 sc, (ch 2, skip 2 sc, sc in next 8 sc) twice, ch 2, skip 2 sc, sc in last 2 sc, turn.

- **Row 4:** Ch 1, sc in each sc and 2 sc in each ch-2 space across, turn.

THE EDGING

- Ch 1, sc in each sc up along right buttonhole band, 3 sc in corner sc, sc in each st across neck edge, 3 sc in corner sc, sc in each sc down along left button band. Fasten off.

THE SLEEVE EDGINGS

- With RS facing and smaller hook, join yarn to armhole at center of underarm with slip st in space between 2 dc, ch 1, sc in each space between 2 dc along left half of underarm edge, sc in next dc space up sleeve edge, ch 1, dc in next dc of sleeve edge, (ch 1, skip next dc, dc in next dc) across sleeve edge, ch 1, sc in next dc space down sleeve edge, sc in each space between 2 dc along remaining half of underarm edge, join with slip st to first sc. Fasten off.

- Repeat sleeve edging on other sleeve.

- Weave in ends. Sew buttons to right front opposite buttonholes.

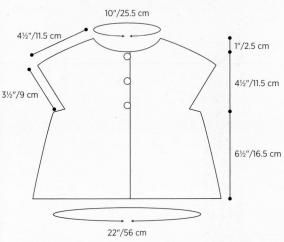

FLORAL LACE CARDIGAN

10"/25.5 cm

4½"/11.5 cm

1"/2.5 cm

4½"/11.5 cm

3½"/9 cm

6½"/16.5 cm

22"/56 cm

April Showers Cape

DESIGNED BY *Christy Hagan*

With fairy gardens and imagination play increasing in popularity, this cape is an ideal addition to any toddler's wardrobe. And it's a great project for beginning crocheters — basic stitches, no shaping, stunning results.

SIZE AND FINISHED MEASUREMENTS
To fit toddler: 14"/35.5 cm center back to neck length

YARN
Red Heart Boutique Unforgettable, 100% acrylic, 280 yds (256 m)/3.5 oz (100 g), Color 3935 Tidal (4)

CROCHET HOOK
US K/10½ (6.5 mm) *or size needed to obtain correct gauge*

GAUGE
13 stitches and 12 rows = 4"/10 cm in half double crochet/single crochet rows

OTHER SUPPLIES
Straight pins, yarn needle, 1"/2.5 cm closure

CROCHETING THE BODY

FIRST PANEL

- Chain 31.
- **Row 1 (WS):** Working into back bump of each ch (see page 276), sc in 2nd ch from hook and each ch across, turn. *You now have* 30 sc.
- **Row 2:** Ch 1 (does not count as st), hdc in each st across, turn.
- **Row 3:** Ch 1, sc into each st across, turn.
- **Rows 4–53:** Repeat Rows 2 and 3.
- **Row 54:** Repeat Row 2; *do not turn*, but rotate to work along edge.

SECOND PANEL

- **Set-Up Row (RS):** Working along side of rows and placing 1 st in each row end, ch 1, 30 hdc along edge, turn, leaving remainder of edge unworked. *You now have* 30 hdc.
- **Row 1:** Ch 1, sc in each st across, turn.
- **Rows 2–23:** Repeat Rows 2 and 3 of first panel.
- **Rnd 24:** Ch 1, sc in each st and row end around all edges of body, placing 3 sc in each exterior corner st, join with slip st to first sc. Fasten off.

CROCHETING THE HOOD

- Chain 40.
- **Row 1:** Working into back bump of each ch, sc in 2nd ch from hook and each ch across, turn. *You now have* 39 sc.
- **Row 2:** Ch 1, hdc in each st across, turn.
- **Row 3:** Ch 1, sc in each st across; turn.
- **Rows 4–21:** Repeat Rows 2 and 3.

- Fold hood in half with RS together, and working through double thickness of previous row and foundation ch, slip st in each st across to seam top of hood.
- Fasten off.

THE EDGING

- **Row 1:** With RS facing, join yarn with slip st to corner of hood, ch 1, working along row ends, work 42 sc evenly spaced across, turn. *You now have* 42 sc.
- **Row 2:** Ch 1, sc in first st, skip 1 sc, *(dc, ch 1, dc, ch 1, dc) in next st, skip 1 sc, sc in next st; repeat from * to last st, sc in last st. *You now have* 10 shells.
- Fasten off.

FINISHING

- Pin hood to body, placing center back of hood on inside corner of body. Whipstitch (see page 276) hood to body. Weave in ends. Sew closure to front corners of body. (See Sewing Buttons on page 91.)

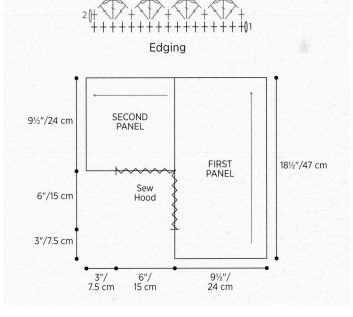

APRIL SHOWERS CAPE

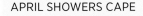

Edging

SECOND PANEL

FIRST PANEL

9½"/24 cm

6"/15 cm

3"/7.5 cm

Sew Hood

18½"/47 cm

3"/7.5 cm   6"/15 cm   9½"/24 cm

Jumper Top

DESIGNED BY *Julie Blagojevich*

Lovely merino, cashmere, and silk yarn will keep your young one cozily comfy. The skirt uses a feather and fan pattern, and the piece is worked in the round with doubled laceweight yarn.

SIZE AND FINISHED MEASUREMENTS

To fit 12 months: 17"/43 cm chest circumference and 13½"/34.5 cm length

YARN

Shalimar Yarns Breathless Single Ply Lace, 75% superwash merino wool/15% cashmere/10% silk, 850 yds (777 m)/3.5 oz (100 g), Color Oyster **⓪**

CROCHET HOOK

US 7 (4.5 mm) *or size needed to obtain correct gauge*

GAUGE

19 stitches and 10 rows = 4"/10 cm in skirt pattern with yarn doubled
18 stitches and 20 rows = 4"/10 cm in bodice pattern with yarn doubled

OTHER SUPPLIES

Straight pins, yarn needle

PATTERN ESSENTIALS

Yarn is used doubled throughout. Prepare the yarn by winding two equal balls and crocheting with one strand from each ball, or wind a center-pull ball and pull from both the inside and the outside of the ball.

CROCHETING THE JUMPER

THE SKIRT

- Fsc 76 (see page 274), join with slip st to form a ring, being careful not to twist the sts.

- **Rnd 1:** Ch 1, sc in each st around, join with slip st to first sc.

- **Rnd 2:** Ch 1, 2 sc each st around, join with slip st to first sc. *You now have* 152 sts.

- **Rnd 3:** Ch 3 (counts as dc here and throughout), 4 dc in same st, *dc in next sc, (skip 1 sc, dc in next sc) eight times, (5 dc in next sc) twice; repeat from * six times, dc in next st, (skip 1 sc, dc in next sc) eight times, 5 dc in last st, join with slip st to top of ch-3.

- **Rnd 4:** Ch 1, sc in each st around, join with slip st to first sc.

- **Rnds 5–16:** Repeat Rnds 3 and 4 six times.

- **Rnd 17:** Ch 1, sc in each st around, join with slip st to first sc.

- **Rnd 18:** Ch 1, slip st in first st, *ch 1, slip st in next sc; repeat from * around, ending last repeat ch 1, join with slip st to first sc. Fasten off.

THE BODICE

- Attach yarn to chain side of foundation rnd at the join.

- **Rnd 1:** Ch 1, sc in same st, sc in each st around, join with slip st to first sc. *You now have* 76 sts.

- **Rnds 2–6:** Ch 1, sc in each st around, join with slip st to first sc.

- **Rnds 7 and 8:** Ch 1, sc in first st, dc in next st, *sc in next st, dc in next st; repeat from * around, join with slip st to first sc.

- **Rnds 9–15:** Repeat Rnds 2–8.

- **Rnds 16–20:** Repeat Rnds 2–6.

- **Rnd 21:** Ch 1, slip st in first st, *ch 1, slip st in next st; repeat from * around, ending last repeat with ch 1, join with slip st to first sc. Fasten off.

THE SHOULDER STRAPS (MAKE 2)

Note: Shoulder straps are worked in rounds to form tubes, giving them double strength and the ability to maintain shape.

- Fsc 14, join with slip st to form a ring, being careful not to twist the sts.

- **Rnds 1–34:** Ch 1, sc in first st and each remaining st around, join with slip st to first sc.

- Fasten off.

ASSEMBLING THE JUMPER

- Pin straps to front and back of bodice, making sure the join lines of the straps run along the center of the undersides. Sew to bodice with doubled yarn. Weave in ends. Block.

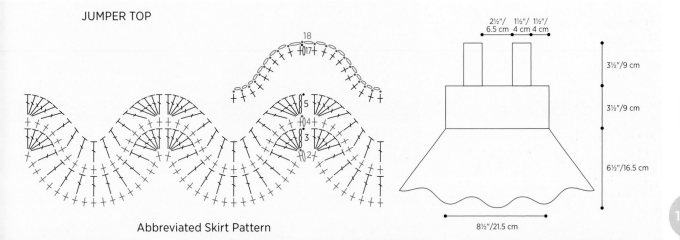

JUMPER TOP

Abbreviated Skirt Pattern

Pistachio Gelato Jacket

DESIGNED BY *Michele DuNaier, MAD Cap Fancies*

This chic and easy-to-slip-on jacket is worked from the neck edge down. There's no end to the fun you can have searching for the perfect buttons.

SIZE AND FINISHED MEASUREMENTS
To fit 12–24 months: 21"/53.5 cm chest circumference

YARN
Lion Brand Baby Soft, 60% acrylic/40% nylon, 459 yds (420 m)/5 oz (141 g), Color 170 Pistachio ③

CROCHET HOOK
US J/10 (6 mm) *or size needed to obtain correct gauge*

GAUGE
15 stitches and 11 rows = 4"/10 cm in double crochet

OTHER SUPPLIES
Eight locking stitch markers, yarn needle, four ⅝"/16 mm buttons, sewing needle and coordinating thread

PATTERN ESSENTIALS

Inc Working into ch-spaces of next large shell, sc in first ch-space, shell in next ch-space, sc in last ch-space.

Large Shell [(Dc, ch 1) three times, dc] in 1 st.

Shell [(Dc, ch 1) twice, dc] in 1 st.

V-st (or half shell) (Dc, ch 1, dc) in 1 st or space.

Pattern Stitch

Row 1: Ch 4 (counts as dc, ch 1 throughout), dc in same st (counts as V-st), sc in center dc of next shell, (shell in next sc, sc in center dc of next shell) across to last shell, V-st in last sc, turn.

Row 2: Ch 1, sc in first st, (shell in next sc, sc in center dc of next shell) across, ending with last sc in 3rd ch of turning ch, turn.

Repeat Rows 1 and 2 for pattern.

PISTACHIO GELATO JACKET

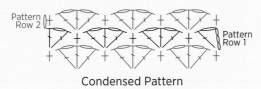

Pattern Row 2

Pattern Row 1

Condensed Pattern

CROCHETING THE JACKET

THE COLLAR AND YOKE

- Chain 50.

- **Row 1:** Sc in 2nd ch from hook and in each ch across, turn. *You now have* 49 sc.

- **Row 2 (large shell row):** Ch 4 (counts as dc and ch 1 here and throughout), dc in same st, skip 1 sc, sc in next sc, skip 1 sc, (shell in next sc, skip 1 sc, sc in next sc, skip 1 sc, large shell in next sc, skip 1 sc, sc in next sc, skip 1 sc) twice, (shell in next sc, skip 1 sc, sc in next sc, skip 1 sc) three times, (large shell in next sc, skip 1 sc, sc in next sc, skip 1 sc, shell in next sc, skip 1 sc, sc in next sc, skip 1 sc) twice, V-st in last st, turn. *You now have* 4 large shells, 7 shells, and 2 half shells.

PISTACHIO GELATO JACKET

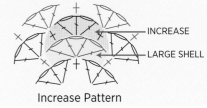

INCREASE

LARGE SHELL

Increase Pattern

- Place a marker in center of each of the 4 large shells; after each row of the yoke, move markers up to center st that was worked in marked st.

- **Row 3 (increase row):** *Work in pattern st Row 2 to marked large shell, inc in large shell; repeat from * across ending last pattern repeat shell in last sc, sc in 3rd ch of beginning ch-4, turn. *You now have* 16 shells.

- **Row 4:** Work in pattern st Row 1. *You now have* 15 shells and 2 half shells.

- **Row 5 (large shell row):** *Work in pattern st Row 2 to next marked sc, large shell in marked sc; repeat from * across to last marker, work in pattern st Row 2 to end, turn. *You now have* 4 large shells and 12 shells.

- **Row 6 (increase row):** *Work in pattern st Row 1 to marked large shell, inc in large shell; repeat from * to last marker, work in pattern st Row 2 to end, turn. *You now have* 19 shells and 2 half shells.

- **Row 7:** Work in pattern st Row 2. *You now have* 20 shells.

- **Row 8 (large shell row):** Work in pattern st Row 1 to marked sc, large shell in marked sc; repeat from * to last marker, work in pattern st Row 1 to end. *You now have* 4 large shells, 15 shells, and 2 half shells.

- **Row 9 (increase row):** *Work in pattern st Row 2 to marked large shell, inc in large shell; repeat from * to last marker, work in pattern st Row 2 to end, turn. *You now have* 24 shells.

- **Row 10:** Work in pattern stitch Row 1. *You now have* 23 shells and 2 half shells.

- **Row 11 (large shell row):** Repeat Row 5. *You now have* 4 large shells and 20 shells.

- **Row 12 (increase row):** Repeat Row 6. *You now have* 27 shells and 2 half shells. Ignoring the half shells at row ends, markers should be at center dc of shells 4, 10, 18, and 24.

Divide for Sleeves

Do not remove markers after next row; they will be used later in the sleeve section.

- **Dividing Row:** Ch 1, sc in first dc, (shell in next sc, sc in next shell) across front, ending with sc in first marked shell, ch 5 for underarm, skip 5 shells, sc in next marked shell, (shell in next sc, sc in next shell) across back, ending with sc in next marked shell, ch 5 for underarm, skip 5 shells, sc in next marked shell, shell in next sc, (sc in next shell, shell in sc) across front, ending with sc in 3rd ch of turning ch, turn. *You now have* 16 shells.

THE BODY

- **Row 1:** Work in pattern st Row 1 to marked sc, shell in marked sc, skip 2 ch of ch-5 space, sc in next ch, skip 2 ch, shell in next marked sc, work in pattern st Row 1 across to next marked sc, shell in next marked sc, skip 2 ch of ch-5 space, sc in next ch, skip 2 ch, shell in next marked sc, work in pattern st Row 1 to end, turn. *You now have* 17 shells and 2 half shells.

- **Rows 2–12:** Starting with pattern st Row 2, work even in pattern, ending with Row 2. *You now have* 18 shells on even-numbered rows, 17 shells and 2 half shells on odd-numbered rows.

The Body Edging

Note: As you work 3 sc in each corner on the following row, place a marker in the center sc.

- **Row 1:** Ch 1, sc in each dc and in each sc across row (skipping ch-spaces); 3 sc in corner; working along right front edge, work 34 sc evenly spaced up edge to corner, 3 sc in corner, work 48 sc evenly spaced along neck edge, 3 sc in corner; working along left front edge, work 34 sc evenly spaced down edge to corner, 3 sc in corner, join with slip st to first sc, turn. *You now have* 201 sts.

- **Row 2:** Ch 3, dc in next sc and in each sc around, placing 3 dc in each of the 4 marked corner sts, join with slip st to 3rd ch of ch-3, turn. *You now have* 209 sts.

- **Row 3:** Ch 1, sc in first dc and in each dc around, placing 3 sc in each of the 4 marked corner sts, join with a slip st to first sc. *You now have* 217 sts.

- Fasten off.

THE SLEEVES

Note: There should still be two markers on each end of the armholes.

- **Rnd 1:** With RS facing, join yarn with slip st in center ch st of underarm chain; (ch 4, dc) in same ch, sc in center dc of marked shell, shell in next sc, (sc in next shell, shell in next sc) around top of armhole, sc in center dc of other marked shell, (dc, ch 1) in center ch where yarn was joined (*completes first shell*), join with slip st to 3rd ch of ch-4, turn. *You now have* 7 shells.

- **Rnd 2:** Ch 1, sc in turning ch of previous row, shell in next sc, (sc in next shell, shell in next sc) around armhole, join with slip st to first sc, turn.

- **Rnd 3:** Ch 4, dc in first sc, sc in next shell, (shell in next sc, sc in next shell) around, (dc, ch 1) in same st as ch-4 to complete shell, join with a slip st to 3rd ch of ch-4, turn.

- **Rnds 4–6:** Repeat Rows 2 and 3 once, then repeat Row 2 once more.

- **Rnd 7 (decrease row):** Ch 3, sc in next shell, (shell in next sc, sc in next shell) around, join with slip st to top of ch-3, turn. *You now have* 6 shells and 1 dc.

- **Rnd 8 (decrease row):** Ch 1, sc in first st, V-st in next sc, sc in next shell, (shell in next sc, sc in next shell) around, ending V-st in last sc, join with slip st to first sc, turn. *You now have* 5 shells and 2 V-sts.

- **Rnd 9:** Ch 1, sc in first sc, sc in ch-space of next V-st, shell in next sc, (sc in next shell, shell in next sc) around, ending sc in ch-space of next V-st, join with slip st to first sc, turn. *You now have* 6 shells.

- **Rnd 10:** Ch 4, dc in first sc, skip next sc, sc in next shell, (shell in next sc, sc in next shell) around, skip last sc, (dc, ch 1) in same sc as beginning ch-4, join with slip st to 3rd ch of ch-4, turn. *You now have* 6 shells.

- **Rnd 11:** Ch 1, sc in first st, shell in next sc, (sc in next shell, shell in next sc) around, join with slip st to first sc, turn. *You now have* 6 shells.

- **Rnd 12:** Ch 4, dc in first sc, sc in next shell, (shell in next sc, sc in next shell) around, (dc, ch 1) in last st, join with slip st to 3rd ch of ch-4, turn.

- **Rnds 13 and 14:** Repeat Rows 11 and 12.

The Sleeve Edging

- **Row 1:** Ch 1, sc in each sc and dc around, skipping all ch-spaces, join with slip st to first sc, turn. *You now have* 24 sc.

- **Row 2:** Ch 3, dc in next sc and in each sc around, join with slip st to top of ch-3, turn. *You now have* 24 dc.

- **Row 3:** Ch 1, sc in each dc around, join with slip st to first sc. Fasten off.

- Repeat for other sleeve.

FINISHING

- Remove all markers. Weave in ends. Fold lapels down. Sew buttons evenly spaced from collar to bottom edging, on one side of body. Use gap between dc on other side of body edging as buttonhole. (See Sewing Buttons on page 91.)

PISTACHIO GELATO JACKET

Justin's Jacket

DESIGNED BY *Edie Eckman*

Worked side to side with minimal shaping, this is a perfect project for beginning crocheters. Let your toddler help you "make" the sweater by picking out cute buttons.

SIZE AND FINISHED MEASUREMENTS
To fit 2–4 years: 26"/66 cm chest circumference, buttoned

YARN
Plymouth Yarn Worsted Merino Superwash Kettle Dyed, 100% superwash fine merino wool, 436 yds (398 m)/7 oz (200 g), Color 1003 Kettle Wisteria (4)

CROCHET HOOK
US I/9 (5.5 mm) *or size needed to obtain correct gauge*

GAUGE
13 stitches and 11 rows = 4"/10 cm in half double crochet

OTHER SUPPLIES
Yarn needle, five ⅞"/22 mm buttons, sewing needle and coordinating thread

CROCHETING THE JACKET

THE FIRST SLEEVE

- Chain 31.

- **Row 1 (RS):** Working into the back bump of each ch (see page 276), hdc in 3rd ch from hook and in each ch across, turn. *You now have* 29 hdc. Mark this side as RS.

- **Rows 2–4:** Ch 2 (does not count as hdc here and throughout), hdc in each hdc across, turn.

- **Row 5 (increase row):** Ch 2, 2 hdc in first st, hdc in each hdc to last st, 2 hdc in last st, turn. *You now have* 31 hdc.

- **Rows 6–9:** Repeat Row 2 four times.

- **Row 10:** Repeat Row 5. *You now have* 33 sts.

- **Rows 11–18:** Repeat Row 2 eight times.

- **Row 19:** Ch 2, hdc in each hdc across, ch 22, turn.

THE BODY

- **Row 1:** Hdc in 3rd ch from hook and in each ch across, hdc in each st across sleeve, fhdc 20 (see page 274), starting first hdc in base of previous hdc, turn. *You now have* 73 sts.

- **Rows 2–10:** Ch 2, hdc in each hdc across, turn.

Divide for Back Neck

- **Row 1 (WS):** Ch 2, hdc in next 34 sts, turn, leaving remaining sts unworked. *You now have* 34 hdc.

- **Rows 2–15:** Ch 2, hdc in each hdc across, turn.

- Fasten off.

The First Front

- **Row 1 (WS):** With back just worked held to the right, skip 7 sts, join yarn with standing hdc in next st, hdc in each st to end, turn. *You now have* 32 hdc.

- **Rows 2–8:** Ch 2, hdc in each hdc across, turn.

- Fasten off. Set aside.

The Second Front

- Loosely chain 34.

- **Row 1 (RS):** Working into the back bump of each ch, hdc in 3rd ch from hook and in each ch across, turn. *You now have* 32 hdc.

- **Rows 2–8:** Ch 2, hdc in each hdc across, turn.

- **Row 9 (joining row):** Ch 2, hdc in each hdc across; fhdc 7; beginning at back neck edge with RS facing, hdc in each hdc across back, turn. *You now have* 73 hdc.

- **Rows 10–18:** Ch 2, hdc in each hdc across, turn.

- Fasten off.

JUSTIN'S JACKET

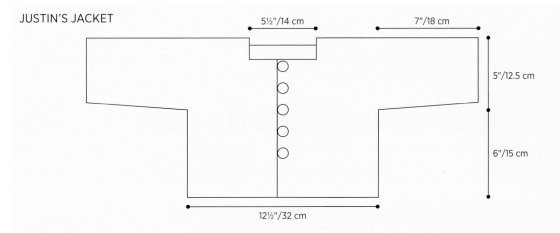

5½"/14 cm   7"/18 cm

5"/12.5 cm

6"/15 cm

12½"/32 cm

THE SECOND SLEEVE

- **Row 1 (RS):** Skip 20 sts, join yarn with standing hdc in next st, hdc in next 32 sts, turn, leaving remaining 20 sts unworked. *You now have* 33 hdc.

- **Rows 2–11:** Ch 2, hdc in each hdc across, turn.

- **Row 12:** Ch 2, hdc2tog, hdc to last 2 sts, hdc2tog, turn. *You now have* 31 hdc.

- **Rows 13–16:** Repeat Row 2 four times.

- **Row 17:** Repeat Row 11. *You now have* 29 hdc.

- **Rows 18–20:** Repeat Row 2 three times.

- Fasten off.

FINISHING

- Fold sweater in half at shoulders with WS together. Working through both layers from lower left underarm to left cuff, join yarn at bottom edge, ch 1, sc across side to sleeve, sc across bottom of sleeve. Fasten off. Repeat for other side, working from right cuff to lower right underarm; *do not fasten off.*

- Place markers for five buttons spaced as desired along left front (or right front) edge.

- **Sweater Edging:** With RS facing and continuing with yarn at right underarm, ch 1, sc evenly around bottom, fronts, and neck edges, working 3 sc in each exterior corner and working sc2tog over each interior corner, and working buttonholes at each marker as follows: (ch 2, skip 2 sts, sc in each st to next marker); join with slip st to first sc. Fasten off.

- Weave in ends. Sew buttons opposite buttonholes. (See Sewing Buttons on page 91.)

JUSTIN'S JACKET

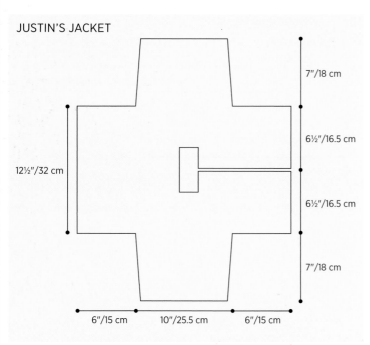

12½"/32 cm

7"/18 cm

6½"/16.5 cm

6½"/16.5 cm

7"/18 cm

6"/15 cm   10"/25.5 cm   6"/15 cm

CHAPTER FOUR

LITTLE
Bottoms

Ruffled Diaper Cover

DESIGNED BY *Corley Groves*

This pattern is worked as one continuous piece from front to back, crocheted in worsted-weight cotton. Crocodile stitch creates the ruffles on the bottom.

SIZES
To cover disposable diaper size 8–14 (12–18) lbs

YARN
Lily Sugar 'n Cream, 100% cotton, 120 yds (109 m)/2.5 oz (71 g), Color 01215 Robins Egg Blue ▨

CROCHET HOOK
US H/8 (5 mm) *or size needed to obtain correct gauge*

GAUGE
14 stitches and 11 rows = 4"/10 cm in half double crochet

OTHER SUPPLIES
Two ¾"/19 mm buttons, sewing needle and coordinating thread, yarn needle

PATTERN ESSENTIALS

Crocodile Ruffle

Instructions are given for right-handed crocheters with left-handed instructions in brackets: Holding piece with first st to be worked rotated to the 3 o'clock [9 o'clock] position and working from right to left [left to right], 5 dc around post of next dc; rotate piece 180° to the 9 o'clock [3 o'clock] position, 5 dc around post of next dc.

CROCHETING THE COVER

See chart on following page.

- Chain 28.
- **Row 1:** Hdc in 3rd chain from hook and in each chain across, turn. *You now have* 27 sts.
- **Rows 2–4:** Ch 2 (counts as hdc here and throughout), hdc in each hdc across, turn.
- **Rows 5–10:** Ch 2, hdc2tog, hdc in each hdc across to last 3 sts, hdc2tog, hdc in last st, turn. *You now have* 15 sts.
- **Row 11:** Ch 2, hdc in each hdc across, turn.
- Repeat Row 11 until piece measures 8 (8½)"/20.5 (21.5) cm from beginning.
- **Increase Row:** Ch 2, hdc in same st, hdc in each hdc to last st, 2 hdc in last st, turn. *You now have* 17 sts.
- Repeat Increase Row. *You now have* 19 sts.

THE RUFFLES

- **Row 1:** Ch 3 (counts as dc here and throughout), dc in same st, *ch 1, skip next 2 sts, 2 dc in next st, ch 1, skip next 2 sts, dc in next st; repeat from * across, ending with 2 dc in last st, turn. *You now have* 12 dc and 6 ch-1 spaces.
- **Row 2:** Ch 1, 2 slip sts in first st, slip st in next st; (Crocodile Ruffle around next pair of dc, slip st in top of next dc) three times, 2 slip sts in last st, turn.
- **Row 3:** Ch 3, dc in next slip st, ch 1, (2 dc in next slip st, ch 1, dc in next space at center of ruffle, ch 1) three times, 2 dc in next slip st, ch 1, skip 1 slip st, 2 dc in last slip st, turn. *You now have* 15 dc and 6 ch-1 spaces.
- **Row 4:** Ch 1, 2 slip st in first st, 1 slip st in next dc, (Crocodile Ruffle around next pair of dc, slip st in next dc) four times, 2 slip st in last st, turn.
- **Row 5:** Ch 3, dc in next slip st, ch 1, (2 dc in next slip st, ch 1, dc in next space at center of ruffle, ch 1) four times, 2 dc in next slip st, ch 1, skip 1 slip st, 2 dc in last slip st; ch 10, turn.
- **Row 6:** Slip st in 2nd ch from hook and in each of next 8 ch, slip st in next 2 dc, (Crocodile Ruffle around next pair of dc, slip st in next dc) five times, slip st in last dc, ch 11, turn.
- **Row 7:** Dc in 4th ch from hook and next 7 ch, dc in next slip st, ch 1, (2 dc in next slip st, ch 1, dc in next space at center of

ruffle, ch 1) five times, 2 dc in next slip st, ch 1, dc in last 10 slip sts, turn. *You now have* 37 dc and 12 ch-1 spaces.

- **Row 8:** Ch 1, slip st in next 10 dc, (Crocodile Ruffle around next pair of dc, slip st in next dc) six times, slip st in last 9 dc, turn.
- **Row 9:** Ch 3, dc in same st, dc in next 8 dc, ch 1, (2 dc in next slip st, ch 1, dc in next space at center of ruffle, ch 1) six times, ch 1, 2 dc in next slip st, ch 1, dc in next 8 dc, 2 dc in last dc, turn. *You now have* 40 dc and 14 ch-1 spaces.
- **Row 10:** Ch 1, slip st in first 10 sts, (Crocodile Ruffle around next pair of dc, slip st in next dc) seven times, slip st in next 9 sts, turn.
- **Row 11:** Ch 2, hdc in same st, hdc in next st, ch 2, skip 2 sts, hdc in next 6 sts, (3 hdc in next space at center of ruffle, hdc in next slip stitch) seven times, hdc in next 5 sts, ch 2, skip 2 sts, hdc in next st, 2 hdc in last st, turn.

- **Row 12:** Ch 2, hdc in next 2 hdc, 2 hdc in ch-2 space, hdc in next 12 sts, (BPhdc in next st, FPhdc in next st) seven times, BPhdc in next st, hdc in next 12 sts, 2 hdc in ch-2 space, hdc in last 3 sts, turn.
- **Row 13:** Ch 2, hdc in next 16 sts, (FPhdc in next st, BPhdc in next st) seven times, FPhdc in next st, hdc in next 17 sts.
- Fasten off.

FINISHING

- Fold in front flaps. Wrap back flaps around the front and align buttons on front band to where the button holes line up. You can adjust the size of the diaper waist by positioning the buttons closer together or farther apart. Sew an additional button on each side to make an adjustable size.
- Weave in ends and block if desired.

RUFFLED DIAPER COVER

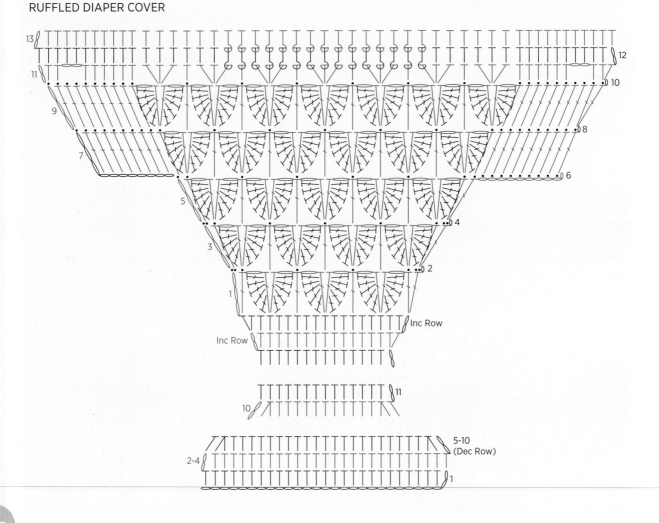

Buttoned-Up Diaper Cover

DESIGNED BY *Gwen Steege*

Cover up that cloth or disposable diaper with a little panache. The soft cotton yarn is machine washable, and the row of double crochet in the waistband makes it adjustable — just insert the buttons in the holes that make the best fit.

SIZE AND FINISHED MEASUREMENTS
To fit 0–3 months: 6½"/16.5 cm wide and 7"/18 cm long (waist to crotch)

YARN
Rowan Siena, 100% mercerized cotton, 153 yds (140 m)/1.76 oz (50 g), Color 656 Lido ⬛①

CROCHET HOOK
US E/4 (3.5 mm) crochet hook *or size needed to obtain correct gauge*

GAUGE
19 stitches and 18 rows = 4"/10 cm in pattern stitch

OTHER SUPPLIES
Stitch markers, yarn needle, two ⁹⁄₁₆"/14 mm buttons, sewing needle and coordinating thread

PATTERN ESSENTIALS

Pattern Stitch (multiple of 2 stitches + 1)

Row 1: Ch 3 (counts as dc), *sc in next dc, dc in next sc; repeat from * across, turn.

Row 2: Ch 1, sc in first dc, *dc in next sc, sc in next dc; repeat from * across, turn.

Repeat Rows 1 and 2 for pattern.

BUTTONED-UP DIAPER COVER

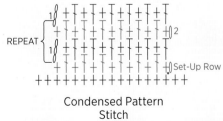

Condensed Pattern
Stitch

CROCHETING THE COVER

THE WAISTBAND

- Fsc 77 (see page 274).
- **Row 1:** Ch 3 (counts as dc here and throughout), dc in each sc across, turn.
- **Rows 2 and 3:** Ch 3, dc in each dc across, turn.
- **Row 4:** Ch 1, sc in each dc across, turn. Fasten off.

THE BODY

- **Set-Up Row:** Skip first 22 dc, join yarn with slip st in next st, ch 1, sc in same st, *dc in next sc, sc in next sc; repeat from * 15 times, turn, leaving remaining 22 dc unworked. *You now have* 16 dc and 17 sc.
- Work Rows 1 and 2 of pattern st until piece measures 5"/12.5 cm from top of band, ending with Row 1 of pattern.

Shape the Crotch

- **Row 1 (decrease row):** Ch 2 (does not count as st), (sc2tog) twice, work pattern st as established to last 4 sts, (sc2tog) twice. *You now have* 29 sts.
- **Row 2:** Repeat Row 1. *You now have* 25 sts.
- **Rows 3–6:** Work Rows 1 and 2 of pattern st twice.
- **Row 7 (increase row):** Ch 2 (does not count as st), 2 sc in next 2 sts, work pattern st as established to last 2 sts, 2 sc in next 2 sts. *You now have* 29 sts.
- Work even in established pattern st until piece measures 13½"/34.5 cm from top of band. Fasten off.
- Weave in ends. Block.

CROCHETING THE FLOWERS (MAKE 2 OR MORE)

- Begin with an adjustable ring (see page 272).
- **Rnd 1:** Ch 1, 16 sc in ring, join with slip st to first sc. *You now have* 16 sc.
- **Rnd 2:** Ch 5 (counts as dc and ch 3), skip next sc, *dc in next sc, ch 3, skip next sc; repeat from * around, join with slip st to 2nd ch of ch-5.
- **Rnd 3:** (Sc, hdc, dc, hdc, sc) in each space around, join with slip st to first sc. Fasten off, leaving a sewing length.

FINISHING

- With yarn needle, sew flowers on back of cover. With needle and thread, sew buttons to center front. Button each side of waistband through the middle dc row.

BUTTONED-UP DIAPER COVER

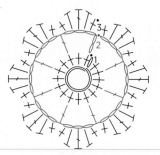

Flower

Octagon Pants

DESIGNED BY *Linda Rommerdahl, Yarntrepeneur.com*

These two versions of Octagon Pants are worked from the center outward in one piece using your choice of stitch pattern: back loop single crochet or double crochet with openwork. The fabric will almost magically fold itself into a pair of pants. The waistband and cuffs on the yellow sample are knitted, but you can substitute the crocheted waistband on the Blue Pants if you like.

SIZE AND FINISHED MEASUREMENTS
To fit 12–24 months: 20″/51 cm waist, 13″/33 cm length, 14″/35.5 cm (including 1″/2.5 cm waistband) rise (center back, to crotch, to center front)

YARN
Red Heart Super Saver, 100% acrylic, 364 yds (333 m)/7 oz (198 g), Color 0324 Bright Yellow or Color 0885 Delft Blue (**4**)

CROCHET HOOK
US I/9 (5.5 mm) *or size needed to obtain correct gauge*

KNITTING NEEDLES (OPTIONAL)
Set of four or five US 9 (5 mm) double-pointed needles

GAUGE
17½ stitches and 15 rounds = 4″/10 cm in back loop single crochet
14 stitches and 8 rounds = 4″/10 cm in double crochet

OTHER SUPPLIES
Stitch marker, yarn needle

PATTERN ESSENTIALS

Pick Up and Knit

With RS facing, insert the needle under both strands of the edge st, then wrap the yarn around the needle and knit the picked-up st.

CROCHETING THE YELLOW PANTS

- Ch 8, join with slip st to form a ring.
- **Rnd 1:** Ch 1, sc in ring, (ch 2, 2 sc) seven times in ring, ch 2, sc in ring, join with slip st to first sc. *You now have* 16 sc and 8 ch-2 corner spaces.

OCTAGON PANTS

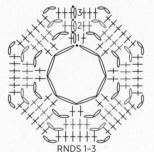

Yellow Pants Pattern

RNDS 1-3

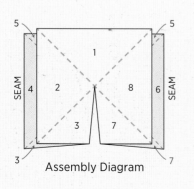

Assembly Diagram

- **Rnd 2:** Ch 1, sc in next sc, (sc, ch 2, sc) in next corner space, *sc in next 2 sc, (sc, ch 2, sc) in next corner space; repeat from * around, ending sc in last sc, join with slip st to first sc.
- **Rnd 3:** Ch 1, *sc in each sc to next corner space, (sc, ch 2, sc) in corner space; repeat from * around, ending sc in each sc to end of rnd, join with slip st to first sc.
- Repeat Rnd 3 until piece measures 6"/15 cm from center ring. *You now have* eight triangular sections.
- Section 1 is the center back and contains the beginning/ending of rnds. Counting in the direction of your stitching, pm in center top edge of triangular section 5.

FINISHING

- With RS together, fold the marked edge up so that marker meets the beginning of the rnd and edges of sections 1 and 5 are parallel.
- Sew outside leg seams, side 2 to side 4, and side 6 to side 8. Turn right-side out. Weave in ends.

THE WAISTBAND AND CUFFS (OPTION 1)

- With double-pointed needles and RS facing, pick up and knit 84 sts evenly spaced around waist opening.
- **Rnds 1–4:** (K2, p2) around.
- Bind off loosely.
- With double-pointed needles and RS facing, pick up and knit 44 sts evenly spaced around one leg opening. Work as for waistband. Repeat for other leg opening. Weave in ends.

THE WAISTBAND AND CUFFS (OPTION 2)

- **Rnd 1:** With RS facing, join yarn at center back waist, ch 1, sc evenly around waistband, join with slip st to first sc.
- **Rnds 2–4:** Ch 1, sc in each sc around, join with slip st to first sc. Fasten off.
- Repeat for leg openings, if desired.

CROCHETING THE BLUE PANTS

- Ch 8, join with slip st to form a ring.
- **Rnd 1:** Ch 3 (counts as dc here and throughout), (ch 2, 2 dc) seven times in ring, ch 2, dc in ring, join with slip st to top of ch-3. *You now have* 16 dc and 8 ch-2 corners.
- **Rnd 2:** Ch 3, dc in next ch, ch 2, dc in next ch, *dc in next 2 dc and in next ch, ch 2, dc in next ch; repeat from * around, ending dc in last dc, join with slip st to top of ch-3.
- **Rnd 3:** Ch 3, *dc in each dc to ch-2, dc in next ch, ch 2, dc in next ch; repeat from * around, ending dc in each dc to end of rnd, join with slip st to top of ch-3.
- Repeat Rnd 3 until piece measures 10"/25.5 cm from center ring. *You now have* eight triangular sections. Section 1 is the center back and contains the beginning/ending of rnds. Counting in the direction of your stitching, pm in center top edge of triangular section 5.
- Finish pants as for yellow version.

OCTAGON PANTS

Blue Pants Pattern

NOTE: After Rnd 1, corner dcs are worked into the ch sts, not into the corner spaces.

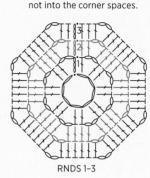

RNDS 1–3

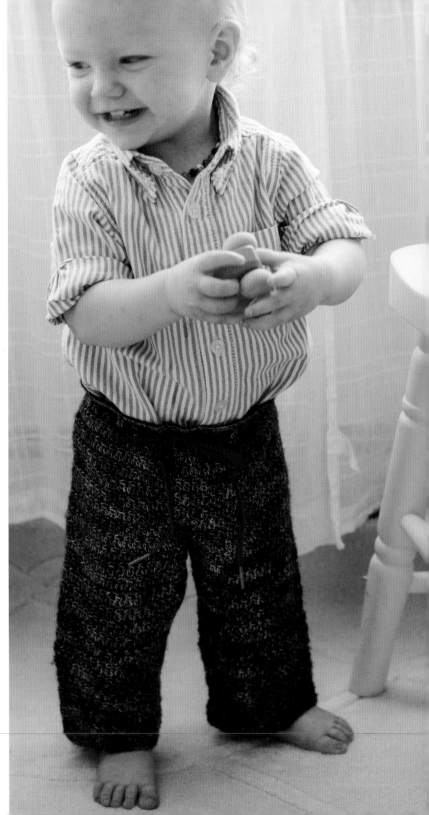

Drawstring Pants

DESIGNED BY *Judith Durant*

Keep baby snug but mobile in these tie-at-the-waist pants. Work the two legs separately in the round, work a few rows back and forth on each, then join the legs together in the round to finish the seat to the waist. If you have enough yarn left over, work an I-cord for the top; if not, use a shoelace or ribbon.

SIZE AND FINISHED MEASUREMENTS
To fit 6–12 months: 20"/51 cm waist, 7½"/19 cm inseam, and 12"/30.5 cm front-to-back through crotch

YARN
Madelinetosh Tosh Merino Light, 100% superwash merino wool, 420 yds (384 m)/3.5 oz (100 g), Spectrum 🔳

CROCHET HOOK
US G/6 (4 mm) *or size needed to obtain correct gauge*

GAUGE
26 stitches and 14 rows/rounds = 4"/10 cm in pattern

OTHER SUPPLIES
Yarn needle, 40"/101.5 cm length of ⅜"/9.5 mm shoelace or ribbon (optional)

CROCHETING THE PANTS

THE LEGS

- **Rnd 1:** Fdc 66 (see page 273); join with slip st to first fdc to form a rnd.

- **Rnd 2:** Work Rnd 2 of pattern st. *You now have* 33 sc and 33 spaces.

- **Rnd 3:** Work Rnd 3 of pattern st.

- **Rnd 4:** Work Rnd 4 of pattern st.

- **Rnd 5:** Repeat Rnd 3.

- **Rnd 6 (increase rnd):** Ch 1, sc in first st, *ch 1, skip next st, sc in next space; repeat from * around, ending with sc in top of beginning ch, ch 1, join with slip st to beginning ch-1. *You now have* 68 sts.

- **Rnd 7:** Repeat Rnd 3.

- **Rnds 8–25:** Repeat Rnds 6 and 7 nine more times. At the end of Rnd 25, *you will have* 86 sts.

- **Rnds 26–29:** Repeat Rnds 4–7. *You now have* 88 sts.

- **Rnds 30 and 31:** Repeat Rnds 4 and 5.

- **Rnd 32:** Slip st in next 6 sts, ch 1 sc in same space, ch 1, *sc in next ch-1 space, ch 1, skip next st; repeat from * to last 7 sts, sc in next ch-1 space, turn, leaving remaining sts unworked. *You now have* 78 sts.

PATTERN ESSENTIALS

Pattern Stitch (multiple of 2 stitches)

Rnd 1: Work an even number of fdc; join with slip st to first fdc to form a rnd.

Rnd 2: Ch 1, skip first st, *sc in next st, ch 1, skip next st; repeat from * around to last st, sc in last st, ch 1, join with slip st to beginning ch-1.

Rnd 3: Ch 3, work dc2tog over same st and next ch-space, ch 1, *dc2tog over same and next space, ch 1; repeat from * around, join with slip st to top of beginning ch-3.

Rnd 4: Ch 1, skip next st, *sc in next space, ch 1, skip next st; repeat from * to last space, sc in last space, ch 1, join with slip st to beginning ch-1.

Repeat Rnds 3 and 4 for pattern.

Begin working back and forth in rows.

- **Row 33:** Ch 3, dc2tog over same st and next ch-space, ch 1, *dc2tog over same and next ch-space, ch 1; repeat from * across, ending with dc in beginning ch-1. *You now have* 78 sts.

- **Row 34:** Slip st in first 2 sts (*2 sts decreased*), slip st in next st, ch 1, *sc in next space, ch 1, skip next st; repeat from * to last 4 sts (the dc2tog, ch 1, dc2tog, ch-3), turn, leaving remaining st unworked. *You now have* 72 sts.

- **Rows 35 and 36:** Repeat Rows 33 and 34. *You now have* 68 sts.

- Fasten off and set aside.

- Repeat to make a second leg. *Do not fasten off.*

DRAWSTRING PANTS

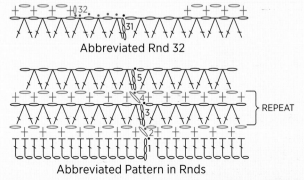

Abbreviated Rnd 32

Abbreviated Pattern in Rnds

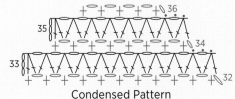

Condensed Pattern
in Rows (Decrease Rows)

147

JOIN THE LEGS

- **Rnd 1 (joining rnd):** Ch 3, work dc2tog inserting hook in sc at base of ch-3 and then in next ch-1 space, ch 1, *dc2tog inserting hook into same sp as previous st and then in next ch-1 space, ch 1*; repeat from * to * across current leg, ending with dc2tog into same space as previous st at end of row and then in first ch-1 space on last row of other leg (making sure the join is snug), repeat from * to * across second leg, ending with dc2tog into same space as previous st at end of row and then in first ch-1 space on last row of first leg, ch 1, join with slip st to beginning ch-3 (center back). *You now have* 136 sts and are working in the rnd.

- Repeat Rnds 4 and 5 from Crocheting the Legs on 136 sts until piece measures 5½"/14 cm from Rnd 1 (joining rnd).

- **Final Rnd:** Ch 1, sc in each st around, join with slip st to first sc. Fasten off.

FINISHING

- Use tails at beginning of legs to join the first and last fdc sts. Sew crotch seam. Block.

- Weave I-cord (see page 150), lacing, or ribbon through every other dc cluster in the 2nd rnd from the waist so that the ends meet at the center front. With sewing needle and thread, tack cord in place at center back so baby cannot remove it.

DRAWSTRING PANTS

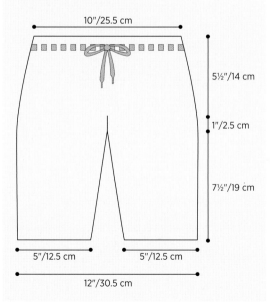

10"/25.5 cm

5½"/14 cm

1"/2.5 cm

7½"/19 cm

5"/12.5 cm   5"/12.5 cm

12"/30.5 cm

All Grow'd Up Skirt

DESIGNED BY *Judith Durant*

A crocheted skirt can be part of your little girl's wardrobe for more than a couple of months when it has an adjustable waist. This one can go from a midi to a mini.

SIZE AND FINISHED MEASUREMENTS
To fit 12–24 months: 18–20"/45.5–51 cm waist and 9"/23 cm length

YARN
Shelridge Yarns Soft Touch DK, 100% superwash merino wool, 265 yds (242 m)/3.5 oz (100 g), Color 1306-058 Straw ❸

CROCHET HOOKS
US I/9 (5.5 mm) *or size needed to obtain correct gauge* and US G/6 (4.25 mm)

GAUGE
20 stitches (2 pattern repeats) and 9 rows = 4"/10 cm in Chevron Pattern on larger hook

OTHER SUPPLIES
One US 5 (3.75 mm) knitting needle, yarn needle

PATTERN ESSENTIALS

Chevron Pattern (multiple of 10 stitches)

Set-Up Rnd: Fsc a multiple of 10, join with slip st to beginning st.

Rnd 1: Ch 3 (counts as dc here and throughout), dc in same st, *dc in next 3 sts, dc3tog, dc in next 3 sts**, 3 dc in next st; repeat from * around ending last repeat at **, dc in joining st, join with slip st to top of ch-3.

Repeat Rnd 1 for pattern.

149

CROCHETING THE SKIRT

- **Set-Up Rnd:** With larger hook, fsc 120 (see page 274). Join with slip st to beginning st, being careful not to twist the sts.

- Work Rnd 1 of Chevron Pattern 17 times or until piece measures approximately 7½"/19 cm.

- With smaller hook, ch 3, dc2tog, *dc in next st, dc2tog; repeat from * around, join with slip st to top of ch-3. *You now have 80 sts.*

THE WAISTBAND

- **Rnds 1–3:** Ch 3, dc in each st to end of rnd, join with slip st to top of ch-3.

- Fasten off.

ALL GROW'D UP SKIRT

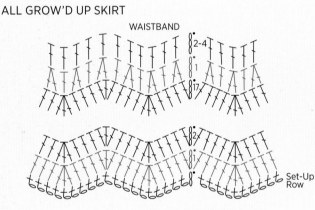

Abbreviated Skirt Pattern

FINISHING

THE BOTTOM EDGING

- With smaller hook, attach yarn at beginning of rnd and work 2 sc in each fsc around, join with slip st to first sc. Fasten off.

CROCHETING THE I-CORD

- Leaving a 4"/10 cm tail, ch 3. Insert hook in 2nd ch from hook and pull up a loop, pull up a loop in next ch; *slip last 2 loops from hook to knitting needle (*1 loop remains on hook*), (yo and pull through 1 loop on hook, slip next st from needle to hook) twice, yo and pull through 1 loop on hook; repeat from * until cord measures 34"/86.5 cm or desired length. ***Note:*** You can eliminate the knitting needle and simply drop and hold the 2 sts from the hook and chain through them one at a time.

- Beginning and ending at the center front, thread cord through 2nd rnd of waistband, weaving under and over 2 dc at a time. Weave in ends.

CHAPTER FIVE

LITTLE
Bibs
+
Washcloths

Little Star Bib and Washcloth

DESIGNED BY *Donna Barranti*

Two designs in one! Crochet a square, then add an edging all around for a washcloth, or add an edging to three sides and a strap to the top for a bib.

....

FINISHED MEASUREMENTS
7"/18 cm square

....

YARN
Knit Picks Brava Sport, 100% premium acrylic, 273 yds (250 m)/3.5 oz (100 g), Color 26380 Fig ②

....

CROCHET HOOK
US F/5 (3.75 mm) *or size needed to obtain correct gauge*

....

GAUGE
10 Star Stitches and 10 rows = 4"/10 cm in Star Stitch pattern

....

OTHER SUPPLIES
Yarn needle, one ⅜"/9.5 mm button for bib, sewing needle and coordinating thread

CROCHETING THE WASHCLOTH

THE SQUARE

- Chain 38.

- **Set-Up Row (RS):** Yo, insert hook in 2nd ch from hook, yo and pull up a loop, yo, skip 1 ch, insert hook in next ch, yo and pull up a loop, yo and draw through all 5 loops on hook, ch 1 (*eyelet made*), *yo, insert hook in same ch as last leg of star st just made, yo and pull up a loop, yo, skip 1 ch, insert hook in next ch, yo and pull up a loop, yo and draw through all 5 loops on hook, ch 1; repeat from * across, turn. *You now have* 18 star sts.

- **Rows 1–20:** Ch 1, beg star st, work star st across, ending with ending star st, turn. *Do not turn at end of last row.*

THE PICOT EDGE

- Working across side edge, ch 1, 3 sc in corner st, slip st in next row-end st, [(sc, ch 3, sc) in next eyelet, slip st in next row-end st] to next corner, 3 sc in next corner, working across bottom edge, slip st in next ch, skip next ch, [(sc, ch 3, sc) in next ch, skip next ch, slip st in next ch] to next corner, 3 sc in corner, slip st in next row-end st, [(sc, ch 3, sc) in next eyelet, slip st in next row-end st] to next corner**, 3 sc in next corner, working across top edge, slip st in next star st, [(sc, ch 3, sc) in next eyelet, slip st in next star st] across, join with slip st to first sc. Fasten off. Weave in ends.

CROCHETING THE BIB

THE SQUARE

- Work Square as for Washcloth.

THE PICOT EDGE

- Work as for Washcloth, ending at **, sc in next corner. *Do not fasten off.*

THE BUTTON TAB

- **Row 1 (RS):** Working across top of bib, (sc in next star st, sc in next eyelet) six times, turn. *You now have* 12 sc.

- **Row 2 (WS):** Ch 1, sc2tog, sc in each sc across, turn. *You now have* 11 sc.

- **Row 3:** Ch 1, sc in each sc across, turn.

- **Rows 4–7:** Repeat Rows 2 and 3 twice. *You now have* 9 sc.

PATTERN ESSENTIALS

Beg Star St (beginning star stitch)
Yo, insert hook in 2nd ch from hook (*eyelet made*), yo and pull up a loop, yo, insert hook in eyelet of next star st, yo and pull up a loop, yo and draw through all 5 loops on hook, ch 1 to close star st and form eyelet.

Ending Star St (ending star stitch) Yo, insert hook in same eyelet as last leg of last star st made, yo and pull up a loop, yo, insert hook in space created by eyelet and ch 1 of previous row, yo and pull up a loop, yo and draw through all 5 loops on hook, ch 1 to close star st and form eyelet.

Star St (star stitch) Yo, insert hook in same eyelet as last leg of last star st made, yo and pull up a loop, yo, insert hook in eyelet of next star st, yo and pull up a loop, yo and draw through all 5 loops on hook, ch 1 to close star st and form eyelet.

LITTLE STAR BIB AND WASHCLOTH

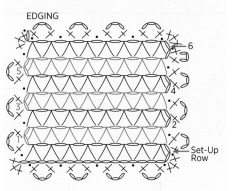

Condensed Washcloth Pattern

- **Row 8:** Repeat Row 2. *You now have 8 sc.*
- **Row 9 (RS):** Ch 1, sc in each sc across to last st, 3 sc in last st.
- Continue working sc evenly along row ends of button tab, then work (sc in next star st, sc in next eyelet), ending with sc in corner, turn.

THE STRAP AND BUTTONHOLE (RIGHT SHOULDER)

- **Row 1 (WS):** Ch 1, sc in next 12 sc, turn. *You now have 12 sc.*
- **Row 2 (RS):** Ch 1, sc2tog, sc in each sc across, turn. *You now have 11 sc.*
- **Row 3:** Ch 1, sc in each sc across, turn.
- **Rows 4–7:** Repeat Rows 2 and 3 twice. *You now have 9 sc.*
- **Row 8:** Repeat Row 2. *You now have 8 sc.*
- **Rows 9–37:** Ch 1, BLsc in each st across, turn.
- **Row 38 and 39:** Ch 1, sc2tog, sc in each sc across, turn. *You now have 6 sc.*
- **Row 40 (WS):** Ch 1, sc in first 2 sts, ch 2, skip 2 sc, sc in last 2 sc, turn.
- **Row 41 (RS):** Ch 1, sc2tog, 2 sc in ch-2 space, sc2tog. *You now have 4 sc.* Fasten off.
- Weave in ends. Sew button securely on tab (see Sewing Buttons on page 91).

Bib Trio

DESIGNED BY *Edie Eckman*

Having three coordinating bibs means you can switch them out frequently when they become soiled. Each bib takes just 10 grams of yarn, so you could get a fourth and maybe a fifth bib out of a single skein, if you like.

CROCHETING THE FIRST BIB

See chart on page 156.

- Ch 4, join with slip st to form a ring.
- **Row 1 (WS):** Ch 3 (counts as dc here and throughout), 10 dc in ring, turn. *You now have 11 dc.*
- **Row 2:** Ch 1, sc in each dc across, turn.
- **Row 3:** Ch 4 (counts as dc and ch 1), (2-dc cluster in next sc, ch 2) eight times, 2-dc cluster in next sc, ch 1, dc in last sc, turn. *You now have 9 clusters and 2 dc.*
- **Row 4:** Ch 1, sc in first dc, sc in next space, (sc in next cluster, 2 sc in next space) eight times, sc in next cluster, sc in next ch-1 space, sc in 3rd ch of ch-4, turn. *You now have 29 sc.*
- **Row 5:** Ch 2 (does not count as hdc throughout), hdc in next 4 sts, (2 hdc in next st, hdc in next 4 sts) five times, turn. *You now have 34 hdc.*
- **Row 6:** Ch 1, sc in each sc across, turn.
- **Row 7:** Ch 2, hdc in next 4 sts, (2 hdc in next st, hdc in next 5 sts) five times. *You now have 39 hdc.*
- **Row 8:** Repeat Row 6.
- **Row 9:** Ch 2, hdc in first 4 sc, (2 hdc in next sc, hdc in next 6 sc) five times, turn. *You now have 44 hdc.*
- **Row 10:** Ch 1, sc in first 4 hdc, (2 sc in next sc, sc in next 5 sc) six times, 2 sc in next sc, sc in last 3 sc, turn. *You now have 51 sc.*

THE TIES AND EDGING

- **Row 11:** *Ch 50 loosely, slip st in back bump (see page 276) of 2nd ch from hook and in each ch across**; sc evenly spaced along row ends, repeat from * to ** once; working across Row 10, sc in next 4 sc, 2 sc in next sc, (sc in next 9 sc, 2 sc in next sc) four times, sc in each sc to base of first tie, slip st in next st; *do not turn.*

- **Row 12:** Ch 1, reverse sc in each sc across to corner, slip st in next st. Fasten off. Weave in ends.

CROCHETING THE SECOND BIB

See chart on page 157.

- Ch 4, join with slip st to form a ring.
- **Row 1 (RS):** Ch 3 (counts as dc here and throughout), 11 dc in ring, turn. *You now have* 12 dc.
- **Row 2:** Ch 1, sc in each dc across, turn.
- **Row 3:** Ch 3, 2 BLdc in each st across to last st, BLdc in last st, turn. *You now have* 22 sts.
- **Row 4:** Ch 1, FLsc in each st across, turn.
- **Row 5:** Ch 1, BLsc in first st, *2 BLsc in next st, BLsc in next st; repeat from * to last st, sc in last st, turn. *You now have* 32 sc.

FINISHED MEASUREMENTS
Approximately 6¼"/16 cm wide and 3¼"/8 cm long, excluding ties

YARN
Plymouth Yarns Bio Sesia 5, 100% cotton, 196 yds (180 m)/1.75 oz (50 g), Color 2859 (1)

CROCHET HOOK
US G/6 (4 mm) *or size needed to obtain correct gauge*

GAUGE
Rows 1–3 of first bib = 2¾"/7 cm across in pattern

OTHER SUPPLIES
Yarn needle

First Bib

Second Bib

Third Bib

- **Row 6:** Repeat Row 4.
- **Row 7:** Ch 1, BLsc in first 2 sts, *2 BLsc in next st, BLsc in next 2 sts; repeat from * across, turn. *You now have* 42 sc.
- **Row 8:** Repeat Row 4.
- **Row 9:** Ch 1, BLsc in first 2 sts, *2 BLsc in next st, BLsc in next 3 sts; repeat from * across, turn. *You now have* 52 sc.
- **Row 10:** Ch 1, FLsc in each st across; do not turn.

THE TIES AND EDGING

- **Row 11:** *Ch 50 loosely, slip st in back bump of 2nd ch from hook and in each ch across**; sc evenly spaced along row ends, repeat from * to ** once; sc in each sc to base of first tie, slip st in base of first tie; *do not turn.*

- **Row 12:** Ch 1, reverse sc in each sc across to base of second tie, slip st in next st. Fasten off. Weave in ends.

CROCHETING THE THIRD BIB

- Ch 4, join with slip st to form a ring.
- **Row 1 (RS):** Ch 3 (counts as dc here and throughout), 8 dc in ring, turn. *You now have* 9 dc.
- **Row 2:** Ch 3, dc in same st, 2 dc in each dc to last st, dc in last st, turn. *You now have* 17 dc.
- **Row 3:** Ch 3, dc in same st, (FPtr in next st, 2 dc in next st) seven times, FPtr in next st, dc in last st. *You now have* 25 sts.
- **Row 4:** Ch 3, dc in same st, dc in each st across, turn. *You now have* 26 dc.
- **Row 5:** Ch 1, sc in same st, *tr in next dc, sc in next dc, (tr, sc) in next st; repeat from * to last st, sc in last st. *You now have* 34 sts.
- **Row 6:** Ch 3, dc in same st, dc in each st across, turn. *You now have* 35 dc.

BIB TRIO

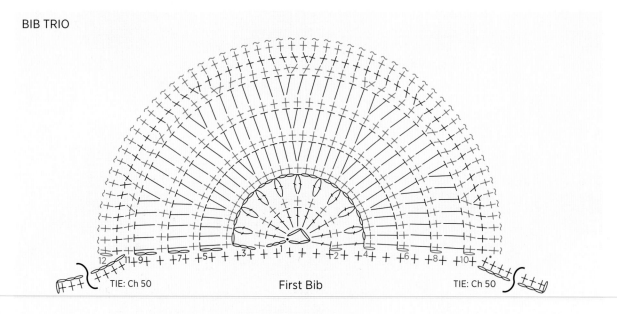

TIE: Ch 50   First Bib   TIE: Ch 50

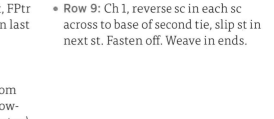

- **Row 7:** Ch 3, dc in same st, *FPtr in next st, dc in next st, FPtr in next st, 2 dc in next st; repeat from * to last 2 sts, dc in last 2 sts, turn. *You now have* 44 sts.

THE TIES AND EDGING

- **Row 8:** *Ch 50 loosely, slip st in back bump of 2nd ch from hook and in each ch across**; sc evenly spaced across row-ends, repeat from * to ** once; (sc in next 3 sc, 2 sc in next sc) 10 times, sc in next 4 sc, slip st in base of first tie; *do not turn.*

- **Row 9:** Ch 1, reverse sc in each sc across to base of second tie, slip st in next st. Fasten off. Weave in ends.

BIB TRIO

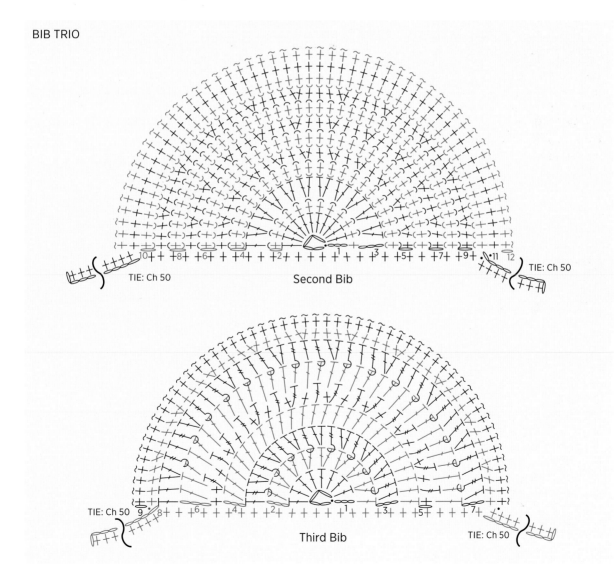

Second Bib

TIE: Ch 50

TIE: Ch 50

Third Bib

TIE: Ch 50

TIE: Ch 50

157

Sweet Pea Bib

DESIGNED BY *Lorna Miser, Lorna Miser Designs*

This sweet bib is worked neck-down from a no-chain foundation. The Shell Stitch is delicate yet substantial enough to catch baby's drips, and one accent button makes the bib easy to put on and take off.

FINISHED MEASUREMENTS
Approximately 7½"/19 cm wide and 6½"/16.5 cm long, excluding neck band

YARN
Universal Yarns Cotton Supreme Splash, 100% cotton, 180 yds (165 m)/3.5 oz (100 g), Color 206 Plum Blanket (4)

CROCHET HOOK
US I/9 (5.5 mm) *or size needed to obtain correct gauge*

GAUGE
17 stitches and 10 rows = 4"/10 cm in Shell Stitch pattern

OTHER SUPPLIES
Yarn needle, one ⅝"/16 mm button, sewing needle and coordinating thread

---

SWEET PEA BIB

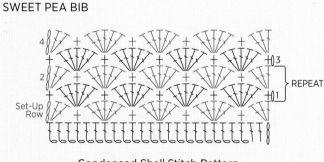

Condensed Shell Stitch Pattern

PATTERN ESSENTIALS

Shell Stitch (multiple of 6 stitches + 1)

Set-Up Row: Ch 3 (counts as dc here and throughout), 2 dc in same st, *skip 2 sts, sc in next st, skip 2 sts**, 5 dc in next st; repeat from * across, ending last repeat at **, 3 dc in last st, turn.

Row 1: Ch 1, sc in same st, *5 dc in next sc, skip 2 dc, sc in next dc; repeat from * across, turn.

Row 2: Ch 3, 2 dc in same st, *skip 2 dc, sc in next dc**, 5 dc in next sc; repeat from * across, ending last repeat at **, 3 dc in last sc, turn.

Repeat Rows 1 and 2 for pattern.

CROCHETING THE BIB

THE STRAP

- Fdc 38 (see page 273), ch 5 for button loop, turn, dc in base of each fdc across.

- Turn strap sideways.

THE BIB

- Ch 3, work 2 dc across end of strap, fdc 28, turn. *You now have* 31 sts.

- Work in Shell Stitch pattern until bib measures 6½"/16.5 cm from beginning. Fasten off. Weave in ends. Sew button to top left-hand corner on RS. See Sewing Buttons on page 91.

Ribbed Baby Bib

DESIGNED BY *René E. Wells, Granny an Me Designs*

Babies always need a little something to catch the drips, and this bib is suitable for any occasion. Crocheted in washable wool with a simple pattern, you can make one to match every outfit.

FINISHED MEASUREMENTS
7½"/19 cm wide and 8½"/21.5 cm long

YARN
Patons Kroy Socks FX, 75% superwash wool/25% nylon, 166 yds (152 m)/1.75 oz (50 g), 57110 Cadet Colors ①

CROCHET HOOK
US E/4 (3.5 mm) *or size needed to obtain correct gauge*

GAUGE
24 stitches and 16 rows = 4"/10 cm in pattern

OTHER SUPPLIES
Yarn needle

CROCHETING THE BIB

- Fdc 45 (see page 273), turn.

- **Row 1 (WS):** Ch 1, sc in first st, *ch 4, skip 3 sts, sc in next st; repeat from * across, ending sc in last st, turn. *You now have* 11 ch-4 spaces.

- **Row 2:** Ch 3 (counts as dc here and throughout), *3 dc in next space, FPtr in st below next sc; repeat from * to last space, 3 dc in last space, dc in last sc, turn. *You now have* 45 sts.

- Repeat Rows 1 and 2 eleven times, then work Row 1 once more.

THE LEFT FRONT

- **Row 1 (RS):** Ch 3, (3 dc in next space, FPtr in next FPtr 2 rows below) three times, 3 dc in next space, dc in last sc, turn, leaving remaining sts unworked. *You now have* 17 sts.

Continue on these 17 sts only.

- **Row 2:** Ch 1, sc in first st, ch 3, skip next 3 dc, (sc in next st, ch 4, skip next 3 dc) three times, sc in last st, turn.

- **Row 3:** Ch 3, (dc2tog, dc) in first space, (FPtr in next FPtr 2 rows below, 3 dc in next space) twice, FPtr in next FPtr 2 rows below, 2 dc in last space, dc2tog over same space and last sc, turn. *You now have* 15 sts.

- **Row 4:** Ch 1, sc in first st, ch 3, skip next 2 dc, (sc in next st, ch 4, skip next 3 dc) twice, sc in next st, ch 2, skip next 2 sts, sc in last st, turn.

- **Row 5:** Ch 3, dc in first space, (FPtr in next FPtr 2 rows below, 3 dc in next space) twice, FPtr in next FPtr 2 rows below, dc2tog over next ch-space and last sc, turn. *You now have* 12 sts.

- **Row 6:** Ch 1, skip first st, sc in next FPtr, (ch 3, skip next 3 dc, sc in next st) twice, turn, leaving remaining sts unworked.

- **Row 7:** Ch 2, dc2tog in first space, dc in same space, FPtr in next FPtr 2 rows below, dc in next space, dc2tog in same space, turn. *You now have* 5 sts.

THE NECK EDGING

- Slip st evenly down left neck edge to front edge, (3 sc in next ch-3 space, sc in next sc) three times.

THE RIGHT FRONT

- **Row 1 (RS):** Ch 2, (3 dc in next ch-3 space, FPtr in next FPtr 2 rows below) three times, 3 dc in last space, dc in last sc, turn. *You now have* 17 sts.

- Repeat Rows 2–7 of left front. *Do not turn.*

FINISHING

- With RS facing and working along outer edge, sc evenly around to top inner edge of left front, working 2 sc in each lower corner.

THE TIES AND OUTER EDGING

- Ch 60, turn; slip st in 2nd ch from hook and in each ch to shoulder. *Do not turn.*

- With RS facing, work reverse sc along outer left side, bottom, and up to top inner edge of right front.

- Ch 60, turn; slip st in 2nd ch from hook and each ch to shoulder, then sc evenly along inner neck edge, slip st to inside corner of neck, slip st in each sc to base of next tie. Fasten off.

- Weave in ends.

RIBBED BABY BIB

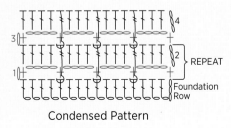

Condensed Pattern

Baby's Bath Set

DESIGNED BY *Judith Durant*

The wonderfully soft and absorbent cotton yarn used here is perfect for the bath. Slide your favorite soap into the mitt, wash baby, and use the towelette for rinsing or for drying.

FINISHED MEASUREMENTS
Mitt: 7"/18 cm circumference and 4½"/11.5 cm tall
Towelette: Approximately 9"/23 cm square

YARN
Classic Elite Yarns Sandpiper, 100% cotton, 114 yds (104 m)/1.75 oz (50 g), Color 1918 Faded Brick ④

CROCHET HOOK
US J/10 (6 mm) *or size needed to obtain correct gauge*

GAUGE
15 stitches and 13 rows = 4"/10 cm in Towelette pattern
16 stitches and 16 rows = 4"/10 cm in Soap Mitt pattern

OTHER SUPPLIES
Yarn needle

PATTERN ESSENTIALS

Towelette Pattern (multiple of 2 stitches + 1, worked on fsc)

Row 1 (WS): Ch 1, sc in first st, *tr in next st, sc in next st; repeat from * across, turn.

Row 2: Ch 1, sc in each st across, turn.

Repeat Rows 1 and 2 for pattern.

Soap Mitt Pattern (multiple of 2 stitches + 1, worked on fsc)

Row 1: Ch 1, sc in first st, *ch 1, skip 1 st, sc in next st; rep from * across, turn.

Repeat Row 1 for pattern.

CROCHETING THE TOWELETTE

- Fsc 33 (see page 274).

- Work Rows 1 and 2 of Towelette pattern 14 times (28 rows). Fasten off. Weave in ends.

CROCHETING THE SOAP MITT

- Fsc 25.

- Work Row 1 of Soap Mitt pattern 20 times. Fasten off, leaving a sewing length.

- With RS together, sew side and bottom seams, leaving foundation row open. Turn right side out. Cut two 16"/40.5 cm lengths of yarn. Thread doubled yarn onto yarn needle and thread the lengths in and out of fsc sts. Knot ends of doubled yarn. Insert soap, then cinch opening closed and secure with a bow knot.

BABY'S BATH SET

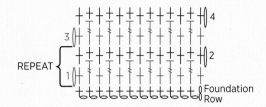

Condensed Towelette Pattern

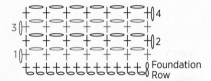

Condensed Soap Mitt Pattern

Waves and Patchwork Washcloths

DESIGNED BY *Melinda A. Slaving*

Mercerized cotton is the perfect choice for washcloths — strong and mildew resistant, it will hold its shape through many washings. Here are two simple cloths with sweet stitch patterns.

FINISHED MEASUREMENTS
Each cloth is 6"/15 cm by 7"/18 cm

YARN
Classic Elite Yarns Provence, 100% Egyptian mercerized cotton, 205 yds (186 m)/3.75 oz (100 g), Color 2625 Rosa Rugosa ③
Note: One skein will make three washcloths.

CROCHET HOOK
US G/6 (4 mm) *or size needed to obtain correct gauge*

GAUGE
20 stitches and 18 rows = 4"/10 cm in wave pattern
16 stitches and 32 rows = 4"/10 cm in patchwork pattern

OTHER SUPPLIES
Yarn needle

CROCHETING THE WAVES WASHCLOTH

- Chain 31.

- **Row 1:** Sc in 2nd ch from hook and in each chain across, turn. *You now have 30 sc.*

- **Rows 2–4:** Ch 1, sc in each sc across, turn.

- **Row 5:** Ch 1, sc in first 2 sc, *skip 2 sc, 5 sc in next sc, skip 2 sts, sc in next 2 sc; repeat from * across, turn.

- **Row 6:** Ch 1, sc in each sc across, turn.

- **Rows 7–30:** Repeat Rows 5 and 6 twelve times.

- **Row 31:** Ch 1, sc in each sc across, turn.

- **Row 32:** Ch 1, reverse sc in each st across.

- Fasten off. Weave in ends.

CROCHETING THE PATCHWORK WASHCLOTH

- Chain 25.

- **Row 1:** Sc in 2nd ch from hook and in each ch across. *You now have 24 sc.*

- **Rows 2–5:** Ch 1, *FLsc in next 4 sts, BLsc in next 4 sts; repeat from * across, turn.

- **Rows 6–9:** Ch 1, *BLsc in next 4 sts, FLsc in next 4 sts; repeat from * across, turn.

- **Rows 10–33:** Repeat Rows 2–9 three more times.

- Fasten off. Weave in ends.

WAVES AND PATCHWORK WASHCLOTHS

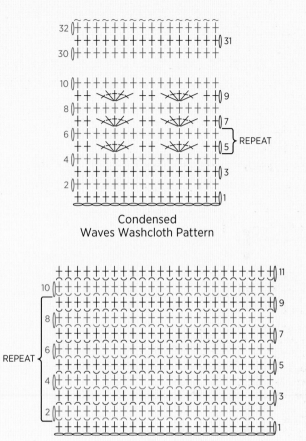

Condensed
Waves Washcloth Pattern

Patchwork Washcloth Pattern

Burp Cloth

DESIGNED BY *Diane McKee*

Mitered squares and colorful variegated cotton yarn combine in this eye-catching shoulder cover. It will keep your clothing clean and dry.

FINISHED MEASUREMENTS
6"/15 cm wide by 12¾"/32 cm long

YARN
Adriafil Kimera, 100% Egyptian mercerized cotton, 148 yds (135 m)/1.75 oz (50 g), Color 016 Proust Fancy 🧶❷

CROCHET HOOK
US G/6 (4 mm) *or size needed to obtain correct gauge*

GAUGE
16 stitches and 14 rows = 4"/10 cm in half double crochet

OTHER SUPPLIES
Stitch marker, yarn needle

PATTERN ESSENTIALS

Surface chain Holding yarn on WS of fabric, insert hook from front to back into next st and pull up a loop through fabric and through loop on hook.

CROCHETING THE FRONT

SQUARE 1

- **Row 1 (RS):** Fsc 25 (see page 274), turn. Pm in center st.
- **Row 2:** Ch 1, sc in each sc to 1 st before marked st, sc3tog, sc in each sc to end. *You now have 23 sts.*
- **Rows 3–12:** Repeat Row 2. *You now have 3 sc.*
- **Row 13:** Ch 1, sc3tog. Fasten off.

SQUARE 2

- **Row 1 (RS):** Holding Square 1 with RS facing and Row 13 at lower right, standing sc in base of first st of Square 1, sc in base of next 11 sc; fsc 1, inserting hook in base of same st, mark this st as center st, fsc 12, turn. *You now have* 25 sc.
- **Rows 2–13:** Work as for Square 1.

SQUARE 3

- **Row 1 (RS):** Holding joined squares with RS facing and Row 13 of Square 2 at lower right, standing sc in base of first st of Square 2, sc in base of next 11 sc; fsc 1, inserting hook in base of same st, mark this st as center st, fsc 12, turn. *You now have* 25 sc.
- **Rows 2–13:** Work as for Square 1.

SQUARE 4

- **Row 1 (RS):** Holding joined squares with RS facing and Row 13 of Square 3 at lower right, standing sc in base of first st of Square 3, sc in base of next 11 sc; sc in corner where squares meet, mark this st as center st; sc in next 12 sts of Square 1, turn. *You now have* 25 sc.
- **Rows 2–13:** Work as for Square 1, but *do not fasten off.*

BURP CLOTH

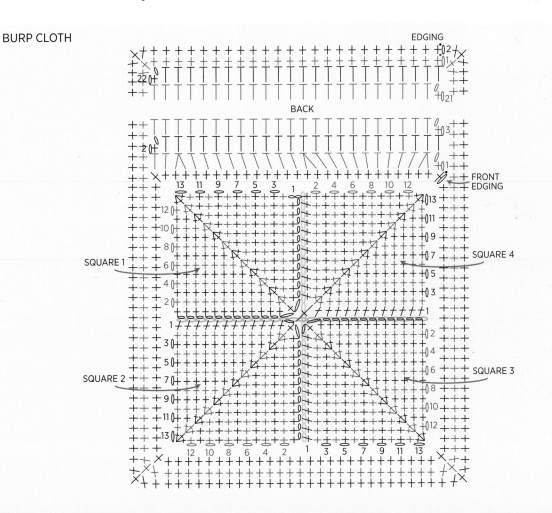

EDGING

- Ch 1, 2 sc in same st, work 25 sc evenly spaced along top edges of squares 4 and 1, *3 sc in corner, work 25 sc evenly spaced to corner; repeat from * twice, sc in beginning st, join with slip st to first sc. *You now have* 112 sc.

CROCHETING THE BACK

- **Row 1 (RS):** Ch 1, sc in same st, ch 1 (sc, ch 1 counts as hdc here and throughout), hdc2tog, *hdc in next 9 sc, hdc2tog; repeat from * once, hdc in last 2 sts, turn. *You now have* 24 hdc.

- **Row 2:** Ch 1, sc in same st, ch 1, hdc in each hdc across, turn.

- **Rows 3–22:** Repeat Row 2. *Do not fasten off.*

FINISHING

EDGING

- **Rnd 1:** Ch 1, sc in same st, sc in each sc to corner, 3 sc in corner, sc evenly down edge of back; sc in each sc around front, placing 2 or 3 sc in each corner st to allow edge to lie flat; sc evenly up edge of back to beginning, ending 2 sc in same st as beginning of rnd, join with slip st to first sc.

- **Rnd 2:** Ch 1, sc in first st, sc in each sc around, placing 2 or 3 sc in each corner st, ending sc in same st as beginning of rnd, join with slip st to first sc. Fasten off.

- Work a surface chain along both the horizontal and vertical "seams" of front. Weave in ends.

CHAPTER SIX

LITTLE
Toys

Benjamin Bear

DESIGNED BY *Ida Herter, Herter Crochet Designs*

This wonderfully huggable teddy bear is made in classic amigurumi style — single crochet worked in continuous rounds. The super-bulky yarn is easy to work with and amazingly soft.

FINISHED MEASUREMENTS
11"/28 cm, seated

YARN
Bernat Blanket, 100% polyester, 258 yds (236 m)/10.5 oz (300 g), Color 10006 Vintage White (MC) 🔟

CROCHET HOOKS
US J/10 (6 mm) *or size needed to obtain correct gauge* and F/5 (3.75 mm)

GAUGE
Head rounds 1–5 = 4"/10 cm on larger hook

OTHER SUPPLIES
Stitch marker, polyester fiberfill, small amount of worsted weight yarn for bow tie (A, optional), yarn needle, scraps of black worsted weight yarn for features (B), two 15 mm safety eyes

CROCHETING THE HEAD

- With MC and larger hook, ch 2.
- **Rnd 1:** 8 sc in 2nd ch from hook; *do not join. You now have* 8 sc. Pm in the first st of the rnd and move it up as you work the rnds.
- **Rnd 2:** 2 sc in each sc around. *You now have* 16 sc.
- **Rnd 3:** *Sc in next sc, 2 sc in next sc; repeat from * around. *You now have* 24 sc.
- **Rnd 4:** *Sc in next 2 sc, 2 sc in next sc; repeat from * around. *You now have* 32 sc.
- **Rnd 5:** *Sc in next 3 sc, 2 sc in next sc; repeat from * around. *You now have* 40 sc.
- **Rnd 6:** *Sc in next 4 sc, 2 sc in next sc; repeat from * around. *You now have* 48 sc.
- **Rnds 7–14:** Sc in each sc around.
- **Rnd 15:** *Sc in next 4 sc, sc2tog; repeat from * around. *You now have* 40 sc.
- **Rnd 16:** *Sc in next 3 sc, sc2tog; repeat from * around. *You now have* 32 sc.
- **Rnd 17:** *Sc in next 2 sc, sc2tog; repeat from * around, join with slip st to first sc. *You now have* 24 sc.
- Fasten off, leaving a long sewing length.

CROCHETING THE BODY

- With MC and larger hook, ch 2.
- **Rnds 1–6:** Repeat Rnds 1–6 of head. *You now have* 48 sc.
- **Rnds 7–11:** Sc in each sc around.
- **Rnd 12:** *Sc in next 6 sc, sc2tog; repeat from * around. *You now have* 42 sc.
- **Rnds 13–15:** Sc in each sc around.
- **Rnd 16:** *Sc in next 5 sc, sc2tog; repeat from * around. *You now have* 36 sc.
- **Rnds 17 and 18:** Sc in each sc around.
- **Rnd 19:** *Sc in next 4 sc, sc2tog; repeat from * around. *You now have* 30 sc.
- **Rnd 20:** *Sc in next 3 sc, sc2tog; repeat from * around, join with slip st to first sc. *You now have* 24 sc.
- Fasten off. Fill firmly with fiberfill.

CROCHETING THE SNOUT

- With MC and larger hook, ch 2.

- **Rnd 1:** 6 sc in 2nd ch from hook; *do not join. You now have* 6 sc. Pm in the first st of the rnd and move it up as you work the rnds.

- **Rnd 2:** 2 sc in each sc around. *You now have* 12 sc.

- **Rnd 3:** *Sc in next sc, 2 sc in next sc; repeat from * around. *You now have* 18 sc.

- **Rnd 4:** Sc in each sc around, join with slip st to first sc.

- Fasten off, leaving a long sewing length.

CROCHETING THE ARMS (MAKE 2)

- With MC and larger hook, ch 2.

- **Rnds 1 and 2:** Repeat Rnds 1 and 2 of snout. *You now have* 12 sc.

- **Rnd 3:** *Sc in next 3 sc, 2 sc in next sc; repeat from * around. *You now have* 15 sc.

- **Rnds 4–11:** Sc in each sc around.

- Fill arm with fiberfill, stuffing bottom of arm firmly and gradually decreasing the amount of fiberfill toward the top of the arm.

- **Rnd 12:** *Sc in next 3 sc, sc2tog; repeat from * around. *You now have* 12 sc.

Toy Safety

Toys are made to be held, and babies will put anything they can hold into their mouths. Here are some things to keep in mind.

- We strongly recommend using safety eyes or embroidery techniques to add eyes and other features to baby toys.
- Don't use novelty yarn with sequins or bits of fiber that can easily be separated from the main yarn.
- Stuff toys with fiberfill rather than poly-pellets, which can come out through the knitted stitches.
- Secure all ribbons and ties with a few stitches to prevent baby from pulling them out.

- **Rnd 13:** *Sc in next 2 sc, sc2tog; repeat from * around. *You now have* 9 sc.

- Fasten off, leaving a long sewing length.

CROCHETING THE FEET AND LEGS (MAKE 2)

- With MC and larger hook, ch 5.

THE SOLE

- **Rnd 1:** 2 sc in 2nd ch from hook, sc in next 2 ch, 4 sc in last ch; working on opposite side of foundation ch, sc in next 2 ch, 2 sc in last ch; *do not join. You now have* 12 sc. Pm in the first st of the rnd and move it up as you work the rnds.

- **Rnd 2:** (2 sc in next sc, sc in next 4 sc, 2 sc in next sc) twice. *You now have* 16 sc.

- **Rnd 3:** Sc in first sc, 2 sc in next sc, sc in next 3 sc, 2 sc in next 6 sc, sc in next 3 sc, 2 sc in next sc, sc in last sc. *You now have* 24 sc.

- **Rnd 4:** (2 sc in next sc, sc in next sc) twice, sc in next 2 sc, (2 sc in next sc, sc in next sc) twice, 2 sc in next sc, sc in next 2 sc, 2 sc in next sc, (sc in next sc, 2 sc in next sc) twice, sc in next 2 sc, (sc in next sc, 2 sc in next sc) twice. *You now have* 34 sc.

THE FOOT

- **Rnds 5 and 6:** Sc in each sc around. *You now have* 34 sc.

- **Rnd 7:** Sc in next 8 sc, (sc2tog, sc in next sc) twice, sc2tog, sc in next 2 sc, (sc2tog, sc in next sc) twice, sc2tog, sc in last 8 sc. *You now have* 28 sc.

- **Rnd 8:** Sc in next 8 sc, (sc2tog) 6 times, sc in last 8 sc. *You now have* 22 sc.
- **Rnd 9:** Sc in each sc around.
- **Rnd 10:** Sc in next 8 sc, (sc3tog) twice, sc in last 8 sc. *You now have* 18 sc.

THE LEG

- **Rnds 11–16:** Sc in each sc around.
- **Rnd 17:** *Sc in next 7 sc, sc2tog; repeat from * around, join with a slip st to first sc of rnd. *You now have* 16 sc.
- Fasten off, leaving a long tail of yarn for sewing. Stuff foot portion firmly and gradually decrease the amount of fiberfill as leg is filled.

CROCHETING THE EARS (MAKE 2)

- With MC and larger hook, ch 2.
- **Rnds 1–3:** Work as for snout. *You now have* 18 sc.
- **Rnds 4 and 5:** Sc in each sc around, join last rnd with slip st to first sc.
- Fasten off, leaving a long tail of yarn for sewing.

CROCHETING THE BOW TIE (OPTIONAL)

- With A and smaller hook, ch 31 (or until desired length is reached).
- **Row 1:** Sc in 2nd ch from hook and in each ch across, turn. *You now have* 30 sc.
- **Row 2:** Ch 1, sc in each sc across, turn.
- **Rows 3–5:** Repeat Row 2; do not turn.
- Fasten off, leaving a 24"/61 cm tail. Weave in the beginning tail.

- Seam the sides of the fabric together to create a loop. Center the seam on the back of the loop and flatten the fabric. Wrap the 24"/61 cm yarn tail tightly around the middle of the loop several times to create the center of the bow. Secure the end and leave the remaining tail of yarn for assembly.

FINISHING

- Using yarn needle and B, embroider the nose by making a V with satin stitches (see page 276) on the snout. Fill in the V with straight satin stitches. Make a small straight stitch from the bottom center of the nose down. Embroider the mouth by making one long stitch to the left of the snout. Gently pull the curve downward and stitch over the center of the curve to secure it in place. Repeat this step on the opposite side of the snout.
- Following manufacturers' instructions, place safety eyes on Rnd 10 of the head, approximately 5 sts apart.
- Using the long tail of yarn attached to the snout, sew the snout to the face. There should be 1 rnd of sts between the eyes and the top of the snout.
- Fill the head with fiberfill and sew bottom of head to top of body.
- Flatten the last rnd of the arms and whipstitch (see page 276) them to the body using the sewing lengths. Arms should be attached between Rnds 18 and 19 on the body. Flatten the last rnd of the legs and, with feet facing forward, whipstitch them to Rnd 7 of the body. Make sure all limbs are centered.
- Flatten the ears and curve them slightly. Whipstitch the ears to the side of the head.
- Using the long tail of yarn attached to the back of the bow tie, sew the bow under the bear's neck, centering the bow with the bear's nose.
- Weave in ends.

Lil' Miss Lilly

DESIGNED BY *Anastasia Popova*

This adorable little piggy will make a wonderful friend for any baby, and may just stick around through the toddling years and beyond. She is crocheted in the traditional amigurumi style of single crochet in spirals.

FINISHED MEASUREMENTS
Approximately 3½"/9 cm long

YARN
Lily Sugar 'n Cream, 100% cotton, 120 yds (109 m)/2.5 oz (71 g), Color 0046 Rose Pink (4)

CROCHET HOOK
US G/6 (4 mm) *or size needed to obtain correct gauge*

GAUGE
16 stitches and 16 rounds = 4"/10 cm in single crochet

OTHER SUPPLIES
Stitch marker, polyester fiberfill, yarn needle, scraps of black and white yarn

CROCHETING THE BODY

- Make an adjustable ring (see page 272).
- **Rnd 1:** Ch 1, 5 sc in ring, pull on beginning yarn tail to tighten loop. *You now have* 5 sts. Do not join. Pm in the first st of the rnd and move it up as you work the rnds.
- **Rnd 2:** 2 sc in each st around. *You now have* 10 sts.
- **Rnds 3 and 4:** Sc in each st around.
- **Rnd 5:** (Sc in next st, 2 sc in next st) around. *You now have* 15 sts.
- **Rnd 6:** (Sc in next 2 sts, 2 sc in next st) around. *You now have* 20 sts.
- **Rnd 7:** (Sc in next 3 sts, 2 sc in next st) around. *You now have* 25 sts.
- **Rnds 8–13:** Sc in each st around.
- **Rnd 14:** (Sc in next 3 sts, sc2tog) around. *You now have* 20 sts.
- **Rnd 15:** (Sc in next 2 sts, sc2tog) around. *You now have* 15 sts.
- **Rnd 16:** (Sc in next st, sc2tog) around. *You now have* 10 sts.
- Stuff the body with fiberfill.
- **Rnd 17:** Sc2tog around. *You now have* 5 sts.
- Fasten off, leaving a 10"/25.5 cm tail. Using yarn needle, weave the tail through the remaining 5 sts and pull tight to close the opening. Using hook, form a loop with yarn tail and ch 6 to create a tail. Fasten off. Trim yarn tail to ¼"/6 mm.

CROCHETING THE EARS (MAKE 2)

- Chain 3.
- **Row 1:** Sc in 2nd ch from hook and next ch, turn. *You now have* 2 sts.
- **Row 2:** Ch 1, sc in same st, 2 sc in next st, turn. *You now have* 3 sts.
- **Row 3:** Ch 1, sc in each st across.
- Fasten off, leaving 10"/25.5 cm sewing length.

CROCHETING THE FEET (MAKE 4)

- Make an adjustable ring.
- **Rnd 1:** Ch 1, 5 sc in ring, pull on beginning yarn tail to tighten loop. *You now have* 5 sts.
- **Rnd 2:** 2 sc in each st around. *You now have* 10 sts.
- **Rnds 3 and 4:** Sc in each st around.
- Fasten off, leaving a 10"/25.5 cm sewing length.

FINISHING

- Using yarn needle and yarn tails, sew ears in place. Stuff feet with fiberfill and sew into place. Weave in ends. Using photograph as a guide, embroider the eyes with black yarn and the snout with white yarn.

Kitty Kat Lovey

DESIGNED BY *Aurelia Mae Delaney*

This adorable stuffed animal and security blanket combo features a classic granny square blankie and a single crochet kitty. Very cute, don't you agree?

....
FINISHED MEASUREMENTS
13"/33 cm by 13"/33 cm square; kitty 2¼"/5.5 cm tall
....
YARN
Freia Fine Handpaints Ombré Sport, 100% wool, 217 yds (198 m)/2.5 oz (75 g), South Beach (2)
....
CROCHET HOOK
US G/6 (4 mm) *or size needed to obtain correct gauge*
....
GAUGE
16 stitches = 4"/10 cm in single crochet
20 sts and 10 rows = 4"/10 cm in granny pattern
....
OTHER SUPPLIES
Stitch markers, polyester fiberfill, yarn needle, scraps of yarn for face

CROCHETING THE KITTY

THE EARS (MAKE 2)

- Chain 6.

- Row 1: Sc in 2nd ch from hook and in each ch across, turn. *You now have* 5 sc.

- Row 2: Ch 1, sc2tog, sc in next st, sc2tog, turn. *You now have* 3 sts.

- Row 3: Ch 1, sc in each st across, turn.

- Row 4: Ch 1, sc2tog over first and last st (skipping middle st), turn. *You now have* 1 st.

- Row 5: Ch 1, sc in first st. Fasten off.

THE HEAD

- Make an adjustable ring (see page 272).

- Rnd 1: Ch 2, 6 sc into ring, do not join. *You now have* 6 sc. Pm in the first st of the rnd and move it up as you work the rnds.

- Rnd 2: 2 sc in each st around. *You now have* 12 sc.

- Rnd 3: *Sc in next sc, 2 sc in next sc; repeat from * around. *You now have* 18 sc.

- Rnd 4: *Sc in next 2 sc, 2 sc in next sc; repeat from * around. *You now have* 24 sc.

KITTY KAT LOVEY

Blanket Rnds 1–3
Granny Square Rnds 1–3

- Rnd 5: *Sc in next 3 sc, 2 sc in next sc; repeat from * around. *You now have* 30 sc.

- Rnds 6–10: Sc in each sc around.

- Rnd 11: *Sc in next 3 sc, sc2tog; repeat from * around. *You now have* 24 sc.

- Rnd 12: *Sc in next 2 sc, sc2tog; repeat from * around. *You now have* 18 sc.

- Stuff the head with fiberfill.

- Rnd 13: *Sc in next sc, sc2tog; repeat from * around. *You now have* 12 sc.

- Rnd 14: Sc2tog around. *You now have* 6 sc.

- Cut yarn, but do not fasten off. Set head aside.

THE ARMS (MAKE 2)

- Make an adjustable ring.

- Rnd 1: Ch 2, 6 sc into ring, do not join. *You now have* 6 sc. Pm in the first st of the rnd and move it up as you work the rnds.

- Rnd 2: *Sc in next sc, 2 sc in next sc; repeat from * two more times. *You now have* 9 sc.

- Rnd 3: Sc in each sc around.

- Rnd 4: 2 sc in next 3 sts, sc in next 6 sts. *You now have* 12 sc.

- Rnd 5: Sc in each sc around.

- Rnd 6: (Sc2tog) three times, sc in next 6 sts. *You now have* 9 sc.

- Rnds 7–16: Sc in each sc around.

- Fasten off, leaving a 12"/30.5 cm tail. Stuff lightly and sew hole closed.

CROCHETING THE BLANKET

- Place dropped loop from head onto hook. Continue on head sts.

- Rnd 1: 2 sc in each sc around. *You now have* 12 sc.

- **Rnd 2:** *Sc in next st, 2 sc in next sc; repeat from * around. *You now have 18 sc.*

- **Rnd 3:** *Hdc in next 2 sts, 2 hdc in next st; repeat from * around. *You now have 24 hdc.*

THE GRANNY SQUARE

- **Rnd 1:** Ch 3 (counts as dc throughout), (2 dc, ch 3, 3 dc) in same st, ch 1, skip 2 sts, 3 dc in next st, ch 1, skip 2 sts, *(3 dc, ch 3, 3 dc) in next st, ch 1, skip 2 sts, 3 dc in next st, ch 1, skip 2 sts; repeat from * around, join with a slip st to top of ch-3.

- **Rnd 2:** Slip st to next ch-3 space, ch 3, (2 dc, ch 3, 3 dc) in same space, ch 1, (3 dc, ch 1) in next 2 ch-1 spaces, *(3 dc, ch 3, 3 dc) in next ch-3 space, ch 1, (3 dc, ch 1) in next 2 ch-1 spaces; repeat from * around, join with slip st to top of ch-3.

- **Rnd 3:** Slip st to next ch-3 space, ch 3, (2 dc, ch 3, 3 dc) in same space, ch 1, (3 dc, ch 1) in each ch-1 space across to next corner ch-3 space, *(3 dc, ch 3, 3 dc) in next ch-3 space, ch 1, (3 dc, ch 1) in each ch-1 space across to next corner ch-3 space; repeat from * around, join with a slip st to top of ch-3.

- Repeat Rnd 3 of granny square pattern until your yarn runs out, ending with a complete rnd. Fasten off.

FINISHING

- Using the photograph as a guide, sew the ears onto the head, and the arms onto the sides of the neck. Weave in ends. Sew hole closed at base of head (under blanket). Use separate colored yarn scraps to embroider the face.

Owl Puppet

DESIGNED BY *Bronislava Slagle*

This little puppet is sure to elicit many giggles. The body is worked in puff stitch, and the other body parts are worked in double crochet.

FINISHED MEASUREMENTS
10"/25.5 cm circumference and
8"/20.5 cm tall

YARN
Loops & Threads Impeccable, Ombré
100% acrylic, 192 yds (175 m)/3.5 oz
(100 g), Color 02015 Adobe (4)

CROCHET HOOK
US G/6 (4 mm) *or size needed to
obtain correct gauge*

GAUGE
7 stitches and 6½ rows = 4"/10 cm in
puff stitch

OTHER SUPPLIES
Yarn needle, two purchased 3"/7.5 cm
flowers, two ⅞"/22 mm buttons, sewing needle and coordinating thread

PATTERN ESSENTIALS

Exch (extended chain) Chain st pulled
longer than usual, up to the height of
the first st of the row or rnd.

Puff st Yo, insert hook into st or
space indicated and pull up a loop
(yo, insert hook into same st or
space and pull up a loop) three
times, yo and pull through 8 loops
on hook, yo and pull through
2 loops on hook.

CROCHETING THE OWL

- Chain 32. Join with a slip st in first ch,
being careful not to twist ch.

- **Rnd 1:** Ch 1, sc in each ch around, join
with slip st to first sc. *You now have*
32 sc.

- **Rnd 2:** Exch, puff st in first st, ch 1, skip
1 st, *puff st in next st, ch 1, skip 1 st;
repeat from * around, join with slip
st to top of first puff st. *You now have*
16 puff sts and 16 ch-1 spaces.

- **Rnds 3–5:** Slip st in next ch-1 space, exch, puff st in first
space, ch 1, *puff st in next space, ch 1; repeat from * around,
join with slip st to top of first puff st.

- **Rnd 6:** Slip st in next ch-1 space, exch, (puff st, ch 1, puff st) in
first space, ch 1, (puff st in next space, ch 1) seven times, (puff
st, ch 1) twice in next space, (puff st in next space, ch 1) seven
times, join with slip st to top of first puff st. *You now have*
18 puff sts and 18 ch-1 spaces.

- **Rnds 7 and 8:** Repeat Rnd 3.

- **Rnd 9:** Ch 3 (counts as dc here and throughout), dc in next st,
ch 5, skip 5 sts for wing opening, dc in next 13 sts, ch 5, skip
5 sts for wing opening, dc in next 11 sts, join with slip st to top
of ch-3. *You now have* 26 dc and 2 ch-5 spaces.

- **Rnd 10:** Ch 3, dc2tog over next dc and ch, dc in next 4 ch and
in next 2 dc, (dc2tog, dc in next 7 sts) three times, join with
slip st to top of ch-3. *You now have* 32 sts.

- **Rnd 11:** Ch 3, skip next st, dc2tog, dc in next 16 dc, dc2tog,
skip next st, dc in next dc, turn, leaving remaining sts
unworked. *You now have* 20 sts.

- **Row 12 (WS):** Ch 3, skip 1 st, dc2tog, dc in next 12 dc, dc2tog,
skip next st, dc in next dc, turn. *You now have* 16 sts.

- **Row 13:** Ch 3, dc in next 15 dc, turn.

- **Row 14:** Ch 3, dc in same st, dc in next 14 dc, 2 dc in last st,
turn. *You now have* 18 sts.

- **Row 15:** Ch 3, dc in same st, dc in next 16 dc, 2 dc in last st,
turn. *You now have* 20 sts.

- Fasten off.

THE EYES (MAKE 2)

- Ch 5, join with slip st to form a ring.

- **Row 1:** Ch 3, 13 dc in ring, join with slip st to top of ch-3. *You
now have* 14 dc.

- **Row 2:** Ch 3, dc in same st, 2 dc in each dc around. *You now
have* 28 sts. Fasten off, leaving a 12"/30.5 cm tail for sewing.

- Place the circles on top of each other with WS together and
line up the sts. Referring to the assembly diagram, sew both
circles (eyes) together under both loops of 6 sts, allowing top
Vs of sts to fold outward. Place circles with RS facing up. Line
up the seam with the center of the top of head/body and sew
them to the head/body, leaving 3 sts on the bottom of each
eye and 2 sts on the body unsewn for the owl's beak.

THE BEAK

- **Rnd 1:** With RS facing, join yarn with slip st in first free st of right eye, ch 1, sc in each of first 3 free sts on right eye; on left eye, dc in next 3 free sts; on body, sc in next 2 free sts, join with slip st to first sc. *You now have* 8 sts.

- **Rnd 2:** Ch 1, sc in first 6 sc, sc2tog, join with slip st to first st. *You now have* 7 sts.

- **Rnd 3:** Ch 1, sc in first st, (sc2tog) three times, join with slip st to first st. *You now have* 4 sts.

- Fasten off. Use yarn tail to close opening at tip of beak. Weave in ends.

THE WINGS (MAKE 2)

- Leaving a long tail for sewing, ch 15, join with slip st to form a circle.

- **Rnd 1:** Ch 3, dc in next 14 dc, join with slip st to top of ch-3. *You now have* 15 dc.

- **Rnd 2:** Ch 3, dc2tog, dc in next 10 dc, dc2tog, join with slip st to top of ch-3. *You now have* 13 dc.

- **Rnd 3:** Ch 3, dc2tog, dc in next 8 dc, dc2tog, join with slip st to top of ch-3. *You now have* 11 dc.

- **Rnd 4:** Ch 3, dc2tog, dc in next 6 dc, dc2tog, join with slip st to top of ch-3. *You now have* 9 dc.

- **Rnd 5:** Ch 3, dc2tog, dc in next 4 dc, dc2tog, join with slip st to top of ch-3. *You now have* 7 dc.

- **Rnd 6:** Ch 3, dc2tog around, join with slip st to top of ch-3. *You now have* 4 dc. Fasten off.

THE EARS (MAKE 2)

- Cut twelve 7"/18 cm pieces of yarn. Holding six strands together, pull strands through one top corner of head; fold strands in half and make a tight overhand knot. Trim ends about 1"/2.5 cm from knot.

FINISHING

- Using photo as a guide, with yarn length and yarn needle sew the wings onto the body. Remove pistils from center of purchased flowers. Layer one button over each flower head and use sewing needle and thread to sew to center of eye circles. See Sewing Buttons on page 91.

- Weave in ends.

OWL PUPPET

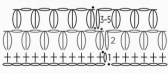

Abbreviated Body Pattern

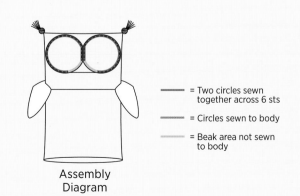

Assembly Diagram

= Two circles sewn together across 6 sts

= Circles sewn to body

= Beak area not sewn to body

Ellie Bear

DESIGNED BY *Laura Biondi, Black Sheep Crochet*

Make a whole family of bears by varying your yarn and gauge — anything goes! Just be sure your tension is tight enough that the fiberfill stays inside, where it belongs.

FINISHED MEASUREMENTS
Approximately 13"/33 cm tall

YARN
Lion Brand Homespun Thick & Quick, 98% acrylic/2% polyester, 185 yds (169 m)/6 oz (170 g), Wild Fire (5)

CROCHET HOOK
US K/10½ (6.5 mm) and US G/6 (4 mm) *or size needed to obtain correct gauge*

GAUGE
12 stitches and 12 rounds = 4"/10 cm in single crochet on larger hook

OTHER SUPPLIES
Stitch markers, polyester fiberfill, yarn needle, small amount of black yarn for features

CROCHETING THE BEAR

THE BODY

- With larger hook, ch 3, join with slip st to form a ring.
- **Rnd 1:** Ch 1, 6 sc in ring. *You now have* 6 sc. Do not join. Pm in the first st of the rnd and move it up as you work the rnds.
- **Rnd 2:** 2 sc in each sc around. *You now have* 12 sc.
- **Rnd 3:** *Sc in next sc, 2 sc in next sc; repeat from * around. *You now have* 18 sts.
- **Rnd 4:** *Sc in next 2 sc, 2 sc in next sc; repeat from * around. *You now have* 24 sts.
- **Rnd 5:** *Sc in next 3 sc, 2 sc in next sc; repeat from * around. *You now have* 30 sts.
- **Rnd 6:** *Sc in next 4 sc, 2 sc in next sc; repeat from * around. *You now have* 36 sts.
- **Rnd 7:** *Sc in next 5 sc, 2 sc in next sc; repeat from * around. *You now have* 42 sts.
- **Rnds 8–10:** Sc in each sc around.
- **Rnd 11:** *Sc in next 5 sc, sc2tog; repeat from * around. *You now have* 36 sc.
- **Rnds 12 and 13:** Sc in each sc around.

- **Rnd 14:** *Sc in next 4 sc, sc2tog; repeat from * around. *You now have* 30 sc.

- **Rnds 15 and 16:** Sc in each sc around.

- **Rnd 17:** *Sc in next 3 sc, sc2tog; repeat from * around. *You now have* 24 sc.

- **Rnds 18 and 19:** Sc in each sc around.

- **Rnd 20:** *Sc in next 2 sc, sc2tog; repeat from * around. *You now have* 18 sc.

- **Rnd 21:** *Sc in next sc, sc2tog; repeat from * around. *You now have* 12 sc.

- Fasten off.

THE ARMS AND LEGS (MAKE 4)

- Ch 3, join with slip st to form a ring.

- **Rnds 1 and 2:** Work as for body. *You now have* 12 sc.

- **Rnds 3–13:** Sc in each sc around.

- Fasten off, leaving a long tail for sewing.

THE HEAD

- Ch 3, join with slip st to form a ring.

- **Rnds 1–6:** Work as for body. *You now have* 36 sc.

- **Rnds 7–11:** Sc in each sc around.

- **Rnd 12:** *Sc in next 4 sc, sc2tog; repeat from * around. *You now have* 30 sc.

- **Rnd 13:** *Sc in next 3 sc, sc2tog; repeat from * around. *You now have* 24 sc.

- **Rnd 14:** *Sc in next 2 sc, sc2tog; repeat from * around. *You now have* 18 sc.

- **Rnd 15:** *Sc in next sc, sc2tog; repeat from * around. *You now have* 12 sc.

- Fasten off, leaving a long tail for sewing.

THE EARS (MAKE 2)

- Ch 3, join with slip st to form a ring.

- **Rnds 1–3:** Work as for body. *You now have* 18 sc.

- **Rnds 4–6:** Sc in each sc around.

- Fasten off, leaving a long tail for sewing.

THE MUZZLE

- Ch 3, join with slip st to form a ring.

- **Rnds 1–3:** Work as for body. *You now have* 18 sc.

- **Rnd 4:** Sc in each sc around.

- Fasten off, leaving a long tail for sewing.

THE EYES (MAKE 2)

- With smaller hook and black yarn, ch 3, join with slip st to form a ring.

- Place a st marker in the first st and move it up as you begin each rnd.

- **Rnds 1 and 2:** Work as for body. *You now have* 12 sc.

- Fasten off, leaving a long tail for sewing.

FINISHING

- Stuff head and body somewhat firmly. Attach head to body using yarn needle, matching stitches evenly around. Attach ears to top of head, about 3 rnds from the top, bending them into a crescent shape. Sew the muzzle onto the lower front half of the face, stuffing lightly before completing seam. Sew eyes to face on either side of and slightly above muzzle.

- Stuff arms and legs lightly, concentrating stuffing at the bottom of each limb. Sew top of arms closed and attach arms to body 2 rnds down from neck. Sew top of legs closed and attach legs in a straight line about 2 rnds up from the center of the bottom of the body.

- With black yarn and using photo as a guide, embroider nose with satin stitch (see page 276).

Zip, Snap, and Button It!

DESIGNED BY *Gwen Steege*

This activity book will provide you and your toddler hours of fun discovering not only zippers, buttons, and snaps, but a pocket, magnets, hooks, and even a hidden picture. Because it's all worked in single crochet, beginning crocheters who also like to sew a little can easily make this fun toy.

FINISHED MEASUREMENTS
5½"/14 cm by 5"/12.5 cm, after gentle felting, folded

YARN
Cascade 220, 100% Peruvian Highland wool, 220 yds (200 m)/3.5 oz (100 g), Color 8895 Christmas Red ④

CROCHET HOOK
US H/8 (5 mm) *or size needed to obtain correct gauge*

GAUGE
16 stitches and 18 rows = 4"/10 cm in single crochet, after light felting

OTHER SUPPLIES
Stitch markers, yarn needle, polyester fiberfill, multicolor sock yarn for trim (optional), one 7"/18 cm patterned zipper, sewing needle and coordinating thread, two 1⅜"/35 mm buttons, one extra-large hook-and-eye closure, one 30 mm sew-on snap, small amount of patterned fabric (for appliqué), one 1⅛"/29 mm sew-on magnetic snap

PATTERN ESSENTIALS

Pages are reversible, but are marked as "right side" (RS) and "wrong side" (WS) for clarity.

CROCHETING THE PAGES

THE INSIDE PAGES

- Fsc 20 (see page 274). Pm to mark this as RS.
- Row 1: Ch 1 (counts as sc here and throughout), sc in next sc and in each sc across, turn. *You now have* 20 sc.
- Repeat Row 1, working last sc of each row in the top of beginning ch, until piece measures 11"/28 cm.
- Fasten off. Weave in ends.

THE OUTSIDE PAGES

- Work as for inside pages until piece measures 2"/5 cm, ending with a WS row.
- Next Row (zipper opening, RS): Ch 1, sc in next 6 sc, ch 14, turn.
- Next Row (WS): Sc in 2nd ch from hook, sc in next 12 ch, sc in next 6 sc, turn. *You now have* 20 sc.
- Work even in sc until piece measures about 7"/18 cm from beginning, ending with a RS row.
- Next Row (top edge of pocket opening, WS): Ch 1, sc in next 7 sc, turn. *You now have* 8 sc.
- Work even in sc on these 8 sc only until piece measures 9½"/24 cm from beginning, ending with a WS row. Fasten off.
- Next Row (bottom edge of pocket opening, WS): With WS facing, join yarn in same st as last st of previous section, ch 1, sc in next 12 sc, turn. *You now have* 13 sc.
- Work even on these 13 sc only until bottom of opening measures same as top of opening, ending with a WS row, turn.
- Joining Row (RS): Ch 1, sc in next 11 sc, insert hook into next st and into first st on other side of opening and sc these 2 sts together, sc in next 7 sc, turn. *You now have* 20 sc.
- Work even until piece measures 11½"/29 cm from beginning, or the same as the inside pages. Fasten off.

THE POCKET

- **Row 1:** Hold outside pages with WS facing and zipper opening at left; attach yarn at the corner of the pocket opening and, working along the top edge of the pocket opening, ch 1, work 8 sc evenly spaced across, turn. *You now have* 9 sc.

- **Row 2:** Ch 1, sc in each sc across, turn.

- Work even until back of pocket measures 2¾"/7 cm.

- **Next Row (turning row):** Ch 1, FLsc in each sc across, turn.

- Repeat Row 2 until front of pocket measures same as back of pocket. Fold pocket to align with lower edge of pocket opening, and working through double thickness of pocket and lower edge of pocket opening, sc in each st across to attach front of pocket to remaining edge of pocket opening.

- Whipstitch (see page 276) sides of the pocket closed. Take an extra stitch on each side to tack corners closed.

CROCHETING THE DOODADS ON INSIDE PAGES

THE HOOK-AND-EYE TAB

Note: All tabs are attached to the *inside pages* of the book. The tabs will fold over to the other side (RS/WS) once completed.

- **Row 1:** With RS facing and short edge at the top, join yarn with slip st on right edge 4"/10 cm from top edge, ch 1, work 8 sc evenly spaced along edge to 1¾"/4.5 cm from top edge, turn. *You now have 9 sc.*
- **Row 2:** Ch 1, sc in each sc across, turn.
- Work even in sc until tab measures 3½"/9 cm. Fasten off.

THE SNAP FLAP

- **Row 1:** With RS facing and short edge at the top, join yarn with slip st on left edge 4"/10 cm from lower edge, ch 1, work 11 sc evenly spaced along edge to 1¼"/3.2 cm from lower edge, turn. *You now have 12 sc.*
- **Row 2:** Ch 1, sc in each sc across, turn.
- Work even in sc until tab measures 2"/5 cm. Fasten off.

THE BUTTON FLAP

- **Row 1:** With WS facing, working on same end of page as snap flap, join yarn with slip st 4"/10 cm from lower edge. (This is at the opposite end from, but the same edge as, the hook-and-eye flap.) Ch 1, work 11 sc evenly spaced along edge to 1¼"/3.2 cm from lower edge, turn. *You now have 12 sc.*

- **Rows 2–8:** Ch 1, sc in each sc across, turn.
- **Row 9:** Ch 1, sc in next sc, ch 5, skip 5 sc, sc in last 2 sts, turn.
- **Row 10:** Ch 1, sc in each sc and ch across, turn.
- **Rows 11–14:** Repeat Row 2. Fasten off.

THE LARGE BALL

- Begin with an adjustable ring (see page 272).
- **Rnd 1:** Ch 1, 5 sc in ring, join with slip st to beginning ch. *You now have 6 sc.*
- **Rnd 2:** Ch 1, sc in same st, 2 sc in each st around, join with slip st to beginning ch. *You now have 12 sc.*
- **Rnd 3:** Ch 1, sc in same st, sc in next sc, *2 sc in next sc, sc in next sc; repeat from * around, join with slip st to beginning ch. *You now have 18 sc.*
- **Rnds 4 and 5:** Ch 1, sc in each sc around, join with slip st to beginning ch.
- **Rnd 6:** Ch 1, *sc2tog, sc in next sc; repeat from * to last 2 sc, sc2tog, join with slip st to beginning ch. *You now have 12 sc.*

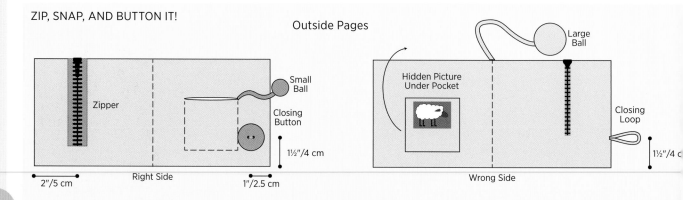

ZIP, SNAP, AND BUTTON IT!

Outside Pages

Zipper

Small Ball

Closing Button

1½"/4 cm

Right Side

2"/5 cm

1"/2.5 cm

Large Ball

Hidden Picture Under Pocket

Closing Loop

1½"/4 c

Wrong Side

- Stuff the ball with a small amount of polyester fiberfill before proceeding.
- Rnd 7: Ch 1, sc2tog five times, skip last st, join with slip st to beginning ch. *You now have* 6 sc.
- Fasten off, leaving a 36"/91 cm tail. Thread the tail through a yarn needle, and run the yarn through the remaining sts to close the hole. Fasten off.
- Use the tail to work a 7"/18 cm chain. Leave tail to attach to book.

THE SMALL BALL

- Using the sock yarn, work same as large ball through Rnd 2. Then work Rnd 7. Fasten off, leaving a 20"/51 cm tail. Use this tail to work a 3"/7.5 cm chain, and then work a row of sc on each side of the chain. Fasten off. Attach this piece to top right-hand of the pocket. Weave in ends.

FINISHING

Note: The sock yarn sc trim is optional, but it does make the project "pop." Felting the completed pages gives them a bit of body and density that will make them stand up to play.

- Edging: If desired, using the sock yarn, work an edging of sc around all edges of the outside pages, as well as around each of the tabs, the top of the pocket, and around the pocket edges on the inside of the front page.
- Felting and blocking: Felt all pieces gently (see page 275). Do not allow pieces to become stiff, but felt them only until slightly fulled. When pages have reached their desired fullness, pin them out flat so that you can even up the edges and square the corners. Allow to dry thoroughly.
- Joining pages: Place outside pages with RS down and pocket on left. Place inside pages on top of outside pages with RS down and hook-and-eye tab on left. With project yarn and yarn needle, sew through center line of both layers together to create book "spine."
- Zipper: With matching sewing thread, machine- or hand-stitch zipper into zipper opening on outside pages.
- Fasteners: Fold tabs inward and use yarn or matching sewing thread to attach the buttons, hook-and-eye, and snap to pages and tabs as pictured.

Continued on next page.

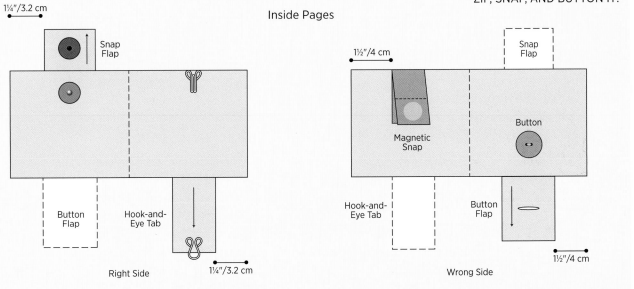

Inside Pages

ZIP, SNAP, AND BUTTON IT!

1¼"/3.2 cm — Snap Flap — Button Flap — Hook-and-Eye Tab — Right Side — 1¼"/3.2 cm

1½"/4 cm — Snap Flap — Magnetic Snap — Button — Hook-and-Eye Tab — Button Flap — Wrong Side — 1½"/4 cm

- **Hidden picture:** Cut a small piece of fabric no larger than 2"/5 cm square. If possible, use fabric with a picture, such as an animal, boat, or flower, that a child will recognize and enjoy. Press under a small seam allowance and use thread to sew to WS of outside pages under pocket flap.

- **Magnetic snap:** Cut two strips of fabric each 6"/15 cm long by 2"/5 cm wide. With WS facing, fold each strip in half to be 2" by 3" (5 × 7.5 cm). Machine- or hand-stitch the long edges, making ¼"/6 mm seams. Place one half of the magnetic snap into each tab. Fold the raw edges at the top of each tab to the inside. Align the tabs with folded edges together, taking care that the magnets are facing in the correct direction to snap closed. Machine- or hand-stitch the tabs to the top edge of the inside page where the hook-and-eye is attached on the other side.

- **Button flap button:** Sew one large button to page to align with button flap.

- **Closing button:** Using photo as a guide, sew one large button to front cover of book.

- **Closing loop:** Join yarn with slip st on outer edge of back cover of book, opposite the button; chain a length long enough to go around button, slip st in same st. Fasten off. Weave in ends.

- **Large ball:** With tail and yarn needle, attach large ball to top edge of spine.

Effie Effalump

DESIGNED BY *Melissa Morgan-Oakes*

Effie's ring handle is perfect for little hands, and her trunk is just right for little teething mouths. A cute face and a subtle jingling noise provide extra interest.

CROCHETING THE HANDLE

- With MC, ch 12, join with slip st to form a ring.

- **Rnd 1:** Ch 1, sc in each ch around; *do not join.* Pm in the first st of the rnd and move it up as you work the rnds.

- Continuing in a spiral, sc in each sc around until tube measures 7"/18 cm long. Roll Mylar lengthwise into a tight tube and insert into crocheted tube; allow Mylar to expand to diameter of crocheted tube. Fill loosely with fiberfill. Bring ends of tube together and stitch all layers closed.

CROCHETING THE TRUNK AND HEAD

- With MC, chain 2.
- Rnd 1: 9 sc in 2nd ch from hook, join with slip st to first sc. *You now have* 9 sts. Pm in the first st of the rnd and move it up as you work the rnds.
- Rnds 2–6: Sc in each sc around, *do not join.*

THE TRUNK

- Rnd 1: Sc in first sc, sc2tog, sc in next sc, sc2tog, 2 sc in next 2 sc, sc in next sc. *You now have* 9 sts.
- Rnd 2: Sc in each st around.
- Repeat Rnds 1 and 2 two more times.

THE HEAD

- Rnd 1: *Sc in first sc, 2 sc in next sc; repeat from * around. *You now have* 12 sts.
- Rnd 2: Sc in each sc around.
- Rnd 3: *Sc in next 2 sc, 2 sc in next sc; repeat from * around. *You now have* 16 sts.
- Rnd 4: Sc in each sc around.
- Rnd 5: 2 sc in each sc around. *You now have* 32 sts.
- Rnds 6 and 7: Sc in each sc around.
- Rnd 8: Sc2tog, sc in each st to last 2 sts, sc2tog. *You now have* 30 sts.
- Rnds 9–11: Repeat Rnd 8. *You now have* 24 sts.
- Rnd 12: Sc in each sc around.
- Clip a locking ring stitch marker in the loop of your live stitch. This will allow you to do some prefinishing without losing your place. Stuff trunk loosely with fiberfill, and attach or embroider eyes where desired. Firmly attach the jingle bell inside the head by tying it to the yarn used to attach or embroider the eyes.
- Place the live stitch back on the hook and proceed. When working the final head shaping below, pause occasionally to stuff the head as you go, tucking fiberfill between the bell and front of face. Do not overstuff.
- Rnd 13: *Sc in next 4 sc, sc2tog; repeat from * around. *You now have* 20 sts.

FINISHED MEASUREMENTS
Approximately 6½"/16.5 cm from tip of trunk to end of ring

YARN
Cascade Yarns Sateen, 100% acrylic, 300 yds (274 m)/3.5 oz (100 g), Color 405 Mist (MC) (3)

CROCHET HOOK
US B/1 (2.25 mm) *or size needed to obtain correct gauge*

GAUGE
22 stitches = 4"/10 cm in single crochet

OTHER SUPPLIES
Locking stitch marker, Mylar coffee bag cut to 6½"/16.5 cm long by 2"/5 cm wide, polyester fiberfill, yarn needle, small black safety eyes or embroidery floss and embroidery needle, jingle bell, small amount of tan yarn (CC) for ruffle (optional)

- Rnd 14: *Sc in next 3 sc, sc2tog; repeat from * around. *You now have* 16 sts.
- Rnd 15: *Sc in next 2 sc, sc2tog; repeat from * around. *You now have* 12 sts.
- Rnd 16: *Sc in next sc, sc2tog; repeat from * around. *You now have* 8 sts.
- Rnd 17: *Sc2tog; repeat from * around. *You now have* 4 sts.
- Fasten off, leaving a sewing length. Thread tail on yarn needle and use to close the back of the head.

CROCHETING THE EARS (MAKE 2)

- With MC, chain 3.
- Row 1: 2 sc in 2nd ch from hook and in next ch, turn. *You now have* 4 sts.
- Row 2: Ch 1, 2 sc in each sc across, turn. *You now have* 8 sts.

- **Row 3:** Ch 1, 2 sc in each sc across, turn. *You now have* 16 sts.

- **Rows 4–6:** Ch 1, sc in each sc across.

- Fasten off. Using photo as a guide, attach ears to sides of head, bending the top of the ear over a bit to give it a little depth.

CROCHETING THE RUFFLE

- With CC, ch 16.

- **Row 1:** 3 dc in 4th ch from hook, 4 dc in each ch across, turn. *You now have* 52 sts.

- **Row 2:** Ch 3 (counts as dc), dc in same st, 2 dc in each dc across, turn. *You now have* 104 sts. Cut CC and join MC.

- **Row 3:** Slip st in each dc across.

- Fasten off, leaving a sewing length.

FINISHING

- Sew head to handle. Place ruffle around Effie's neck and stitch ends of rows together. Weave in ends.

Granny Bunny Buddy

DESIGNED BY *Dana Bincer, Yarnovations.com*

Young ones will love to poke their little fingers through the holes in this playmate, so-named for its granny square body. The ears and arms are the perfect size for little hands to grab and hold onto.

CROCHETING THE BUNNY

THE HEAD

- Chain 2.

- **Rnd 1:** 6 sc in 2nd ch from hook. *You now have* 6 sts. Do not join. Pm in the first st of the rnd and move it up as you work the rnds.

- **Rnd 2:** 2 sc in each sc around. *You now have* 12 sts.

- **Rnd 3:** *Sc in next sc, 2 sc in next sc**, sc in next 2 sc, 2 sc in next sc; repeat from * around, ending last repeat at **. *You now have* 17 sts.

- **Rnd 4:** Sc in next sc, 2 sc in next sc, (sc in next 3 sc, 2 sc in next sc, sc in next 2 sc, 2 sc in next sc) twice, sc in last sc. *You now have* 22 sts.

- **Rnd 5:** Sc in next 3 sc, 2 sc in next sc, sc in next 7 sc, 2 sc in next sc, sc in next 6 sc, 2 sc in next sc, sc in next 3 sc. *You now have* 25 sts.

- **Rnd 6:** Sc in next 7 sc, 2 sc in next sc, sc in next 8 sc, 2 sc in next sc, sc in next 7 sc, 2 sc in next sc. *You now have* 28 sts.

- **Rnd 7:** Sc in next 14 sc, 2 sc in next sc, sc in next 13 sc. *You now have* 29 sts.

- **Rnd 8:** Sc in each sc around.

- **Rnd 9:** Sc in next 13 st, sc2tog, sc in next 14 sc. *You now have* 28 sts.

- **Rnd 10:** Sc2tog, sc in next 7 sc, sc2tog, sc in next 8 sc, sc2tog, sc in next 7 sc. *You now have* 25 sts.

- **Rnd 11:** Sc in next 3 sc, sc2tog, sc in next 6 sc, sc2tog, sc in next 7 sc, sc2tog, sc in next 3 sc. *You now have* 22 sts.

FINISHED MEASUREMENTS
8"/20.5 cm long

YARN
Red Heart Soft Baby Steps, 100% acrylic, 256 yds (234m)/4 oz (113 g), Color 9600 White (4)

CROCHET HOOK
US G/6 (4 mm) *or size needed to obtain correct gauge*

GAUGE
18 stitches and 20 rows = 4"/10 cm in single crochet

OTHER SUPPLIES
Stitch marker, polyester fiberfill, yarn needle, scrap of pink yarn for mouth, two ⅜"/10 mm buttons for eyes, sewing needle and coordinating thread, 12"/30.5 cm of ¼"/6 mm ribbon for bow at neck

- **Rnd 12:** Sc, sc2tog, (sc in next 2 sc, sc2tog, sc in next 3 sc, sc2tog) twice, sc in last sc. *You now have* 17 sts.
- **Rnd 13:** Sc2tog, (sc in next sc, sc2tog, sc in next 2 sc, sc2tog) twice, sc in last sc. *You now have* 12 sts.
- Stuff the head with fiberfill.
- **Rnd 14:** Sc2tog around. *You now have* 6 sts. Fasten off, leaving a long tail for sewing. Weave end through each stitch around and cinch closed. Secure with knot, leaving a long tail for sewing.

THE EARS (MAKE 2)

- Chain 2.
- **Rnd 1:** 8 sc in 2nd ch from hook. *You now have* 8 sts. *Do not join.* Pm in the first st of the rnd and move it up as you work the rnds.
- **Rnd 2:** 2 sc in each sc around. *You now have* 16 sts.
- **Rnds 3–5:** Sc in each sc around.
- **Rnd 6:** (Sc in next 6 sc, sc2tog) twice. *You now have* 14 sts.
- **Rnd 7:** Sc in each sc around.

- **Rnd 8:** (Sc in next 5 sc, sc2tog) twice. *You now have* 12 sts.
- **Rnd 9:** Sc in each sc around.
- **Rnd 10:** (Sc in next 4 sc, sc2tog) twice. *You now have* 10 sts.
- **Rnd 11:** (Sc in next 3 sc, sc2tog) twice. *You now have* 8 sts.
- **Rnds 12–20:** Sc in each sc around.
- **Row 21:** Flatten ear to create two sets of parallel stitches. Holding WS together and working through both thicknesses, sc in next 4 sts to close ear, turn. *You now have* 4 sts.
- **Row 22:** (Sc2tog) twice, turn. *You now have* 2 sts.
- **Row 23:** Sc across.
- Fasten off, leaving a long tail for sewing.

THE ARMS (MAKE 2)

- Chain 2.

- Rnd 1: 6 sc in 2nd ch from hook. *You now have* 6 sc. *Do not join.* Pm in the first st of the rnd and move it up as you work the rnds.

- Rnd 2: 2 sc in each sc around. *You now have* 12 sts.

- Rnds 3 and 4: Sc in each sc around.

- Rnd 5: (Sc2tog, sc in next 4 sc) twice. *You now have* 10 sts.

- Rnd 6: (Sc2tog, sc in next 3 sc) twice. *You now have* 8 sts.

- Rnd 7: (Sc2tog, sc in next 2 sc) twice. *You now have* 6 sts.

- Rnds 8–15: Sc in each sc around.

- Fasten off, leaving a long tail for sewing.

- Stuff lightly.

CROCHETING THE GRANNY BODY

- Ch 4, join with slip st to form a ring.

- Rnd 1: Ch 3 (counts as dc), 3 dc in ring, ch 2, (4 dc, ch 2) three times in ring, join with slip st to top of ch-4. *You now have* 16 dc and 4 ch-2 spaces.

- Rnd 2: Ch 5 (counts as dc and ch 2 here and throughout), (4 dc, ch 2) twice in next 3 spaces, (4 dc, ch 2, 3 dc) in next space, join with slip st to 3rd ch of ch-5.

- Rnd 3: Ch 3 (counts as dc here and throughout), 3 dc in next space, *ch 2, (4 dc, ch 2, 4 dc) in corner space, ch 2**, 4 dc in next space; repeat from * around, ending last repeat at **, join with slip st to top of ch-3.

- Rnd 4: Ch 5, *(4 dc, ch 2) in each space to corner, (4 dc, ch 2) twice in corner space; repeat from * around, ending with 3 dc in last space, join with slip st to 3rd ch of ch-5.

- Rnd 5: Ch 3, 3 dc in next space, ch 2, *(4 dc, ch 2) in each space to corner, (4 dc, ch 2) twice in corner space; repeat from * around, ending (4 dc, ch 2) in each space to beginning of rnd, join with slip st to top of ch-3.

- Rnds 6–9: Repeat Rnds 4 and 5 twice.

- Rnd 10: Ch 1, *sc in next 2 dc, picot, sc in next 2 dc, (2 sc, picot, sc) in next space; repeat from * around, join with slip st to first sc.

- Fasten off. Weave in ends.

FINISHING

- Using photo as a guide, sew ears to top of head. With pink yarn, embroider mouth. With sewing needle and thread, sew on button eyes securely. Sew arms to center of blanket, then sew head assembly to top of arms at blanket center. Weave in ends. Tie ribbon in a bow around bunny's neck and tack in place with sewing thread.

GRANNY BUNNY BUDDY

Granny Body

The Owl and the Pussycat

DESIGNED BY *Lorna Miser, Lorna Miser Designs*

This quirky toy is worked in the round — the owl is on one side, the pussycat is on the other. Further entertain your child by reciting the quirky poem by Edward Lear, about "the land where the Bong-Tree grows."

....
FINISHED MEASUREMENTS
Approximately 8"/20.5 cm tall
....
YARN
Universal Yarns Poems, 100% wool, 109 yds (100 m)/3.5 oz (100 g), Color 588 La Lavande 🔵
....
CROCHET HOOK
US G/6 (4 mm) *or size needed to obtain correct gauge*
....
GAUGE
14 stitches and 10 rows = 4"/10 cm in half double crochet
....
OTHER SUPPLIES
Stitch marker, yarn needle, polyester fiberfill, small amounts of different colored felt, sewing needle and thread, scraps of white and black yarn for features

CROCHETING THE BASE

- Chain 10.

- **Row 1:** Dc in 4th ch from hook and in each ch across, turn. *You now have* 8 dc.

- **Row 2:** Ch 3 (counts as dc here and throughout), dc in each dc across, turn.

- Repeat Row 2 until base measures 5"/12.5 cm from beginning. Fasten off and set aside.

CROCHETING THE BODY

- Ch 50, join with slip st to first ch, being careful not to twist.

- **Rnd 1:** Sc in first ch, hdc in each ch around; *do not join.* Pm in the first st of the rnd and move it up as you work the rnds.

- Continue to hdc in each st around until piece measures 4½"/11.5 cm from beginning. *Do not fasten off.*

- Fasten off, leaving a sewing length. Sew tip of ear closed. Weave in ends.

THE SECOND EAR

- With RS facing, join yarn with standing hdc in first skipped st, hdc in next 24 sts. *You now have* 25 sts.
- Work Rnds 2–10 as for first ear.

FINISHING

- Stuff the body with fiberfill. With RS facing, slip st base to bottom of body. Weave in ends.
- Using templates for eyes and noses, cut out two eyes and one nose for each face from felt. Using photo as a guide, sew features to each side with needle and thread. Embroider whiskers for cat with white yarn. Embroider pupils for all four eyes with black yarn.

THE FIRST EAR

- **Rnd 1:** Skip next 24 sts, hdc in next st. Pm in the first st of the rnd and move it up as you work the rnds.
- **Rnd 2:** Hdc in each hdc around. *You now have* 25 sts.
- **Rnd 3:** Repeat Rnd 2.
- **Rnd 4:** *Hdc in next 3 sts, hdc2tog; repeat from * around. *You now have* 20 sts.
- **Rnd 5:** Repeat Rnd 2.
- **Rnd 6:** *Hdc in next 2 sts, hdc2tog; repeat from * around. *You now have* 15 sts.
- **Rnd 7:** Repeat Rnd 2.
- **Rnd 8:** *Hdc in next st, hdc2tog; repeat from * around. *You now have* 10 sts.
- **Rnd 9:** Repeat Rnd 2.
- **Rnd 10:** Hdc2tog around. *You now have* 5 sts.

THE OWL AND THE PUSSYCAT

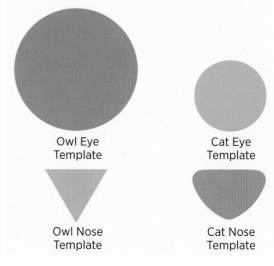

Owl Eye Template

Cat Eye Template

Owl Nose Template

Cat Nose Template

Little Pegasus

DESIGNED BY *Kate Wood*

This Pegasus is glittery white, but since it's a mythological creature, you can stitch it in whatever color you like. The pattern is worked continuously in the round, except where indicated.

FINISHED MEASUREMENTS
Approximately 7"/18 cm long from nose to tail

YARN
Red Heart Shimmer, 97% acrylic/3% metallic, 280 yds (256 m)/3.5 oz (100 g), Color 1010 Snow (4)

CROCHET HOOK
US E/4 (3.5 mm) *or size needed to obtain correct gauge*

GAUGE
20 stitches and 20 rounds = 4"/10 cm in single crochet

OTHER SUPPLIES
Stitch marker, two safety eyes or small amount of black yarn, yarn needle, polyester fiberfill

PATTERN ESSENTIALS

Beg 5-dc cluster (beginning 5-dc cluster) Ch 2, yo, insert hook into first st and pull up a loop, yo and pull through 2 loops on hook, (yo, insert hook into same st and pull up a loop, yo and pull through 2 loops on hook) three times, yo and pull through 5 loops on hook.

CROCHETING THE HEAD

- Make an adjustable ring (see page 272).
- **Rnd 1:** Work 6 sc in ring. Do not join. *You now have* 6 sc. Pm in the first st of the rnd and move it up as you work the rnds.
- **Rnd 2:** 2 sc in each st around. *You now have* 12 sc.
- **Rnd 3:** (Sc in next 3 sc, 2 sc in next sc) around. *You now have* 15 sts.
- **Rnd 4:** Sc in each sc around.
- **Rnd 5:** (Sc in next 3 sc, sc2tog) around. *You now have* 12 sts.
- **Rnd 6:** Sc in each sc around.
- **Rnd 7:** (Sc in next 3 sc, 2 sc in next sc) around. *You now have* 15 sts.
- **Rnd 8:** (Sc in next 4 sc, 2 sc in next sc) around. *You now have* 18 sts.
- **Rnd 9:** (Sc in next 2 sc, 2 sc in next sc) four times, (hdc in next 2 sc, 2 hdc in next sc) twice. *You now have* 24 sts.
- **Rnd 10:** (Sc in next 3 sc, 2 sc in next st) four times, (hdc in next 3 sts, 2 hdc in next st) twice. *You now have* 30 sts.

- **Rnd 11:** (Sc in next 4 sts, 2 sc in next st) four times, (hdc in next 4 sts, 2 hdc in next st) twice. *You now have 36 sts.*
- **Rnds 12–16:** Sc in each st around.
- Embroider or affix eyes at ends of the hdc made in Rnd 10.
- **Rnd 17:** (Sc in next 4 sc, sc2tog) around. *You now have 30 sts.*
- **Rnd 18:** (Sc in next 3 sc, sc2tog) around. *You now have 24 sts.*
- **Rnd 19:** (Sc in next 2 sc, sc2tog) around. *You now have 18 sts.*
- Stuff head with fiberfill.
- **Rnd 20:** (Sc in next sc, sc2tog) around. *You now have 12 sts.*
- **Rnd 21:** Sc2tog around. *You now have 6 sts.*
- Fasten off, leaving a long sewing length. Finish stuffing head. Use yarn needle and tail to sew open end firmly closed.

THE EARS (MAKE 2)

- Leaving a long sewing length, ch 3.
- **Row 1:** 2 sc in 2nd ch from hook and in next ch, turn. *You now have 4 sc.*
- **Row 2:** Ch 1, sc2tog twice, turn. *You now have 2 sts.*
- **Row 3:** Ch 1, sc2tog. *You now have 1 st.*
- Fasten off.
- Using yarn needle and beginning yarn tail, sew ears to head, just behind Rnd 13. Weave in ends.

THE NECK

- Leaving a long sewing length, ch 18.
- **Rnd 1:** Being careful not to twist chain, sc in first ch to form a circle, then sc in each ch around; *do not join.* Pm in the first st of the rnd and move it up as you work the rnds. *You now have 18 sc.*
- **Rnd 2:** Sc in next 16 sc, sc2tog. *You now have 17 sc.*
- **Rnd 3:** Sc in next 15 sc, sc2tog. *You now have 16 sc.*
- **Rnd 4:** Sc in next 14 sc, sc2tog. *You now have 15 sc.*
- **Rnd 5:** Sc in next 13 sc, sc2tog. *You now have 14 sc.*
- **Rnd 6:** Sc in next 12 sc, sc2tog. *You now have 13 sc.*
- **Rnd 7:** Sc in next 11 sc, sc2tog. *You now have 12 sc.*
- Fasten off.

CROCHETING THE BODY

- Make an adjustable ring.
- **Rnd 1:** Work 6 sc in ring. *Do not join. You now have 6 sc.* Pm in the first st of the rnd and move it up as you work the rnds.
- **Rnd 2:** 2 sc in each st around. *You now have 12 sc.*
- **Rnd 3:** (Sc in next sc, 2 sc in next sc) around. *You now have 18 sts.*
- **Rnd 4:** (Sc in next 2 sc, 2 sc in next sc) around. *You now have 24 sts.*
- **Rnd 5:** (Sc in next 3 sc, 2 sc in next sc) around. *You now have 30 sts.*
- **Rnd 6:** (Sc in next 4 sc, 2 sc in next sc) around. *You now have 36 sts.*
- **Rnds 7–11:** Sc in each sc around.
- **Rnd 12:** (Sc in next 10 sc, sc2tog) around. *You now have 33 sts.*
- **Rnd 13:** (Sc in next 9 sc, sc2tog) around. *You now have 30 sts.*
- **Rnds 14 and 15:** Sc in each around.
- **Rnd 16:** (Sc in next 9 sc, 2 sc in next st) around. *You now have 33 sts.*
- **Rnd 17:** (Sc in next 10 sc, 2 sc in next st) around. *You now have 36 sts.*
- **Rnds 18–22:** Sc in each sc around.
- Stuff body with fiberfill.
- **Rnd 23:** (Sc in next 4 sc, sc2tog) around. *You now have 30 sts.*
- **Rnd 24:** (Sc in next 3 sc, sc2tog) around. *You now have 24 sts.*
- **Rnd 25:** (Sc in next 2 sc, sc2tog) around. *You now have 18 sts.*
- **Rnd 26:** (Sc in next sc, sc2tog) around. *You now have 12 sts.*

- Rnd 27: Sc2tog around. *You now have* 6 sts.

- Fasten off, leaving a long sewing length. Finish stuffing body. Use yarn needle and tail to sew open end firmly closed.

THE HIND LEGS (MAKE 2)

- Make an adjustable ring.

- Rnd 1: Work 6 sc in ring. *Do not join. You now have* 6 sc. Pm in the first st of the rnd and move it up as you work the rnds.

- Rnd 2: 2 sc in each st around. *You now have* 12 sc.

- Rnd 3: (Sc in next 3 sc, 2 sc in next sc) around. *You now have* 15 sts.

- Rnd 4: BLsc in each sc around.

- Rnd 5: Sc in next 3 sc, (sc2tog) three times, sc in next 3 sc, 2 sc in next 3 sc. *You now have* 15 sts.

- Rnds 6 and 7: Sc in each sc around.

- Rnd 8: Sc in next 3 sc, sc2tog, sc in next 10 sc. *You now have* 14 sts.

- Rnd 9: Sc in next 4 sc, sc2tog, sc in next 8 sc. *You now have* 13 sts.

- Rnd 10: Sc in next 3 sc, sc2tog, sc in next 8 sc. *You now have* 12 sts.

- Rnds 11–14: Sc in each sc around.

- Rnds 15 and 16: Sc in next 3 sc, slip st in next 3 sts, sc in next 3 sc, hdc in next 3 sts.

- Rnds 17–20: Sc in each st around.

- Rnd 21: Sc in next 6 sc, 2 sc in next sc, sc in next 5 sc. *You now have* 13 sts.

- Rnd 22: Sc in next 6 sc, 2 sc in next sc, sc in next 6 sc. *You now have* 14 sts.

- Rnd 23: Sc in next 8 sc, 2 sc in next sc, sc in next 5 sc. *You now have* 15 sts.

- Rnd 24: Sc in next 8 sc, 2 sc in next st, sc in next 6 sc. *You now have* 16 sts.

- Rnd 25: Sc in each sc around.

- Rnd 26 (first leg only): Hdc in next 8 sc, slip st in next 8 sc.

- Rnd 26 (second leg only): Slip st in next 8 sc, hdc in next 8 sc.

- Fasten off, leaving a long tail for sewing.

THE FRONT LEGS (MAKE 2)

- Work same as hind legs through Rnd 10.

- Rnds 11–20: Sc in each st around.

- Rnds 21–26: Work Rnds 21–26 of hind legs.

- Fasten off, leaving a long sewing length.

THE WINGS (MAKE 2)

- Leaving a long sewing length, ch 1.

- Row 1: (Beg 5-dc cluster, ch 2, 5-dc cluster) in starting ch, turn.

- Row 2: Ch 1, sc in first cluster, ch 1, sc in ch-2 space, ch 1, sc in cluster, turn.

- Row 3: Beg 5-dc cluster in first sc, *ch 2, 5-dc cluster in next sc; repeat from * once more, turn.

- Row 4: Ch 1, sc in first cluster, (ch 1, sc in next ch-2 space, ch 1, sc in next cluster) twice, turn.

- Row 5: Beg 5-dc cluster in first sc, ch 3, slip st in next ch-1 space, beg 5-dc cluster in next sc, ch 3, slip st in next ch-1 space, slip st in next sc, beg 5-dc cluster in next sc, ch 3, slip st in next ch-1 space, beg 5-dc cluster in next sc, ch 3, slip st in same sc.

- Fasten off.

LITTLE PEGASUS

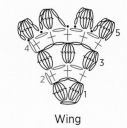

Wing

FINISHING

- Firmly stuff legs and sew to body, placing the hdc side of each leg to the outside of body and the slip st side on the inside of body, creating a smooth transition from legs to body.

- Sew wider edge (first row) of neck to body. Stuff the neck, then sew the narrow end of the neck (last row) to the head.

- Sew the wings to the back.

- For mane, cut pieces of yarn 4"/10 cm long. Fold each in half, and use hook to pull through stitching on the head/neck, creating a loop. Yarnover with both loose ends, pulling them through the loop to attach. Trim to desired length.

- For tail, cut 13 pieces of yarn 9"/23 cm long or desired length. Lay 12 yarn pieces parallel and tie them together at the center with the 13th strand of yarn to create a tassel. Sew tassel to body; trim to desired length.

Cuddly Snuggly Elephant

DESIGNED BY *Kate Wood*

The merino-and-angora blend used for this pachyderm makes him extra soft and cuddly. He's worked in continuous rounds of single crochet and has eyes made from scrap yarn.

CROCHETING THE HEAD

- Make an adjustable ring (see page 272).

- **Rnd 1:** Ch 1, 6 sc in ring. *You now have* 6 sts. *Do not join.* Pm in the first st of the rnd and move it up as you work the rnds.

- **Rnd 2:** 2 sc in each st around. *You now have* 12 sts.

- **Rnd 3:** *Sc in next sc, 2 sc in next sc; repeat from * around. *You now have* 18 sts.

- **Rnd 4:** *Sc in next 2 sc, 2 sc in next sc; repeat from * around. *You now have* 24 sts.

- **Rnd 5:** *Sc in next 3 sc, 2 sc in next sc; repeat from * around. *You now have* 30 sts.

- **Rnds 6–12:** Sc in each sc around.

- Fasten off, leaving a long sewing length.

THE EARS (MAKE 2)

- Make an adjustable ring.

- **Rnd 1:** Ch 1, 6 sc in ring. *You now have* 6 sts. *Do not join.* Pm in the first st of the rnd and move it up as you work the rnds.

- **Rnd 2:** *Sc in next sc, 2 sc in next sc; repeat from * around. *You now have* 9 sts.

- **Rnd 3:** *Sc in next 2 sc, 2 sc in next sc; repeat from * around. *You now have* 12 sts.

- **Rnd 4:** *Sc in next 3 sc, 2 sc in next sc; repeat from * around. *You now have* 15 sts.

- **Rnd 5:** *Sc in next 4 sc, 2 sc in next sc; repeat from * around. *You now have* 18 sts.

- **Rnd 6:** *Sc in next 5 sc, 2 sc in next sc; repeat from * around. *You now have* 21 sts.

- **Rnd 7:** *Sc in next 6 sc, 2 sc in next sc; repeat from * around. *You now have* 24 sts.

- **Rnds 8–10:** Sc in each sc around.

- **Rnd 11:** (Sc2tog) six times, sc in next 4 sc, (sc2tog) four times. *You now have* 14 sts.

- Fasten off, leaving a long sewing length. Flatten the ear; the decreases worked in Rnd 11 will give it a curved shape. Sew the open end closed, leaving a sewing length.

THE TRUNK

- Make an adjustable ring.

- **Rnd 1:** Ch 1, 6 sc in ring. *You now have* 6 sts. *Do not join.* Pm in the first st of the rnd and move it up as you work the rnds. Pull excess yarn through to the right side of work (this yarn tail will be used to curl up the trunk).

FINISHED MEASUREMENTS
Approximately 7"/18 cm long, including trunk

YARN
Lana Gatto Class, 80% extrafine merino wool/20% angora, 136 yds (124 m)/1.75 oz (50 g), Color 5234 Light Grey (4)

CROCHET HOOK
US F/5 (3.75 mm) *or size needed to obtain correct gauge*

GAUGE
20 stitches and 20 rounds = 4"/10 cm in single crochet, unstuffed

OTHER SUPPLIES
Stitch marker, yarn needle, polyester fiberfill, scrap of yarn for eyes

- **Rnds 2–10:** Sc in each sc around.

- **Rnd 11:** Sc in next 5 sc, 2 sc in last sc. *You now have* 7 sts.

- **Rnd 12:** Sc in next 3 sc, 2 sc in next sc, sc in next 3 sc. *You now have* 8 sts.

- **Rnd 13:** Sc in next 7 sc, 2 sc in last sc. *You now have* 9 sts.

- **Rnd 14:** Sc in next 4 sc, 2 sc in next st, sc in last 4 sc. *You now have* 10 sts.

- **Rnd 15:** Sc in next 9 sc, 2 sc in last sc. *You now have* 11 sts.

- **Rnd 16:** Sc in next 5 sc, 2 sc in next sc, sc in last 5 sc. *You now have* 12 sts.

- **Rnd 17:** (Sc in next 3 sc, 2 sc in next sc) three times. *You now have* 15 sts.

- **Rnd 18:** (Sc in next 4 sc, 2 sc in next sc) three times. *You now have* 18 sts.

The shaping in the next rnd will help the trunk attach more cleanly to the head.

- **Rnd 19:** Hdc in next 8 sc, sc in next st, slip st in next 9 sts. *You now have* 18 sts. Slip st to first hdc to join. Fasten off, leaving a long sewing length.

CROCHETING THE TAIL

- Chain 4. Fasten off, leaving a long sewing length to sew to body. Trim other yarn tail to ¼"/6 mm.

CROCHETING THE BODY

- Make an adjustable ring.

- **Rnds 1–5:** Work as for head. *You now have* 30 sts.

- **Rnd 6:** *Sc in next 4 sc, 2 sc in next sc; repeat from * around. *You now have* 36 sts.

- **Rnd 7:** *Sc in next 5 sc, 2 sc in next sc; repeat from * around. *You now have* 42 sts.

- To attach the tail, use hook to pull yarn tail through between Rnds 6 and 7. Using yarn needle, sew yarn tail securely to WS of body. Trim excess.

- **Rnds 8–19:** Sc in each sc around.

- **Rnd 20:** *Sc in next 5 sc, sc2tog; repeat from * around. *You now have* 36 sts.

- **Rnd 21:** *Sc in next 4 sc, sc2tog; repeat from * around. *You now have* 30 sts.

- **Rnd 22:** *Sc in next 3 sc, sc2tog; repeat from * around. *You now have* 24 sts.

- Stuff body with fiberfill.

- **Rnd 23:** *Sc in next 2 sc, sc2tog; repeat from * around. *You now have* 18 sts.

- **Rnd 24:** *Sc in next sc, sc2tog; repeat from * around. *You now have* 12 sts.

- **Rnd 25:** Sc2tog around. *You now have* 6 sts.

- Finish stuffing body. Use yarn needle and tail to sew open end closed.

THE LEGS (MAKE 4)

- Make an adjustable ring.

- **Rnds 1–3:** Work as for head. *You now have* 18 sts.

- **Rnd 4:** BLsc in each sc around. (This makes the transition from hoof to leg.)

- **Rnd 5:** *Sc next 4 sts, sc2tog; repeat from * around. *You now have* 15 sts.

- **Rnds 6–10:** Sc in each sc around.

- **Row 11:** Hdc in next 6 sc, sc next st, slip st in next st, leaving remaining sts unworked.

- Fasten off, leaving a long sewing length.

CUDDLY SNUGGLY ELEPHANT

Assembly Diagram

FINISHING

- Follow diagram for help with assembling the elephant.

- Stuff each leg. Rotate each leg so that the hdc are facing outward, allowing the leg to meet the curve of the body. Sew the elephant's tail at the back and top of the body.

- Flatten the end of the elephant's trunk, and curl it under (toward the slip st). Use the yarn tail that was pulled through to sew the curl in place. Stuff the remainder of trunk. Using yarn tail at open end, sew the trunk to the head. The hdc edge of the trunk should just meet Rnd 2 of the head.

- With scrap yarn, satin stitch (see page 276) two eyes on front of head between Rnds 5 and 6, using the trunk to guide placement.

- Sew the ears to the head, then firmly stuff head. Using yarn needle and tail, sew head to front of body. Weave in ends.

Goldie the Bouncing Fish

DESIGNED BY *Melissa Dallke, The Crochet Experience*

This fish gets its bounce by being crocheted over a tennis ball. Crocheted with wool using single and double crochet, this unique amigurumi is sure to delight.

FINISHED MEASUREMENTS
9"/23 cm circumference with 3"/7.5 cm tail

YARN
Berlini Merino Xtra, 100% extrafine merino wool, 154 yds (141 m)/1.75 oz (50 g), Color 10 Mandarin Orange ②

CROCHET HOOK
US D/3 (3.25 mm) *or size needed to obtain correct gauge*

GAUGE
28 stitches and 28 rounds = 4"/10 cm in single crochet

OTHER SUPPLIES
Stitch marker, tennis ball, yarn needle, scraps of white and black worsted yarn for eyes

CROCHETING THE BODY

- Make an adjustable ring (see page 272).
- Rnd 1: Work 6 sc into ring. Do not join. Pm in the first st of the rnd and move it up as you work the rnds.
- Rnd 2: 2 sc in each st around. *You now have* 12 sts.
- Rnd 3: (Sc in next st, 2 sc in next st) around. *You now have* 18 sts.
- Rnd 4: (Sc in next 2 sts, 2 sc in next st) around. *You now have* 24 sts.
- Rnd 5: (Sc in next 3 sts, 2 sc in next st) around. *You now have* 30 sts.
- Rnd 6: (Sc in next 4 sts, 2 sc in next st) around. *You now have* 36 sts.
- Rnd 7: (Sc in next 5 sts, 2 sc in next st) around. *You now have* 42 sts.
- Rnd 8: (Sc in next 6 sts, 2 sc in next st) around. *You now have* 48 sts.
- Rnd 9: (Sc in next 7 sts, 2 sc in next st) around. *You now have* 54 sts.
- Rnds 10–19: Sc in each st around.

- **Rnd 20:** (Sc in next 7 sts, sc2tog) around. *You now have* 48 sts.
- **Rnd 21:** (Sc in next 6 sts, sc2tog) around. *You now have* 42 sts.
- Insert tennis ball and continue working around ball.
- **Rnd 22:** (Sc in next 5 sts, sc2tog) around. *You now have* 36 sts.
- **Rnd 23:** (Sc in next 4 sts, sc2tog) around. *You now have* 30 sts.
- **Rnd 24:** (Sc in next 3 sts, sc2tog) around. *You now have* 24 sts.
- **Rnd 25:** (Sc in next 2 sts, sc2tog) around. *You now have* 18 sts.
- **Rnd 26:** (Sc in next st, sc2tog) around. *You now have* 12 sts.
- **Rnd 27:** Sc2tog around. *You now have* 6 sts. Remove marker; *do not fasten off.*

THE TAIL

- Ch 22; 3 dc in 2nd ch from hook, 3 dc in each ch across, slip st into body next to beginning ch; repeat from * two more times.
- Fasten off. Weave in ends.

CROCHETING THE SIDE FINS

Note: Use photo as a guide when making fins.

- With tail facing away, join yarn to side of fish by inserting hook between 2 sc and making a slip st.
- **Row 1:** Working up the side of the ball (insert hook between next 2 sc, pull up loop and make 1 sc) four times, turn. *You now have* 5 sts.
- **Row 2:** Ch 3 (counts as dc), dc in same st, (2 dc in next st) four times, turn. *You now have* 10 sts.
- **Row 3:** Ch 1, 2 sc in each st across. *You now have* 20 sts.
- Fasten off. Weave in ends.
- Repeat to make a fin on opposite side of ball.

CROCHETING THE TOP FIN

- With the tail on the right, slip st between 2 sc (about ½"/13 mm from top of ball) as for side fins.
- **Row 1:** Work 6 sc in a line toward face, turn.
- **Row 2:** Ch 3, dc in next st, hdc in next 2 sts, sc in next 2 sts, slip st into body.
- Fasten off. Weave in ends.

CROCHETING THE EYES (MAKE 2)

- With white yarn, make adjustable ring.
- **Rnd 1:** Work 6 sc into ring. *Do not join.* Pm in the first st of the rnd.
- **Rnd 2:** 2 sc in each st around. *You now have* 12 sts. Slip st into marked st.
- Thread a needle with a 24"/61 cm piece of black yarn and tie a knot in one end. Pull needle through center of white circle from WS to RS. Embroider a five-point star by working five evenly spaced straight sts from center, each ¼"/6 mm long, around toward outer edge. Starting in the center of the star, weave yarn in an outward spiral, *working over one ray, then under next ray; repeat from * until you reach the points of the star. Pull yarn to WS. Cut yarn and weave in ends.

GOLDIE THE BOUNCING FISH

START

Eye Embroidery Diagram

- Place eyes close together, ½"/13 mm below top fin and whipstitch (see page 276) to head with white tails. Weave in ends.

CROCHETING THE MOUTH

- Beginning 1"/2.5 cm below center of one eye, slip st between 2 sc; sc between next 2 sts four times, slip st into body. Cut yarn and weave in ends.
- Steam block, pinning fins back.

Pocket Dolly

DESIGNED BY *Gwen Steege*

This soft little dolly, with her flapper hat and flouncy skirt, is likely to become a take-along favorite, tucked into a pocket or wrapped in its own cozy blanket. Crocheted with superwash merino wool, it is carefree for parents, as well. You can make three dolls with one skein of this yarn.

FINISHED MEASUREMENTS
5"/12.5 cm tall

YARN
Madelinetosh Tosh Merino Light, 100% superwash merino wool, 420 yds (384 m)/3.5 oz (100 g), Dachshund

CROCHET HOOK
US E/4 (3.5 mm) crochet hook *or size needed to obtain correct gauge*

GAUGE
24 stitches and 24 rounds = 4"/10 cm in single crochet

OTHER SUPPLIES
Stitch markers, yarn needle, polyester fiberfill, about 4 yds/3.5 m, 5/2 pearl cotton (sample uses Halcyon Yarn's Dark Gold), ½ yd/45.5 cm of ⅜"/1 cm ribbon, sewing needle and coordinating thread

CROCHETING THE DOLL

THE HEAD

- Begin with an adjustable ring (see page 272).
- **Rnd 1:** Ch 1, work 6 sc in ring, join with slip st to first sc. *You now have* 6 sts.
- **Rnd 2:** Ch 1, 2 sc in same st, 2 sc in each st around, join with slip st to first sc. *You now have* 12 sc.
- **Rnd 3:** Ch 1, 2 sc in same st, sc in next sc, *2 sc in next sc, sc in next sc; repeat from * around, join with slip st to first sc. *You now have* 18 sc.
- **Rnd 4:** Ch 1, 2 sc in same st, sc in next 2 sc, *2 sc in next sc, sc in next 2 sc; repeat from * around, join with slip st to first sc. *You now have* 24 sc.
- **Rnd 5:** Ch 1, 2 sc in same st, sc in next 3 sc, *2 sc in next st, sc in next 3 sc; repeat from * around, join with slip st to first sc. *You now have* 30 sc.
- Pm in the first st of the rnd and move it up as you work the rnds. Continuing in rnds without joining, sc in each sc around until piece measures 1½"/4 cm from center ring.
- **Decrease Rnd 1:** *Sc in next 3 sts, sc2tog; repeat from * around. *You now have* 24 sc.
- **Decrease Rnd 2:** *Sc in next 2 sts, sc2tog; repeat from * around. *You now have* 18 sc.
- **Decrease Rnd 3:** *Sc in next st, sc2tog; repeat from* around, join with slip st to first sc. *You now have* 12 sc.

THE UPPER BODY

- Continue in joined rnds.
- **Rnd 1:** Ch 1, 2 sc in same st, sc in next sc, *2 sc in next sc, sc in next sc; repeat from * around, join with slip st to first sc. *You now have* 18 sc.
- **Rnd 2:** Ch 1, 2 sc in same st, sc in next 2 sc, *2 sc in next st, sc in next 2 sc; repeat from * around, join with slip st to first sc. *You now have* 24 sc.
- **Rnd 3:** Ch 1, 2 sc in same st, sc in next 3 sc, *2 sc in next st, sc in next 3 sc; repeat from * around, join with slip st to first sc. *You now have* 30 sc.

- **Rnd 4:** Ch 1, 2 sc in same st, sc in next 4 sc, *2 sc in next st, sc in next 4 sc; repeat from * around, join with slip st to first sc. *You now have* 36 sc.
- **Rnds 5–13:** Ch 1, sc in each sc around, join with slip st to first ch.

THE SKIRT

- **Rnd 1:** Ch 2 (counts as hdc), FLhdc in each sc around, join with slip st to top of ch-2.
- **Rnd 2:** Ch 1, 2 sc in same st, sc in next 3 sc, *2 sc in next sc, sc in next 3 hdc; repeat from * around, join with slip st to first sc. *You now have* 45 sc.
- **Rnd 3:** Ch 1, 2 sc in same st, sc in next 4 sc, *2 sc in next sc, sc in next 4 sc; repeat from * around, join with slip st to first sc. *You now have* 54 sc.
- **Rnd 5:** Ch 1, sc in first st, ch 2, skip 2 sc, *sc in next sc, ch 2, skip 2 sts; repeat from * around, join with slip st to first sc.
- **Rnd 6:** Ch 1, sc in each sc and 2 sc in each ch-2 space around; with pearl cotton, join with slip st to first sc.
- With pearl cotton, ch 1, sc in each sc around, join with slip st to first sc. Fasten off.

CROCHETING THE LOWER BODY

- Fold skirt toward head.
- **Rnd 1:** Join yarn with slip st in back loop of any st in last upper body rnd, ch 1 (counts as sc), BLsc in each sc around. *You now have* 36 sc. *Do not join.* Pm in the first st of the rnd and move it up as you work the rnds.

- Sc in each sc around until lower body measures about 1"/2.5 cm from waist (top of skirt). Lightly stuff the head and upper body with fiberfill.

THE RIGHT LEG

- **Rnd 1:** Sc in next 18 sc, leaving remaining sts unworked. *You now have* 18 sc.

Continue in rnds without joining.

- **Rnd 2:** Skip next 18 sts, sc in each sc around. *You now have* 18 sc.
- Repeat Rnd 2 until leg measures about ½"/13 mm from crotch.
- **Next Rnd:** FLsc in each sc around.
- **Next Rnd:** BLsc in each sc around.
- Lightly stuff the leg with fiberfill.
- **Decrease Rnd 1:** *Sc in next st, sc2tog; repeat from* around. *You now have* 12 sc.
- **Next Rnd:** (Sc2tog) around. *You now have* 6 sc. Fasten off, leaving a 6"/15 cm tail. With yarn needle, weave the tail through remaining 6 sts and pull tight to close. Weave in ends.

THE LEFT LEG

- **Rnd 1:** With RS facing, standing sc in first sc at crotch opening, sc in each sc around remaining body sts. *You now have* 18 sc.
- Complete as for right leg.

CROCHETING THE ARMS

- Mark sides of doll. Beginning just below the neck and working downward toward the waist, join yarn and work 6 sc evenly spaced along center side line, turn, work 6 sc evenly spaced up side toward neck. *You now have* 12 sc. *Do not join.* Pm in the first st of the rnd and move it up as you work the rnds.
- Continuing in rnds without joining, sc in each sc around until arm measures ¾"/2 cm from the body.
- Lightly stuff the arm with fiberfill.

- **Decrease Rnds:** Sc2tog around until 3 sts remain. Fasten off, leaving a 6"/15 cm tail. With yarn needle, thread the tail through the remaining 6 sts and pull tight to close. Weave in ends.
- On opposite side of doll, repeat the above rnds for the second arm.

CROCHETING THE HAT

- Locate the middle round of the head.
- **Rnd 1:** Beginning at center back head with doll's feet toward you and head facing away, standing sc in first sc, sc in each sc around, join with slip st to first sc. *You now have* 30 sc.
- **Rnds 2 and 3:** Ch 1, sc in each sc around, join with slip st to first ch.
- Fasten off.

CROCHETING THE FLOWER (MAKE 2)

- With pearl cotton, make an adjustable ring.
- **Rnd 1:** Ch 1, work 6 sc in ring, join with slip st to first sc. *You now have* 6 sts.
- **Rnd 2:** Ch 1, 2 sc in each st around, join with slip st to first ch. *You now have* 12 sc. Fasten off, leaving a 6"/15 cm tail.

FINISHING

- Use the beginning and ending tails to attach the flowers securely to the head just above the rim of the hat. Weave in ends. Tie the ribbon around the doll's neck and tack in place with needle and thread.

CHAPTER SEVEN

LITTLE
Blankets
+
Sacks

Zucchini Sleep Sack and Cap

DESIGNED BY *Reyna Thera Lorele, YIYO Designs*

Sleep sacks are all the rage, and this one will keep your little one cozy and warm while napping. It also will make for some precious photo ops.

....
SIZE AND FINISHED MEASUREMENTS
For newborn: 21½"/54.5 cm sack circumference and 23"/58.5 cm sack length; 14"/35.5 cm cap circumference and 6"/15 cm cap height

....
YARN
James C. Brett Marble Chunky, 100% acrylic, 341 yds (312 m)/7 oz (200 g), Color 0033 Lemon/Lime 🄻5

....
CROCHET HOOK
US I/9 (5.5 mm) *or size needed to obtain correct gauge*

....
GAUGE
10 stitches and 5 rounds = 4"/10 cm in back loop double crochet

....
OTHER SUPPLIES
Yarn needle

PATTERN ESSENTIALS

FPtr2tog (front post treble 2 together) *(Yo) twice, insert hook from front to back to front around post of FPtr below dc just made and pull up a loop, (yo and pull through 2 loops on hook) twice, skip 1 dc; insert hook from front to back to front around post of next FPtr and pull up a loop (yo and pull through 2 loops on hook), yo and pull through all 3 loops on hook.

CROCHETING THE SACK

- **Rnd 1:** Ch 4, 11 dc in 4th ch from hook, join with slip st to top of beginning ch-4. *You now have* 12 dc.

- **Rnd 2:** Ch 3 (counts as dc here and throughout), dc in same st, 2 dc in each st around, join with slip st to top of ch-3. *You now have* 24 dc.

- **Rnd 3:** Ch 3, 2 dc in next st, *dc in next st, 2 dc in next st; repeat from * around, join with slip st to back loop only in top of ch-3. *You now have* 36 dc.

THE BODY

- **Rnd 1:** Ch 3, 2 BLdc in next st, *BLdc in next st, 2 BLdc in next st; repeat from * around, join with slip st to back loop only in top of ch-3. *You now have* 54 sts.

- **Rnds 2–24:** Ch 3, BLdc in next 4 sts, *FPtr in next st, BLdc in next 5 sts, repeat from * around to last st, FPtr in last st, join with slip st to back loop only in top of ch-3.

- **Rnd 25 (increase rnd):** Ch 3, BLdc in next 4 sts, (FPtr, BLdc, FPtr) in next st, *BLdc in next 5 sts, (FPtr, BLdc, FPtr) in next st; repeat from * around, join with slip st to back loop only in top of ch-3. *You now have* 72 sts.

- **Rnd 26:** Ch 3, BLdc in each BLdc and FPtr around each FPtr around, join with slip st to back loop only in top of ch-3.

- **Rnd 27:** Ch 3, dc in next 5 sts, FPtr2tog, *BLdc in same FPtr and in next 6 sts, FPtr2tog; rep from * around, ending BLdc in same FPtr, join with slip st to both loops at top of ch-3.

ZUCCHINI SLEEP SACK AND CAP

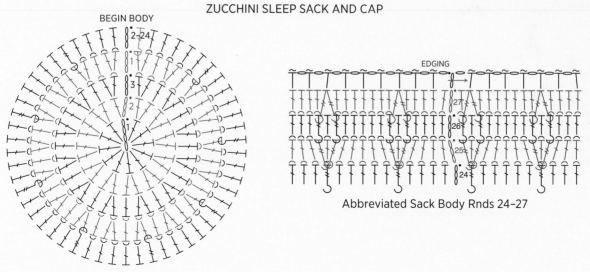

BEGIN BODY

Sack Bottom

EDGING

Abbreviated Sack Body Rnds 24–27

THE EDGING

- Ch 3 (counts as hdc and ch 1), skip next st to the right (left for left-handed crocheters), *reverse hdc in next st, ch 1, skip 1 st, repeat from * around, join with slip st to 2nd ch of ch-2. Fasten off.

THE RUFFLE

- Working in free loops from Rnd 3, join yarn with FLdc in any st, FLdc in same st, 3 FLdc in next st, *2 FLdc in next st, 3 FLdc in next st; repeat from * around, join with slip st to top of first FLdc. *You now have* 90 dc. Fasten off.

CROCHETING THE CURLICUES

- **Large (make 2):** Ch 21, 2 sc in 2nd ch from hook and in each ch across to last 2 sts, 3 sc in last 2 sts. Fasten off.

- **Small (make 1):** Ch 16, work as for large curlicue. Set aside to use on cap.

- Use yarn ends to attach large curlicues to any FPtr on sack body. (On sample shown, they are attached at 7th and 10th rows from top edge.)

CROCHETING THE CAP

- **Rnds 1–3:** Work as for Rnds 1–3 of sack. *You now have* 36 dc.

- **Rnd 4:** Ch 3, dc in each st around, join with slip st to top of ch-3.

- **Rnds 5–8:** Ch 3, BLdc in next 4 sts, *FPtr in next st, BLdc in next 5 sts, repeat from * around to last st, FPtr in last st, join with slip st to back loop only at top of ch-3.

- **Rnd 9:** Ch 3 (counts as hdc, ch 1), skip next st to the right (left for left-handed crocheters), *reverse hdc in next st, ch 1, skip 1 st, repeat from * around, join with slip st to 2nd ch of ch-2. Fasten off.

- Attach small curlicue to top of cap. Weave in ends.

ZUCCHINI SLEEP SACK AND CAP

Sack Ruffle

Condensed Curlique

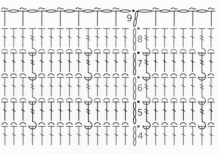

Cap Rnds 4–9

Snuggly Wave Cocoon

DESIGNED BY *Gwen Steege*

Whether you call it a cocoon or a baby sack or bunting, this welcome cover-up is an especially useful gift for a newborn. Crocheted in Madlinetosh's Pashmina, it's luxuriously warm, and machine washable, as well.

SIZE AND FINISHED MEASUREMENTS

For newborn: 18"/45.5 cm circumference and 17"/43 cm length

YARN

Madelinetosh Pashmina, 75% merino wool/15% silk/10% cashmere, 360 yds (329 m)/4 oz (113 g), Fragrant (2)

CROCHET HOOK

US E/4 (3.5 mm) crochet hook *or size needed to obtain correct gauge*

GAUGE

First 4 rounds = 4"/10 cm in diameter 2 pattern repeats and 20 rounds = 5"/12.5 cm in Wave Stitch pattern

OTHER SUPPLIES

Yarn needle

PATTERN ESSENTIALS

Wave Stitch Pattern (multiple of 14 stitches)

Rnd 1: Ch 1, sc in each st around, join with slip st to first sc.

Rnd 2: Ch 3 (counts as dc here and throughout), 3 dc in first st, *skip next 3 sc, sc in next 7 sc, skip next 3 sc**, 7 dc in next sc; repeat from * around, ending last repeat at **, 3 dc in same st as beginning ch-3, join with slip st to top of ch-3.

Rnd 3: Ch 1, sc in each st around, join with slip st to first sc.

Rnd 4: Ch 1, sc in first 4 dc, *skip next 3 sc, 7 dc in next sc, skip next 3 sc**, sc in next 7 sc; repeat from * around, ending last repeat at **, sc in next 3 sc, join with slip st to first sc.

Repeat Rnds 1–4 for pattern.

CROCHETING THE COCOON

THE BOTTOM

- Begin with an adjustable ring (see page 272).

- **Rnd 1:** Ch 1, 12 sc in ring, join with slip st to first sc. *You now have* 12 sc.

- **Rnd 2:** Ch 3 (counts as dc here and throughout), dc in same st, 2 dc in each sc around, join with slip st to top of ch-3. *You now have* 24 dc.

- **Rnd 3:** Ch 3, dc in same st, dc in next dc, *2 dc in next dc, dc in next dc; repeat from * around, join with slip st to top of ch-3. *You now have* 36 dc.

- **Rnd 4:** Ch 3, dc in same st, dc in next 2 dc, *2 dc in next dc, dc in next 2 dc; repeat from * around, join with slip st to top of ch-3. *You now have* 48 dc.

- **Rnd 5:** Ch 3, dc in same st, dc in next 3 dc, *2 dc in next dc, dc in next 3 dc; repeat from * around, join with slip st to top of ch-3. *You now have* 60 dc.

- **Rnd 6:** Ch 3, dc in same st, dc in next 4 dc, *2 dc in next dc, dc in next 4 dc; repeat from * around, join with slip st to top of ch-3. *You now have* 72 dc.

- **Rnd 7:** Ch 3, dc in same st, dc in next 5 dc, *2 dc in next dc, dc in next 5 dc; repeat from * around, join with slip st to top of ch-3. *You now have* 84 dc.

- **Rnd 8:** Ch 3, dc in same st, dc in next 6 dc, *2 dc in next dc, dc in next 6 dc; repeat from * around, join with slip st to top of ch-3. *You now have* 96 dc.

- **Rnd 9:** Ch 1, 2 sc in same st, sc in next 48 dc, 2 sc in next dc, sc in each dc around join with slip st to first sc. *You now have* 98 sc.

THE BODY

- Work Rnds 1–4 of Wave Stitch pattern 14 times.

- **Next Rnd:** Ch 1, sc in each st around, join with slip st to first sc, turn.

- **Final Rnd (WS):** Ch 1, sc in each st around, join with slip st to first sc.

- Weave in ends. Block.

SNUGGLY WAVE COCOON

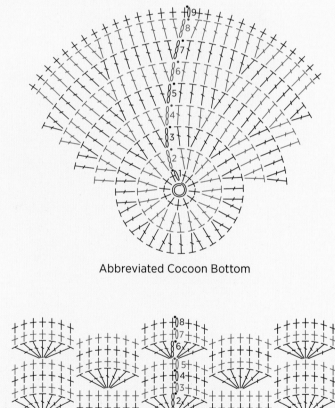

Abbreviated Cocoon Bottom

WAVE STITCH PATTERN REPEAT

Abbreviated Cocoon Body

Cotton Play Mat

DESIGNED BY *Elizabeth Garcia Kalka*

This large cotton square is perfect for laying down on the floor as a surface for baby's tummy time. It can also be used as a stroller or car-seat blanket.

FINISHED MEASUREMENTS
30"/76 cm square, including edging

YARN
Bernat Handicrafter Cotton, 100% cotton, 603 yds (551 m)/12 oz (340 g), Color 90510 Strawberry Cream (4)

CROCHET HOOK
US I/9 (5.5 mm) *or size needed to obtain correct gauge*

GAUGE
13 stitches and 6 rows = 4"/10 cm in pattern
First 2 rounds = 3"/7.5 cm square

OTHER SUPPLIES
Yarn needle

PATTERN ESSENTIALS

Exch (extended chain) Chain st pulled longer than usual, up to level of first st of round.

V-st (Dc, ch 1, dc) in 1 stitch or space.

CROCHETING THE BLANKET

See chart on following page.

- Ch 5, slip st in first ch to form a ring.

- **Rnd 1:** Exch (does not count as st), (3 dc, ch 2) three times in ring, 3 dc in ring, join with hdc to first dc.

- **Rnd 2:** Exch, 2 dc in space formed by joining hdc, dc in each dc to next corner space, *(2 dc, ch 2, 2 dc) in corner space, dc in each dc to next corner space; repeat from * around, ending with 2 dc in beginning space, join with hdc to first dc. *You now have* 7 dc per side and 4 ch-2 spaces.

- **Rnds 3 and 4:** Repeat Rnd 2. *You now have* 15 dc per side and 4 ch-2 spaces.

211

- **Rnd 5:** Exch, 2 dc in space formed by joining hdc, *dc in next dc, (ch 1, skip 1 dc, dc in next 3 dc) three times, ch 1, skip 1 dc, dc in next dc**, (2 dc, ch 2, 2 dc) in corner space; repeat from * around, ending last repeat at **, 2 dc in beginning space, join with hdc to first dc. *You now have* five 3-dc groups per side.

- **Rnd 6:** Exch, 2 dc in space formed by joining hdc, *dc in each st and ch-1 space across to corner**, (2 dc, ch 2, 2 dc) in corner space; repeat from * around, ending last repeat at **, 2 dc in beginning space, join with hdc to first dc. *You now have* 23 dc per side.

- **Rnds 7–18:** Repeat Rnds 3–6 three times. *You now have* 71 dc per side.

- **Rnds 19–21:** Repeat Rnds 3–5. *You now have* twenty-one 3-dc groups per side.

- **Rnd 22:** Exch, dc in space formed by joining hdc, *ch 1, dc in next dc, (ch 1, V-st in next ch-1 space) across to corner, dc in last dc before corner space, ch 1**, (dc, ch 2, dc) in corner space; repeat from * around, ending last repeat at **, dc in beginning space, join with hdc to first dc.

- **Rnd 23:** Ch 1, sc in space formed by joining hdc, (ch 5, sc in next ch-1 space) around, ch 3, join with hdc to first sc.

- **Rnd 24:** Ch 1, sc in space formed by joining hdc, *ch 2, picot, ch 2, sc in next ch-5 space; repeat from * around, omitting last sc, join with slip st to first sc.

- Fasten off. Weave in ends.

COTTON PLAY MAT

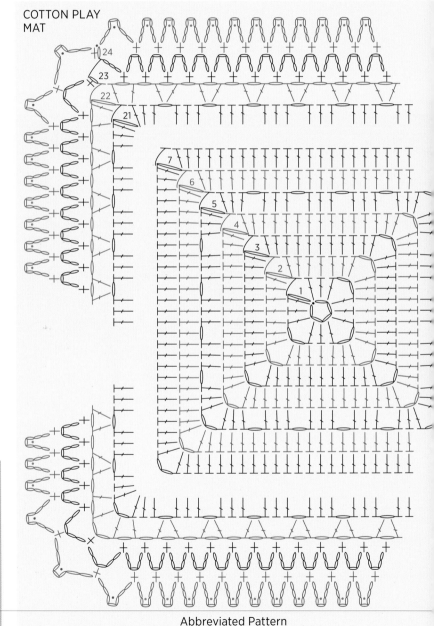

Abbreviated Pattern

Babies and Lace

In general, when knitting lace for babywear or blankets, choose patterns that have holes on the small side. Tiny fingers and toes can easily get tangled in fabric with a large openwork pattern.

Christening Cloud

DESIGNED BY *Reyna Thera Lorele, YIYO Designs*

An openwork body pattern and flouncy border are worked in laceweight yarn for a truly ethereal effect. This lovely blanket should be passed down through generations.

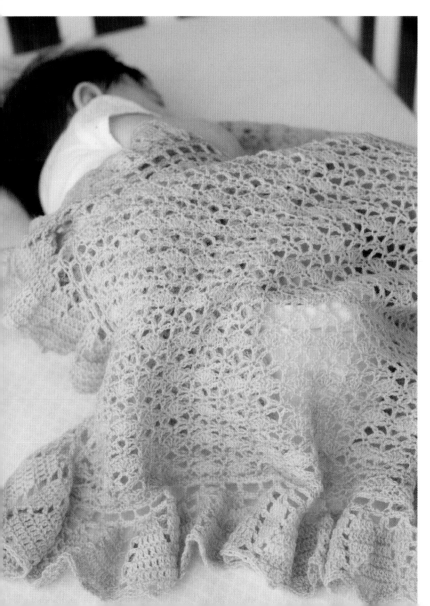

FINISHED MEASUREMENTS
24"/61 cm wide and 29"/73.5 cm long

YARN
Madelinetosh Tosh Lace, 100% superwash merino wool, 950 yds (868 m)/4 oz (113 g), Silver Fox

CROCHET HOOK
US D/3 (3.25 mm) *or size needed to obtain correct gauge*

GAUGE
4 pattern repeats and 12 rows = 3½"/9 cm in pattern before blocking

OTHER SUPPLIES
Yarn needle, pins for blocking

PATTERN ESSENTIALS

Corner shell [Dc, (ch 1, dc) twice] in 1 stitch.

Lacy shell (Dc, ch 3, dc) in 1 stitch.

Shell 5 dc in 1 stitch.

CROCHETING THE BODY

See charts on page 215.

- Chain 122.

- **Row 1:** Sc in 2nd ch from hook, *skip 2 ch, shell in next ch, skip 2 ch, sc in next ch; repeat from * across, turn. *You now have 20 shells.*

- **Row 2:** Ch 5 (counts as dc, ch 2 here and throughout), *sc in center dc of next shell, ch 2, dc in next sc, ch 2; repeat from * across, omitting last ch 2, turn.

- **Row 3:** Ch 1, sc in same st, *lacy shell in next sc, sc in next dc; repeat from *, ending with sc in 3rd ch of beginning ch-5 of previous row, turn.

- **Row 4:** Ch 5, *sc in next ch-3 space, ch 2, dc in next sc, ch 2; repeat from * to last ch-3 space, sc in last ch-3 space, ch 2, dc in last sc, turn.

- **Row 5:** Ch 1, sc in first st, *shell in next sc, sc in next dc, repeat from *, ending with sc in 3rd ch of beginning ch-5, turn.

- **Rows 6–81:** Repeat Rows 2–5 nineteen times, or until piece measures 19"/48.5 cm from beginning.

- **Row 82:** Repeat Row 2 once more.

CROCHETING THE BORDER

- **Rnd 1:** Ch 1, 2 sc in each ch-2 space and sc in each sc and dc across top of blanket, sc in corner, sc in each row-end sc and 2 sc in each row-end dc across side of blanket, sc in corner, sc in each ch across bottom edge of blanket, sc in corner, sc in each row-end sc and 2 sc in each row-end dc across side of blanket, sc in corner, join with slip st to first sc.

- **Rnd 2:** Ch 5, skip next 2 sc, dc in next sc, *(ch 2, skip 2 sc, dc in next sc), to corner, corner shell in corner st; repeat from * around, [(dc, ch 1) twice] in same st as beginning ch-5, join with slip st to 3rd ch of beginning ch-5.

- **Rnd 3:** Ch 1, 2 sc in each ch-2 space and sc in each dc around, placing 3 sc in center dc of each corner shell.

- **Rnd 4:** Ch 4 (counts as dc, ch 1), dc in first st, ch 2, skip 2 sc, *[(dc, ch 1, dc) in next sc, ch 2, skip 2 sc] to corner sc, corner shell in corner sc, ch 2, skip 2 sc; repeat from *, join with slip st to 3rd ch of ch-4.

- **Rnd 5:** Ch 3 (counts as dc here and throughout), dc in same st, dc in next ch-1 space, 2 dc in next dc, ch 2, *(2 dc in next dc, dc in next ch-1 space, 2 dc in next dc, ch 2) to corner shell, 5 dc in first dc of corner shell, ch 2, skip next ch-1 space, 5 dc in center dc of corner shell, ch 2, skip next ch-1 space, 5 dc in 3rd dc of corner shell, ch 2; repeat from * around, join with slip st to top of ch-3.

- **Rnd 6:** Ch 3, dc in each of next 4 dc, ch 2, *dc in next 5 dc, ch 2; repeat from * around; join with slip st to top of ch-3.

- **Rnd 7:** Ch 3, dc in first st, dc in next 3 dc, 2 dc in next dc, ch 2, dc2tog over next 2 dc, dc in next dc, dc2tog over next 2 dc, ch 2, *2 dc in next dc, dc in next 3 dc, 2 dc in next dc, ch 2, dc2tog over next 2 dc, dc in next dc, dc2tog over next 2 dc, ch 2; repeat from * around, join with slip st to top of beginning ch-3.

- **Rnd 8:** Ch 3, dc in first st, dc in next 5 dc, 2 dc in next dc, ch 2, dc3tog over next 3 dc, ch 2, *2 dc in next dc, dc in next 5 dc, 2 dc in next dc, ch 2, dc3tog over next 3 dc, ch 2; repeat from * around, join with slip st to top of beginning ch-3.

- **Rnd 9:** Ch 2, dc in next dc (counts as dc2tog), dc in next 5 dc, dc2tog over next 2 dc, ch 3, sc in top of next dc3tog, ch 3, *dc2tog over next 2 dc, dc in next 5 dc, dc2tog over next 2 dc, ch 3, sc in top of next dc3tog, ch 3; repeat from * around, join with slip st to top of beginning ch-2.

- **Rnd 10:** Ch 2, dc in next dc (counts as dc2tog), dc in next dc, picot, skip 1 dc, dc in next dc, dc2tog over next 2 dc, (ch 3, sc in next space) twice, ch 3, *dc2tog over next 2 dc, dc in next dc, picot, skip 1 dc, dc in next dc, dc2tog over next 2 dc, (ch 3, sc in next space) twice, ch 3; repeat from * around, join with slip st to top of beginning ch-2.

- Fasten off. Weave in ends.

FINISHING

- Block center section to measure 18½"/47 cm wide and 24"/61 cm long, then block the ruffle, pinning the picots to lie a little farther out than the ch-3 sections.

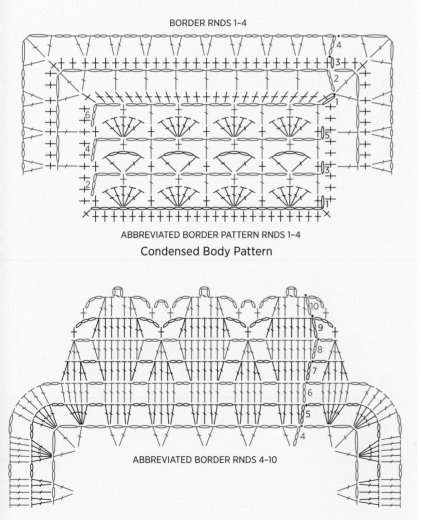

CHRISTENING CLOUD

BORDER RNDS 1–4

ABBREVIATED BORDER PATTERN RNDS 1–4

Condensed Body Pattern

ABBREVIATED BORDER RNDS 4–10

215

Ivory Dreams Blanket

DESIGNED BY *Carrie Carpenter*

The aptly named "Pound of Love" yarn works up quickly into a generously sized blanket. Worked in a simple stitch, the pattern is easy to memorize, and the blanket will delight a boy or a girl.

FINISHED MEASUREMENTS
Approximately 35"/89 cm square

YARN
Lion Brand Pound of Love, 100% premium acrylic, 1,020 yds (932 m)/16 oz (454 g), Color 099 Antique White

CROCHET HOOK
US J/10 (6 mm) *or size needed to obtain correct gauge*

GAUGE
4 pattern repeats and 8 rows = 4"/10 cm
Note: Each (2 dc, ch 2, sc) counts as a pattern repeat.

OTHER SUPPLIES
Yarn needle

PATTERN ESSENTIALS

Pattern Stitch
(multiple of 3 stitches + 1)

Chain a multiple of 3 sts plus 1.

Set-Up Row: (Dc, ch 2, sc) in 4th ch from hook, *skip next 2 chs, (2 dc, ch 2, sc) in next ch; repeat from * across, turn.

Row 1: Ch 3 (counts as dc), (dc, ch 2, sc) in first ch-2 space, (2 dc, ch 2, sc) in each ch-2 space across, turn.

Repeat Row 1 for pattern.

CROCHETING THE BLANKET

- Chain 109. Work in Pattern Stitch (36 repeats per row) until piece is 35"/89 cm or desired length. Fasten off.

FINISHING

- Weave in ends. Block lightly, if desired.

IVORY DREAMS BLANKET

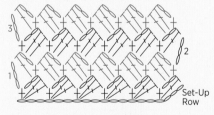

Condensed Pattern

Flouncy Edged Blanket

DESIGNED BY *Judith Durant*

First crochet the body, then pick up around the edges, double the stitch count, and *voilà,* you've got a ruffle. Worked in V-stitch, the flouncy edge is finished with another little edging.

FINISHED MEASUREMENTS
Approximately 22"/56 cm by 29"/73.5 cm

YARN
Maple Creek Farm Sport Weight, 100% superwash merino wool, 770 yds (704 m)/8 oz (225 g), Periwinkle ②

CROCHET HOOK
US H/8 (5 mm) *or size needed to obtain correct gauge*

GAUGE
18 stitches and 18 rows = 4"/10 cm in body pattern before blocking

OTHER SUPPLIES
Stitch markers, yarn needle

PATTERN ESSENTIALS

V-st (Dc, ch 1, dc) in 1 stitch or space.

CROCHETING THE BODY

- Chain 72.
- **Row 1 (WS):** Skip 3 ch (counts as dc), sc in next ch, *dc in next ch, sc in next ch; repeat from * across. *You now have 70 sts.*
- **Row 2:** Ch 3 (counts as dc here and throughout), skip first sc, *sc in next dc, dc in next sc; repeat from * across, sc in top of turning ch.

- Repeat Row 2 ninety-two more times (94 rows total); piece measures approximately 21"/53.5 cm long.

SETTING UP FOR THE RUFFLE

- Turn to work down long edge of blanket.
- **Rnd 1:** Ch 1 (does not count as st), *2 sc in first row edge st, 1 sc in each row edge along side to last st on this side, 2 sc in last row edge st *(you now have 96 sts along side 1)*; ch 2, 2 sc in next st, 1 sc in each st to last st on this edge, 2 sc in last st *(you now have 72 sts along side 2 and a ch-2 space in corner)*, ch 2; repeat from * to end of side 4, join with slip st to first sc. *You now have 336 sc plus ch-2 spaces in each corner.*
- **Rnd 2:** *Ch 3, dc in each sc to corner, 3 dc in corner ch-2 space, pm in center st of these 3 dc to mark corner and move marker as you work the rnds; repeat from * to end of rnd, join with slip st to beginning ch. *You now have 348 dc.*
- **Rnd 3:** *Ch 3, dc in same space, 2 dc in each dc to corner st, 3 dc in corner st; repeat from * around, join with slip st to top of ch-3. *You now have 704 dc.*

FLOUNCY EDGED BLANKET

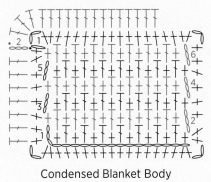

Condensed Blanket Body

CROCHETING THE RUFFLE

Note: To work the corners, do not skip the sts before and after the corner st — V-st into 3 sts, then continue in pattern. The result is that you'll have 5 V-sts together with no slipped sts between.

- **Rnd 1:** Ch 4 (counts as dc and ch-1 throughout), dc in same space (counts as V-st), *(skip 1 dc, V-st in next dc) to corner st, V-st in next 3 dc; repeat from * around, ending skip 1 dc, join with slip st to 3rd ch of ch-4.

- **Rnd 2:** Slip st in first ch-space, ch 4, dc in same space, V-st in each ch-1 space around, join with slip st to 3rd ch of ch-4.

- **Rnd 3:** Slip st in first ch-space, ch 4, dc in same space, *V-st in each ch-1 space to corner, V-st in space before corner V-st, V-st in corner V-st, V-st in space before next V-st, repeat from * around, V-st in each V-st to beginning of rnd, join with slip st to 3rd ch of ch-4.

- **Rnd 4–7:** Repeat Rnds 2 and 3 twice more.

- **Rnd 8:** Ch 1, (sc, ch 2, dc, ch 2, sc) in each ch-space around, join with slip st to first sc. Fasten off.

FINISHING

- Weave in ends. Wet block to finished measurements.

FLOUNCY EDGED BLANKET

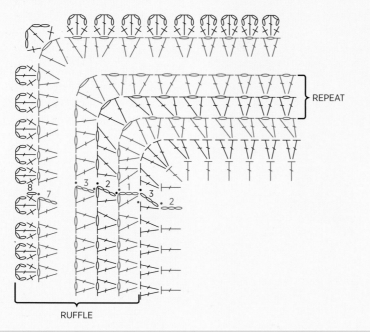

REPEAT

RUFFLE

Vaya con Dios Stroller Blanket

DESIGNED BY *Robin Nickerson*

Beginning with a square motif, this stroller or car-seat blanket is worked outward in bands of texture and lace until the skein is finished. This is a great project for baby yarns with long color changes.

PATTERN ESSENTIALS

Corner V-st (corner V-st) (Dc, ch 2, dc) in 1 stitch or space.

V-st (V-stitch) (Dc, ch 1, dc) in 1 stitch or space.

CROCHETING THE BLANKET

See the chart on page 223.

- Ch 4, join with slip st to first ch to form a ring.

- **Rnd 1:** Ch 3 (counts as dc here and throughout), 15 dc in ring, join with slip st to top of ch-3. *You now have* 16 dc.

- **Rnd 2:** Ch 3, dc in same st, dc in next dc, *2 dc in next dc, dc in next dc; repeat from * around, join with slip st to top of ch-3. *You now have* 24 dc.

- **Rnd 3:** Repeat Rnd 2. *You now have* 36 dc.

- **Rnd 4:** Ch 3, dc in same st, dc in next 2 dc, *2 dc in next dc, dc in next 2 dc; repeat from * around, join with slip st to top of ch-3. *You now have* 48 dc.

FINISHED MEASUREMENTS
Approximately 20"/51 cm square

YARN
James C. Brett Magi-Knit Baby DK, 90% acrylic/10% nylon, 328 yds (300 m)/3.5 oz (100 g), Color 3047 Tans & Blues (3)

CROCHET HOOK
US I/9 (5.5 mm) *or size needed to obtain correct gauge*

GAUGE
Rounds 1–5 = 4½"/11.5 cm square

OTHER SUPPLIES
Yarn needle

- **Rnd 5:** Ch 5 (counts as dc and ch-2 here and throughout), dc in same st, skip next st, *(V-st in next st, skip 1 st) five times, corner V-st in next st; repeat from * around, omitting last corner V-st, join with slip st to 3rd ch of ch-5. *You now have 20 V-sts and 4 corner V-sts.*

- **Rnd 6:** Slip st in next ch-2 space, ch 4 (counts as dc and ch-1 here and throughout), (dc, ch 1, corner V-st, ch 1, V-st) in same space, *dc in next ch-1 space, (ch 1, sc in next space) three times, ch 1, dc in next space**, (V-st, ch 1, corner V-st, ch 1, V-st) in next corner ch-2 space; repeat from * around, ending last repeat at **, join with slip st to 3rd ch of ch-4.

- **Rnd 7:** Ch 3 (counts as dc here and throughout), (dc in next space, dc in next dc) twice, *(2 dc, ch 2, 2 dc) in next corner space**, dc in each dc and ch-1 space to corner space; repeat from * around, ending last repeat at **, dc in each dc and ch-1 space to end, join with slip st to top of ch-3. *You now have 23 dc per side and 4 ch-2 corner spaces.*

- **Rnd 8:** Slip st in next st, ch 4 (counts as dc and ch-1), dc in same st (counts as V-st throughout), skip 2 dc, V-st in next dc, *skip 2 dc, (V-st, ch 2, V-st) in next corner space**, (skip 2 dc, V-st in next dc) to 2 sts before corner space; repeat from * around, ending last repeat at **, (skip 2 dc, V-st in next dc) five times, skip 2 dc, join with slip st to 3rd ch of ch-4.

- **Rnd 9:** Ch 1, sc in each ch-1 space and each dc around, placing (2 sc, ch 2, 2 sc) in each ch-2 corner space, join with slip st to first sc. *You now have 31 sc per side and 4 ch-2 corner spaces.*

- **Rnd 10:** Ch 4 (counts as tr here and throughout), tr in each sc and (tr, ch 3, tr) in each corner space around, join with slip st to top of ch-4. *You now have 33 tr per side and 4 ch-3 corner spaces.*

- **Rnd 11:** Ch 4, tr in next tr, *(ch 2, skip 2 tr, tr in next 3 tr) to corner space, ch 2, 3 tr in corner space, ch 2, tr in next 3 tr; repeat from * around, ending last repeat (ch 3, skip 2 tr, tr in next 3 tr) to last 3 sts, ch 2, skip 2 tr, tr in last tr, join with slip st to top of ch-4.

- **Rnd 12:** Slip st to next space, ch 4, 2 tr in same space, *(ch 2, 3 tr in next space) to corner, *ch 1, skip 1 tr, 2 tr in next corner tr, ch 3, 2 tr in next tr, ch 1, 3 tr in next space; repeat from * around, ending last repeat (ch 2, 3 tr in next space) to end, ch 2, join with slip st to top of ch-4.

- **Rnd 13:** Ch 4, tr in each tr and space around, placing (2 tr, ch 3, 2 tr) in each corner space, join with slip st to top of ch-4. *You now have 41 tr per side.*

- **Rnd 14:** Ch 1, sc in each tr and (2 sc, ch 3, 2 sc) in each corner space around, join with slip to first sc. *You now have 45 sc per side.*

- **Rnd 15:** Slip st in next st, ch 4, dc in same st, *(skip 2 sc, V-st in next sc) to 1 st before corner space, *skip 1 sc, corner V-st in corner space, skip 1 sc, V-st in next sc; repeat from * around, ending (skip 2 sc, V-st in next sc) to last 2 sc, skip 2 sc, join with slip st to 3rd ch of ch-4.

VAYA CON DIOS STROLLER BLANKET

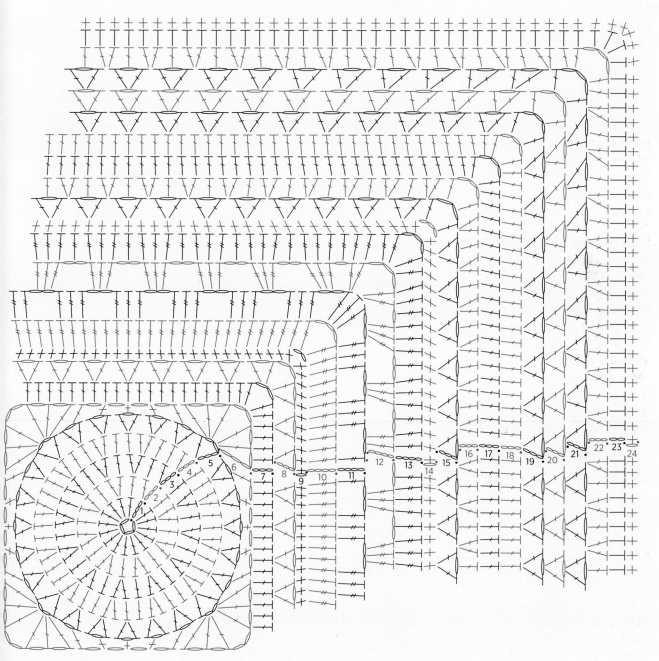

Abbreviated Blanket Pattern

- **Rnd 16:** Slip st in next ch-1 space, ch 3, 2 dc in each space between V-sts and 1 dc in each ch-1 space at center of V-sts around, placing (dc, ch 3, dc) in each corner space, join with slip st to top of ch-3. *You now have* 49 dc per side.

- **Rnds 17–18:** Ch 3 (counts as dc), dc in each st, placing (2 dc, ch 3, 2 dc) in each corner space around, join with slip st to top of ch-3. *You now have* 57 dc per side.

- **Rnd 19:** Ch 4, dc in same st, *(skip 2 dc, V-st in next dc) to 1 st before corner space, *skip 1 dc, (dc, ch 3, dc) in corner space, skip 1 dc, V-st in next dc; repeat from * around, ending (skip 2 dc, V-st in next dc) to last 2 dc, skip 2 dc, join with slip st to 3rd ch of ch-4.

- **Rnds 20–21:** Slip st in next ch-1 space, ch 4, dc in same st, V-st in center of each V-st and (dc, ch 3, dc) in each corner space around, join with slip st to 3rd ch of ch-4.

- **Rnd 22:** Slip st in next ch-1 space, ch 3, 2 dc in each space between V-sts and 1 dc in each ch-1 space at center of V-sts around, placing (2 dc, ch 3, 2 dc) in each corner space, join with slip st to top of ch-3.

- **Rnd 23:** Ch 2 (counts as hdc), hdc in each st and 4 hdc in each corner space around, join with slip st to top of ch-2.

- **Rnd 24:** Ch 1, sc in each st around, placing 2 sc between 2 center hdc's of each 4-hdc corner, join with slip st to first sc.

- Fasten off. Weave in ends.

Sweet Baby James

DESIGNED BY *Sharon Ballsmith*

This sweet little blanket is worked from the center out, turning after each round, in an easy-to-memorize stitch pattern. A border of playful circle fringes adds the finishing touch.

PATTERN ESSENTIALS

Beg cluster (beginning cluster) FLsc in st indicated, (ch 1, dc) in same st.

Circle-fringe Ch 2, work 7 sc in back bump (see page 276) of 2nd ch from hook.

First corner (2-dc cluster, dc, hdc) in st indicated.

Hdc shell (worked over 2 sts) Hdc in first st, 2 BLhdc in next st.

Second corner (Hdc, dc, 2-dc cluster) in st indicated.

CROCHETING THE BLANKET

- Make an adjustable ring (see page 272).

- **Rnd 1 (RS):** Ch 2 (does not count as st), work eight 2-dc clusters (see page 272) in adjustable ring, join with slip st in top of first cluster, turn. *You now have* eight 2-dc clusters.

Note: Do not ch 1 at beginning of the following rnds.

- **Rnd 2 (WS):** (Beg cluster, dc, hdc) in first cluster (counts as first corner), *second corner in next cluster**, first corner in next cluster; repeat from * around, ending last repeat at **, join with slip st to top of dc of beg cluster, turn. *You now have* 4 first corners and 4 second corners.

- **Rnd 3:** (Beg cluster, dc, hdc) in first cluster, *skip next st, hdc shell over next 2 sts, skip next st, second corner in next cluster**, first corner in next cluster; repeat from * around, ending last repeat at **, join with slip st to top of dc of beg cluster, turn. *You now have* 4 first corners, 4 second corners, and 4 hdc shells.

FINISHED MEASUREMENTS

Approximately 31"/79 cm square

YARN

Lion Brand Pound of Love, 100% premium acrylic, 1,020 yds (932 m)/16 oz (454 g), Color 106 Light Baby Blue ④

CROCHET HOOK

US H/8 (5 mm) *or size needed to obtain correct gauge*

GAUGE

Rounds 1–5 = 4"/10 cm square

OTHER SUPPLIES

Yarn needle

- **Rnd 4:** (Beg cluster, dc, hdc) in first cluster, *skip next st, (hdc shell, skip next st) to next cluster, second corner in next cluster**, first corner in next cluster; repeat from * around, ending last repeat at **, join with slip st in top of dc of beg cluster, turn. *You now have* 4 first corners, 4 second corners, and 8 hdc shells.

- **Rnds 5–40:** Repeat Rnd 4. *Do not fasten off. You now have* 4 first corners, 4 second corners, and 152 hdc shells.

SWEET BABY JAMES

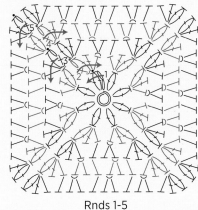

Rnds 1–5

CROCHETING THE EDGING

- With RS facing, (sc, work circle-fringe, sc) in next cluster, skip next st, *[(sc, circle-fringe, sc) in next st, skip next st] across to next cluster, (sc, circle-fringe, sc) in next 2 clusters; repeat from * around, ending last repeat (sc, circle-fringe, sc) in last cluster, join with slip st to first sc. *You now have 164 circle-fringes. Fasten off.*

FINISHING

- Weave in ends.

SWEET BABY JAMES

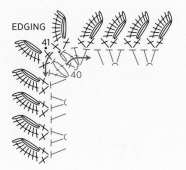

EDGING

41

40

Grey Coverlet

DESIGNED BY *Julie Blagojevich*

Laceweight yarn, a reversible stitch pattern, and an easy-as-pie border combine to make an heirloom-quality, summer-weight blanket.

PATTERN ESSENTIALS

Openwork Pattern (multiple of 2 stitches + 1)

Row 1: Ch 1, sc in first sc, *dc in next dc, sc in next sc; repeat from * across, turn.

Row 2: Ch 1, sc in first sc, *ch 1, skip 1 dc, sc in next sc; repeat from * across, turn.

Row 3: Ch 1, sc in first sc, *dc in ch-1 space, sc in next sc; repeat from * across, turn.

Repeat Rows 1–3 for pattern.

GREY COVERLET

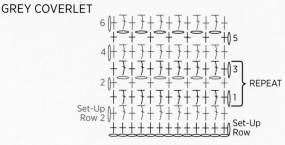

Set-Up Row 2

Set-Up Row

REPEAT

Condensed Pattern

CROCHETING THE BODY

- Chain 100.

- **Set-Up Row 1:** Sc in 2nd ch from hook and in each remaining ch across. *You now have* 99 sc.

- **Set-Up Row 2:** Ch 1, sc in first sc, *dc in next sc, sc in next sc; repeat from * across, turn.

- **Rows 1–126:** Work Rows 1–3 of Openwork pattern 42 times. Do not turn at end of last row.

FINISHED MEASUREMENTS
26"/66 cm wide and 36"/91 cm long, blocked

YARN
Tanis Fiber Arts Pink Label Lace Weight, 100% superwash merino wool, 1,000 yds (914 m)/4 oz (113 g), Chris Grey

CROCHET HOOK
US G/6 (4 mm) *or size needed to obtain correct gauge*

GAUGE
20 stitches and 20 rows = 4"/10 cm in Openwork pattern

OTHER SUPPLIES
Yarn needle, blocking tools

CROCHETING THE EDGING

Notes: The edging will be worked in rounds around the outer edge of the blanket. On the two sides containing row ends, work stitches into spaces by wrapping the stitch around the last stitch in the row. When working into the foundation edge, work clusters over the foundation ch into the sc spaces.

Proceed around blanket as follows.

- **Rnd 1:** Ch 3, dc in the side of the last sc in the previous row (counts as first 2-dc cluster); continuing down side of blanket, 2-dc cluster in each row end until to first corner (*you now have* 128 clusters), ch 2, 2-dc cluster in same space (*corner made*); working along opposite side of foundation ch, 2-dc cluster in each remaining sc space across (*you now have* 99 clusters along this edge), ch 2, 2-dc cluster in same space (*corner made*); 2-dc cluster in each remaining row end along side of blanket, ch 2, 2-dc cluster in same space (*corner made*);

2-dc cluster in each remaining st along final side, placing last cluster in same st as first cluster of rnd, ch 2, join with slip st to top of ch-3. *You now have* 454 clusters and 4 ch-2 corners.

- **Rnd 2:** Ch 3, dc in first cluster (counts as first 2-dc cluster), 2-dc cluster in each cluster and (2-dc cluster) three times each corner space around, join with slip st to top of ch 3. *You now have* 466 clusters.

- **Rnd 3:** Ch 2 (counts as hdc), picot, skip next cluster, *hdc in next cluster, picot, skip next cluster; repeat from * around, join with slip st in top of beginning ch-2.

- **Rnd 4:** Slip st in next space just before the picot, ch 1, sc in same space, ch 3, sc in space just after same picot (the sc are on either side of the picot, and the 3 chains float over the picot), *sc in next space just before the next picot, ch 3, sc in space just after same picot; repeat from * around, join with slip st to first sc.

- **Rnd 5:** Ch 1, sc in same st, picot, sc in next sc, *sc in next sc, picot, sc in next sc; repeat from * around, join with slip st to first sc.

- Fasten off. Weave in ends.

- Block.

GREY COVERLET

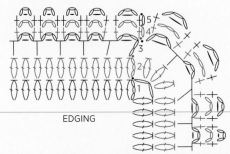

EDGING

Baptism Blanket

DESIGNED BY *Judith Durant*

A winter baptism may call for a little extra warmth, and this blanket will provide that as well as beauty. The pattern works up quickly and is enlarged through blocking.

FINISHED MEASUREMENTS
16"/40.5 cm wide and 18"/45.5 cm long without border, unblocked
22"/56 cm by 24"/61 cm without border, blocked

YARN
Valley Yarns Charlemont, 60% superwash merino wool/20% mulberry silk/20% nylon, 439 yds (401 m)/3.75 oz (100 g), Natural **1**
Note: Blanket used all but 3 yds/3 m of the skein.

CROCHET HOOK
US G/6 (4 mm) *or size needed to obtain correct gauge*

GAUGE
20 stitches and 11 rows = 4"/10 cm in pattern, unblocked

OTHER SUPPLIES
Yarn needle, blocking tools

PATTERN ESSENTIALS

Blanket Pattern (multiple of 3 stitches + 2, add 2 for base chain)

Row 1: 3 dc in 5th chain from hook, *skip 2 ch, 3 dc in next ch; repeat from * to last 2 ch, skip 1 ch, dc in last ch, turn.

Row 2: Ch 3 (counts as dc), skip next dc, 3 dc in next dc, *skip next 2 dc, 3 dc in next dc; repeat from * across, ending with skip 1 dc, dc in top of turning ch, turn.

Repeat Row 2 for pattern.

Tr2tog (treble crochet 2 together) *Yo (twice), insert hook in st or space indicated and pull up a loop, (yo and pull through 2 loops on hook) twice, repeat from * once, yo, draw yarn through 3 loops on hook.

CROCHETING THE BLANKET

- Chain 82.
- Work Blanket pattern over 80 sts for 50 rows total.

THE BORDER

- **Rnd 1:** Ch 1, sc in next st and each st across to corner (80 sts); turn 90°, work 2 sc in each row-end st across to next corner (100 sts); turn 90°, sc in each st across (80 sts), turn 90°, work 2 sc in each row-end st across to next corner (100 sts), join with slip st to first sc. *You now have* 360 sts.

- **Rnd 2:** Ch 4 (counts as first leg of first tr2tog, skip next 3 sts, tr in next st, ch 5, *tr2tog working first leg in same st as previous tr, skip next 3 sts, work next leg in next st, ch 5; repeat from * around, working ch-7 loops at corners instead of ch-5 loops; join with slip st to top of beginning ch-4, slip st in next ch-5 space.

- **Rnd 3:** Ch 1, 5 sc in each ch-5 space and 7 sc in each ch-7 loop around, join with slip st to first sc. Fasten off.

FINISHING

- Weave in ends. Block to finished measurements.

BAPTISM BLANKET

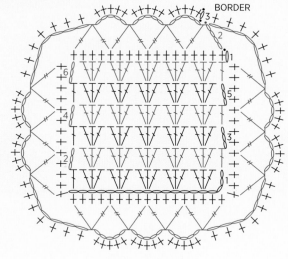

Condensed Pattern

CHAPTER EIGHT

LITTLE

Bags
+
Accessories

Put-and-Take Purse

DESIGNED BY *Gwen Steege*

What little girl doesn't want to play dress up? This colorful little purse is perfect for playing "put-and-take," too — a place to hide and retrieve favorite items. Because of the long drawstrings, this purse is not suitable for children under the age of three.

FINISHED MEASUREMENTS
6"/15 cm tall

YARN
Adriafil Kimera, 100% Egyptian mercerized cotton, 148 yds (135 m)/1.75 oz (50g), Color 16 Proust Fancy 🄸🄸

CROCHET HOOK
US E/4 (3.5 mm) *or size needed to obtain correct gauge*

GAUGE
Rnds 1–5 = 4"/10 cm in diameter

OTHER SUPPLIES
Yarn needle

CROCHETING THE PURSE

- Begin with an adjustable ring (see page 272).
- **Rnd 1:** Ch 3 (counts as dc here and throughout), 11 dc in ring, join with slip st to top of ch-3. *You now have* 12 dc.
- **Rnd 2:** Ch 3, dc in same st, 2 dc in each dc around, join with slip st to top of ch-3. *You now have* 24 dc.
- **Rnd 3:** Ch 3, dc in same st, dc in next dc, *2 dc in next dc, dc in next dc; repeat from * around, join with slip st to top of ch-3. *You now have* 36 dc.
- **Rnd 4:** Ch 1, sc in each dc around, join with slip st to first sc.
- **Rnd 5:** Ch 3, dc in same st, dc in next 2 sc, *2 dc in next sc, dc in next 2 sc; repeat from * around, join with slip st to top of ch-3. *You now have* 48 dc.
- **Rnds 6–8:** Ch 1, sc in each st around, join with slip st to first sc.
- **Rnd 9:** Ch 3, dc in each sc around, join with slip st to top of ch-3.
- **Rnds 10–14:** Ch 1, sc in each st around, join with slip st to first sc.
- **Rnd 15:** Ch 3, dc in each sc around, join with slip st to top of ch-3.
- **Rnds 16–18:** Ch 1, sc in each st around, join with slip st to first sc.
- **Rnd 19:** Ch 3, dc in each sc around, join with slip st to top of ch-3.
- **Rnd 20:** Ch 4 (counts as dc, ch 1), (dc, ch 1) in each dc around, join with slip st to 3rd ch of ch-4.
- **Rnd 21:** Ch 1, sc in same st, ch 3, (sc, ch 3) in each ch-space around, join with slip to first sc. Fasten off. Weave in ends.

CROCHETING THE DRAWSTRINGS

- Leaving 7"/18 cm yarn tails at each end, crochet two lengths of 100 chains each. Thread one chain onto a yarn needle and run it under and over the dc's worked in Rnd 19. Using photo as a guide, knot the ends together on one side of the purse, then knot yarn tails together with four evenly spaced over-hand knots.

- Thread the other chain onto the yarn needle and, beginning at the exact opposite side of the purse, weave it through the same path as the first chain. Knot its ends together.

- To close purse, draw out each loop.

PUT-AND-TAKE PURSE

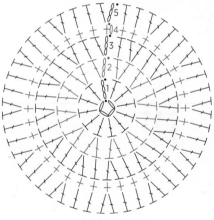

Rnds 1–5

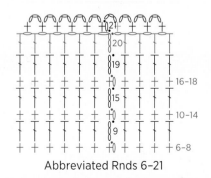

Abbreviated Rnds 6–21

Little Miss Felted Purse

DESIGNED BY *Gwen Buttke McGannon*

The sides of this purse are worked circularly with post stitches to create the visual texture of the spokes of a wheel. After felting, the purse is ready to hold little precious things while your girl is out and about.

FINISHED MEASUREMENTS
Approximately 5"/12.5 cm diameter

YARN
Plymouth Yarn Gina, 100% wool, 109 yds (100 m)/1.75 oz (50 g), Color 0007 ⓸

CROCHET HOOK
US J/10 (6 mm) *or size needed to obtain correct gauge*

GAUGE
16 stitches and 8 rounds = 4"/10 cm in front post double crochet before felting

OTHER SUPPLIES
Yarn needle, snap, sewing needle and coordinating thread

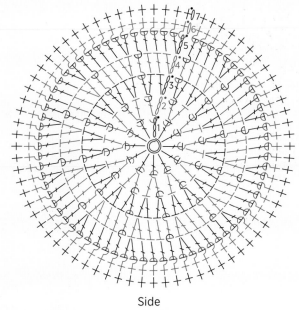

dc in next 3 dc, FPdc in next FPdc; repeat from * around, join with slip st to top of ch-3. *You now have* 72 sts.

- **Rnd 6:** Ch 1, BPsc in each st around, join with slip st to first sc.
- **Rnd 7:** Ch 1, sc in each st around, join with slip st to first sc. Fasten off.
- Repeat to make a second side but do not fasten off.

FINISHING

JOIN THE SIDES

- Holding both pieces with RS together, ch 1, sc through double thickness in each sc to last 18 sts; stitching only into one piece, ch 1, hdc in next 18 sts, turn, continue working the across remaining sts on opposite side, hdc in each of the 18 sts, slip st in next hdc. *Do not fasten off.* Turn RS out.

THE HANDLE

- Fsc 45, join to opposite side of opening with slip st. Fasten off.
- Weave in ends. Felt (see page 275).

CROCHETING THE SIDES

- Make an adjustable ring (see page 272).
- **Rnd 1:** Ch 3 (counts as dc here and throughout), ch 3, 11 dc in ring, join with slip st to top of ch-3. *You now have* 12 sts.
- **Rnd 2:** Ch 3, FPdc in same st, *dc in next st, FPdc in same st; repeat from * around, join with slip st to top of ch-3. *You now have* 24 sts.
- **Rnd 3:** Ch 3, dc in same st, (dc, FPdc) in next FPdc, *2 dc in next dc, (dc, FPdc) in next FPdc; repeat from * around, join with slip st to top of ch-3. *You now have* 48 sts.
- **Rnd 4:** Ch 3, dc in same st and in next 2 dc, FPdc in next FPdc, *2 dc in next dc, dc in next 2 dc, FPdc in next FPdc; repeat from * around, join with slip st to top of ch-3. *You now have* 60 sts.
- **Rnd 5:** Ch 3, dc in same st and in next 3 dc, FPdc in next FPdc, *2 dc in next dc,

LITTLE MISS FELTED PURSE

Side

Max's Backpack

DESIGNED BY *LeAnna Nocita-Lyons,*
The Eccentric Haus Frau

This little backpack is perfect for transporting favorite toys for a trip to the park or to Grandma's house. Stitched with single, double, and front post double crochet, the pack works up quickly and requires no extra notions. Because of the long drawstrings, this backpack is not suitable for children under the age of three.

FINISHED MEASUREMENTS
5½"/14 cm wide, 7"/18 cm tall, and 5½"/14 cm deep

YARN
Red Heart With Love, 100% acrylic, 370 yds (338 m)/7 oz (198 g), Color 1803 Blue Hawaii (4)

CROCHET HOOK
US G/6 (4 mm) *or size needed to obtain correct gauge*

GAUGE
16 stitches and 18 rows = 5"/12.5 cm in single crochet
16 stitches and 11 rows = 5"/12.5 cm in half double crochet

OTHER SUPPLIES
Stitch marker, yarn needle

CROCHETING THE BAG

THE BOTTOM

- Chain 21.
- **Row 1:** Sc in 2nd st from hook and in each ch across, turn. *You now have* 20 sc.
- **Row 2:** Ch 1, sc in each sc across, turn.
- **Rows 3–20:** Repeat Row 2 eighteen times. At end of Row 20, do not turn.

THE SIDES

- **Rnd 1:** Ch 1, working along the side of Rows 20–1, 1 sc in each row to corner, 2 sc in corner st; working along opposite side of foundation ch, sc in each ch across, 2 sc in corner st; working along side of Rows 1–20, 1 sc in each row to corner, 2 sc in corner st, sc in each sc across to last st, 2 sc in corner. *You now have* 84 sc.
- **Rnd 2:** Ch 1, BPsc around post of each sc around, join with slip st to first sc.
- **Rnd 3:** Ch 2 (counts as hdc), hdc in each st around. Do not join. Pm in the first st of the rnd and move it up as you work the rnds.
- **Rnd 4:** (Hdc in next 19 sts, hdc2tog) four times. *You now have* 80 sts.
- **Rnd 5:** FPdc in first BPsc in Rnd 2, *hdc in next 19 sts, FPdc in next corresponding st in Rnd 2; repeat from * around. *You now have* 80 hdc and 4 FPdc.
- **Rnd 6:** *Hdc in next 19 sts, FPdc in next FPdc of rnd below; repeat from * around. *You now have* 80 hdc and 4 fpdc.
- **Rnds 7–15:** Repeat Rnd 6.
- **Rnd 16:** *Dc in first st, ch 1, skip 1 st; repeat from * around, join with slip st to first dc. *You now have* 40 dc and 40 ch-spaces.
- **Rnd 17:** Slip st in each st and ch-space around. Fasten off. Weave in ends.

CROCHETING THE DRAWSTRING

- Leaving a 2"/5 cm tail, ch 120. Fasten off, leaving a 2"/5 cm tail. Fray 2"/5 cm of tails, and trim if necessary to make even. Tie an overhand knot at each ends of chain, leaving the frayed tassels below the knots. Thread through Rnd 16. Once the drawstring has been woven through and evened out, tack with a few stitches to the back of the pack.

CROCHETING THE TOP COVER

THE TOP

- Chain 21.
- Repeat Rnds 1–20 of bottom.

THE SIDES

- **Rnds 1–4:** Repeat Rnds 1–4 of sides.

- **Rnd 5 (front of top cover):** Sc in next 8 st, ch 5, skip 2 st, sc in each st around.

- **Rnd 6:** Slip st in each st to ch-5 space, sc in next 5 ch of ch-space, slip st in each st around. Fasten off. Weave in ends.

ATTACH TOP COVER TO BACKPACK

- With yarn needle and approximately 20"/51 cm of yarn, sew edge of back top to the back edge of Rnd 15 using a whipstitch (see page 276) in each hdc. Fasten off and weave in ends.

THE BACK LOOP

- Attach yarn with slip st to 6th st on back of top cover, ch 10, skip 4 sts, slip st in next st (*loop made*). Turn, slip st in loop just made, 23 sc in same loop, slip st in loop. Fasten off. Weave in ends.

CROCHETING THE BACK STRAPS

Note: Strap will measure approximately 32"/81 cm before being folded in half and stitched to back of pack.

- Chain 116.

- **Row 1:** Dc in 4th ch from hook, dc in next ch; work FPdc around posts of last 2 dc's, *dc in next 2 ch, FPdc around posts of last 2 dc's; repeat from * to last st, dc in last st. Do not turn. *You now have* 56 FPdc.

- **Row 2:** Ch 1, work 3 sc around the dc post at end of row; working across

opposite side of foundation ch, sc in chain at base of next 3 dc, *FPdc around base of the posts of last and next dc's; from the previous row (one dc from each 2-dc pair, to form a V with the dc's), sc in next ch at base of 2 dc; repeat from * to last dc, sc in chain at base of last dc, 3 sc in beginning ch-3, join with slip st to first st of Row 1. Fasten off. Weave in ends.

FINISHING

- Fold strap in half and, with yarn needle and approximately 20"/51 cm of yarn, sew center of strap to the center back bottom. Making sure not to twist the strap, sew ends of straps to the top left and right corners at Row 15. Fasten off. Weave in ends.

Optional: Add a lining to the backpack and sew on a large button that will fit the loop of the top cover.

MAX'S BACKPACK

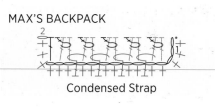

Condensed Strap

Dad's Diaper Bag

DESIGNED BY *Dana Bincer, Yarnovations.com*

While we don't see a problem, some men just don't like walking in public carrying pink-flowered diaper bags. Problem solved with this masculine tote. Straps, buckles, and bias tape give the simple-to-crochet bag an industrial feel.

CROCHETING THE FRONT PANEL

- Chain 38.
- **Row 1:** Hdc in 2nd ch from hook and in each ch across, turn. *You now have 37 hdc.*
- **Rows 2–30:** Ch 1, hdc in each hdc across, turn.
- Fasten off.

CROCHETING THE BACK PANEL

- Repeat instructions for front panel but *do not cut yarn*. Continue as follows.
- **Rows 31–46:** Repeat Row 2 from front panel.
- **Row 47:** Ch 1, hdc in next 20 hdc, turn, leaving remaining sts unworked. *You now have 20 hdc.*
- **Row 48:** Ch 2 (does not count as st), skip first st, hdc in each across, turn. *You now have 19 hdc.*
- **Row 49:** Ch 1, hdc in next 18 hdc, turn. *You now have 18 hdc.*

....
FINISHED MEASUREMENTS
12"/30.5 cm wide, 11"/28 cm tall, and 2"/5 cm deep
....
YARN
Caron Jumbo, 100% acrylic, 659 yds (602 m)/12 oz (340 g), Color 09012 Dalmation (4)
....
CROCHET HOOK
US J/10 (6 mm) *or size needed to obtain correct gauge*
....
GAUGE
13 stitches and 11 rows = 4"/10 cm in half double crochet
....
OTHER SUPPLIES
Yarn needle, 1 yd/1 m lining fabric, sewing needle and coordinating thread, 12"/30.5 cm metal zipper, 5"/12.5 cm of ¼"/6 mm elastic (optional), 5 yds/4.5 m of ½"/13 mm extra-wide double-fold bias tape, 50"/127 cm of 1"/2.5 cm nylon strapping, two 1"/2.5 cm plastic side release buckles, straight pins

- **Rows 50–56:** Ch 1, hdc in each hdc across, turn.
- **Row 57:** Ch 2, skip first st, hdc in next 16 hdc, turn. *You now have* 16 hdc.
- **Row 58:** Ch 2, skip first st, hdc in next 14 hdc, slip st in next st. *You now have* 15 hdc.
- Fasten off.

CROCHETING THE GUSSET

- Chain 149.
- **Row 1:** Hdc in 2nd ch from hook and in each ch across, turn. *You now have* 148 hdc.
- **Row 2:** Ch 1, hdc in each hdc across, turn.
- **Row 3:** Ch 1, hdc in next 111 sts, ch 38 to form zipper opening, turn.
- **Row 4:** Ch 1, hdc in 2nd ch from hook and each ch and st across. *You now have* 148 hdc.
- **Row 5:** Repeat Row 2.
- Fasten off. Weave in ends.

CROCHETING THE BOTTLE POCKET

- Chain 14.
- **Row 1:** Hdc in 2nd ch from hook and in each ch across, turn. *You now have* 13 hdc.
- **Rows 2–14:** Ch 1, hdc in each hdc across, turn.
- **Row 15:** Ch 1, hdc in each hdc across; do not turn.
- **Row 16:** Ch 1, working along side of Rows 15–1, work 20 hdc across; working along opposite side of foundation ch, hdc in each ch across; working along side of Rows 1–15, work 20 hdc across, turn. *You now have* 53 hdc.
- **Row 17:** Ch 1, hdc in each hdc across.
- Fasten off, leaving a long tail for sewing. Weave in ends.

CROCHETING THE FLAT POCKET

- Chain 17.
- **Row 1:** Hdc in 2nd ch from hook and in each ch across, turn. *You now have* 16 hdc.
- **Rows 2–15:** Ch 1, hdc in each hdc across, turn.
- Fasten off, leaving a long tail for sewing.

ASSEMBLING THE BAG

- Referring to assembly diagrams, pin gusset to top, bottom, and sides of front panel and to bottom and Rows 1–30 of back panel, placing opening for zipper at center top of bag. Rows 31–58 of back panel serve as a flap.
- Working from RS, slip st through both thicknesses around to join gusset to front panel. Fasten off. Repeat to join gusset to 3 sides of back panel. Sew remaining side of gusset to Row 30 of back panel. Fasten off. Weave in ends.

DAD'S DIAPER BAG

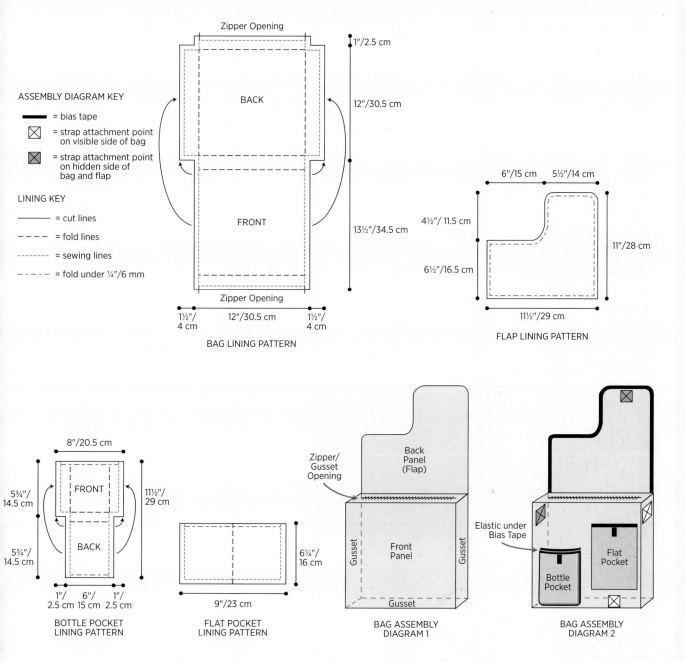

ASSEMBLY DIAGRAM KEY

▬ = bias tape

⊠ = strap attachment point on visible side of bag

⬚ = strap attachment point on hidden side of bag and flap

LINING KEY

— = cut lines

– – – = fold lines

· · · · = sewing lines

– · – · = fold under ¼"/6 mm

Zipper Opening

BACK

FRONT

Zipper Opening

1"/2.5 cm

12"/30.5 cm

13½"/34.5 cm

1½"/4 cm   12"/30.5 cm   1½"/4 cm

BAG LINING PATTERN

6"/15 cm   5½"/14 cm

4½"/11.5 cm

6½"/16.5 cm

11"/28 cm

11½"/29 cm

FLAP LINING PATTERN

8"/20.5 cm

FRONT

BACK

5¾"/14.5 cm

5¾"/14.5 cm

11½"/29 cm

1"/2.5 cm   6"/15 cm   1"/2.5 cm

BOTTLE POCKET LINING PATTERN

9"/23 cm

6¼"/16 cm

FLAT POCKET LINING PATTERN

Zipper/Gusset Opening

Back Panel (Flap)

Front Panel

Gusset

Gusset

Gusset

BAG ASSEMBLY DIAGRAM 1

Elastic under Bias Tape

Bottle Pocket

Flat Pocket

BAG ASSEMBLY DIAGRAM 2

- Pin bottle pocket to front of bag in area not covered by the front flap. With yarn and yarn needle, attach with whipstitch (see page 276) across sides and bottom, leaving top open. Pin flat pocket to front of bag in area to be covered by front flap. Attach with whipstitch on sides and bottom.

- Attach a 2"/5 cm loop of strapping to the non-adjustable part of one buckle and sew it to one side of the gusset, near the top. Attach one end of a 40"/101.5 cm piece of strapping to the adjustable part of the buckle and snap the strap in place. Sew the other end of the strap to the other side of the gusset, opposite the end with the buckle.

- Attach a 2"/5 cm loop of strapping to the non-adjustable part of the other buckle and sew it to the front flap. Sew one end of the remaining 6"/15 cm piece of strapping to the lower front, in line with the buckle on the front flap. Attach the adjustable part of the buckle to the other end of this strap.

- Place a folded piece of bias tape over all strapping ends sewn to bag and machine- or hand-sew securely in place. Wrap all remaining ends of strapping with bias tape and sew the tape securely to the strapping to prevent fraying.

- Cut linings from each lining pattern. With sewing needle and thread, sew bag lining together with ½"/13 mm seam allowances, leaving top open. Hand-sew zipper into opening at top of lining. Hand-sew lining into bag.

- Fold down edges of flap lining ¼"/6 mm and sew to inside of flap with needle and thread.

- With needle and thread, sew linings for two front pockets and hand-sew linings into pockets.

- Hand-sew elastic to top inside of bottle pocket, if desired, using a length that's half the width of the pocket opening.

- Folding it in half, sew bias tape around outer edge of flap.

- Folding it in half, sew bias tape to top of pockets; add a 2"/5 cm folded piece of bias tape in the center of each binding to act as a pull tab.

- Wrap ends of strapping with bias tape and sew in place to prevent fraying.

Cady's Cowl

DESIGNED BY *Gwen Buttke McGannon*

A lovely cowl of Catherine wheel and shell stitches is worked from beginning to end in one piece — no extra ends to weave it. It will delight and warm your child. (And if you borrow it for yourself, we won't tell.)

FINISHED MEASUREMENTS
21"/53.5 cm circumference and 8½"/21.5 cm deep

YARN
Lang Mille Colori Baby, 100% superwash merino wool, 207 yds (190 cm)/1.75 oz (50 g), Color 53 Macaw ❶

CROCHET HOOK
US H/8 (5 mm) *or size needed to obtain correct gauge*

GAUGE
2 shells = 4¼"/11 cm
8 rows = 4"/10 cm

OTHER SUPPLIES
Yarn needle

PATTERN ESSENTIALS

Cluster (Yo, insert hook and pull up a loop, yo, pull through 2 loops on hook) over designated number of stitches, yo and pull through all loops on hook.

CROCHETING THE COWL

See chart on next page.

- Chain 37.

- **Row 1:** Sc in 2nd ch from hook, sc in next ch, *skip 3 ch, 7 dc in next ch, skip 3 ch, sc in next 3 ch; repeat from * to last 4 ch, skip 3 ch, 4 dc in last ch, turn.

- **Row 2:** Ch 1, sc in first 2 dc, *ch 3, cluster over next 7 sts, ch 3, sc in next 3 sts, repeat from * to last 4 sts, ch 3, cluster over last 4 sts, turn.

- **Row 3:** Ch 3 (counts as dc here and throughout), 3 dc in first st, *skip 3 ch, sc in next 3 sc, skip 3 ch, 7 dc in top of next cluster; repeat from *, ending last repeat skip 3 ch, sc in last 2 sc, turn.

- **Row 4:** Ch 3, cluster over next 3 sts, *ch 3, sc in next 3 sts, ch 3, cluster over next 7 sts; repeat from * across, ending with ch 3, sc in last 2 sts, turn.
- **Row 5:** Ch 1, sc in first 2 sts, *skip 3 ch, 7 dc in next st, skip 3 ch, sc in next 3 sc; repeat from * across, ending with skip 3 ch, 4 dc in last st, turn.
- Repeat Rows 2–5 until piece measures 21"/53.5 cm, ending with Row 4 of pattern.

THE EDGING

- Working evenly along long edge of cowl, ch 1, sc in same st, (7 dc in edge of next pattern Row 3, sc in edge of next pattern Row 2) to corner, ending with sc in last st of edge. Holding both short ends of cowl together and working through both layers, ch 1, sc in first st, sc in next st, skip next 3 sts, (7 dc in next st, skip next 3 sts, sc in next 3 sts) across, ending 7 dc in last st. Working across the other long edge of cowl, (sc in edge of next pattern Row 3, 7 dc in edge of next pattern Row 5) around, ending 7 dc in last pattern Row 5, join with slip st to first sc.
- Fasten off. Weave in ends.

CADY'S COWL

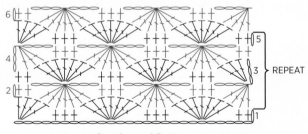

Condensed Pattern

Dewdrop Flower Pin

DESIGNED BY *Alla Koval, Alla Koval Designs*

A double layer of crochet surrounds a purchased spray of stamen and is trimmed with purchased green satin leaves. Pin this to a favorite garment, or make it a hair accessory.

CROCHETING THE FLOWER

- Ch 5, join with slip st to form a ring.
- **Rnd 1 (RS):** Ch 1, (sc, ch 3) five times in ring, join with slip st to first sc. *You now have* 5 ch-3 spaces and 5 sc.
- **Rnd 2:** Ch 1, (sc, hdc, 5 dc, hdc, sc) in each ch-3 space around, join with slip st to first sc. *You now have five petals.*
- **Rnd 3:** Ch 1, working behind petals of Rnd 2, (sc in next sc of Rnd 1, ch 5) around, join with slip st to first sc.
- **Rnd 4:** Ch 1, (sc, hdc, 9 dc, hdc, sc) in each ch-5 space around, join with slip st to first sc. Fasten off. Weave in ends.

CROCHETING THE BACKING

- Make an adjustable ring (see page 272).
- **Rnd 1:** Ch 2 (counts as hdc here and throughout), 11 hdc in ring. *You now have* 12 hdc.
- **Rnd 2:** Ch 2, hdc in same st, 2 hdc in each st around, join with slip st to top of ch-2. *You now have* 24 hdc.

- **Rnd 3:** Ch 2, 2 hdc in next st, (hdc in next st, 2 hdc in next st) around, join with slip st to top of ch-2. *You now have* 36 hdc.
- Fasten off.

FINISHING

- Referring to photograph for placement and using needle and thread or hot glue, attach stamen to center front of flower. Attach leaves to WS of flower. With WS facing, attach backing to back of flower, then attach backing pin or hair clip to backing.

FINISHED MEASUREMENTS
3"/7.5 cm in diameter

YARN
Cascade Yarns Avalon, 50% cotton/ 50% acrylic, 175 yds (160 m)/3.5 oz (100 g), Color 01 White **(4)**

CROCHET HOOK
US G/6 (4 mm) *or size needed to obtain correct gauge*

GAUGE
Rounds 1 and 2 = 2¼"/5.5 cm in diameter

OTHER SUPPLIES
Yarn needle; sewing needle and coordinating thread or hot glue; purchased leaves, stamen, and backing pin or hair clip

DEWDROP FLOWER PIN

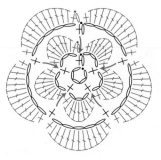

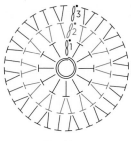

Backing

Diaper Stacker

DESIGNED BY *Deborah Bagley,*
Yarnovations.com

This innovative stacker will
add a touch of class as well as
practicality to your nursery.
The design maximizes stitch
characteristics in terms of
shaping and stretching, and the
ribbon edge adds to its looks and
functionality.

FINISHED MEASUREMENTS
10"/25.5 cm wide and 15"/38 cm tall

YARN
Caron Simply Soft, 100% acrylic,
315 yds (288 m)/6 oz (170 g),
Color 0003 Pistachio (4)

CROCHET HOOK
US J/10 (6 mm) *or size needed to*
obtain correct gauge

GAUGE
12 stitches and 10 rows = 4"/10 cm in
half double crochet

OTHER SUPPLIES
Stitch markers, yarn needle, 2 yds/2 m
double-fold bias tape binding or
2"/5 cm ribbon (fold ribbon in half
lengthwise), straight pins, sewing
needle and coordinating thread

CROCHETING THE BASE

- Chain 31.
- **Row 1 (RS):** Working in the back bump across row (see page 276), hdc in 2nd ch from hook and each ch across, turn. *You now have* 30 sts.
- **Rows 2–11:** Ch 1 (does not count as st throughout), hdc in each across, turn.
- **Rnd 12:** Ch 1, BLhdc in next 30 hdc; working across side edge of base, hdc in each row-end st across to next corner; working across opposite side of foundation ch, BLhdc in st across to next corner; working across side edge, hdc in each row-end st across to next corner, join with slip st to first hdc. Fasten off. *You now have* 82 sts.

CROCHETING THE SIDES

- **Row 1:** With RS facing, skip 16 sts, standing hdc in next st, hdc in next 79 hdc, turn, leaving last 2 sts unworked. *You now have* 80 sts.
- **Row 2:** Ch 1, working under frontmost bar of sts, hdc in next 4 sts, (picot, hdc in next 4 sts) across, turn.
- **Row 3:** Ch 1, hdc in each hdc across, pushing each picot to RS, turn.
- **Row 4:** Ch 1, hdc in each hdc across, turn.
- **Row 5:** Ch 1, hdc under backmost bar of each hdc across, turn.
- **Row 6:** Ch 1, hdc in each hdc across, turn.
- **Row 7:** Ch 5, skip first 3 hdc, sc in next hdc, picot, (ch 5, skip 3 hdc, sc in next hdc, picot) to last 4 sts, ch 5, skip 3 hdc, sc in last hdc, turn. *You now have* 20 ch-5 spaces and 19 picots.
- **Rows 8–13:** (Ch 5, sc in next ch-5 space, picot) to last space, ch 5, sc in 3rd ch of beginning ch-5, turn.
- **Row 14:** Ch 5, sc in 3rd ch of next ch-5, (ch 3, sc in third ch of next ch-5) across, turn.
- **Row 15:** Ch 1, (hdc in next sc, 3 hdc in next space) across, turn. *You now have* 80 sc.
- **Rows 16–19:** Repeat Rows 2–5.
- **Row 20:** Repeat Row 7.
- **Row 21–26:** Repeat Row 8.

PATTERN ESSENTIALS

Hdc under backmost bar Yo, insert hook from bottom to top under the horizontal bar that lies behind and just below the V at the top of the next st and pull up a loop, yo and pull through 3 loops on hook.

Hdc under frontmost bar Yo, insert hook from bottom to top under the horizontal bar that lies in front of and just below the V at the top of the next st and pull up a loop, yo and pull through 3 loops on hook.

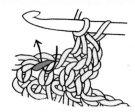

DIAPER STACKER

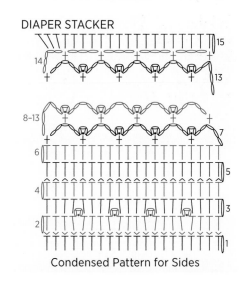

Condensed Pattern for Sides

- **Rnd 27:** Ch 5, sc in 3rd ch of next ch-5, (ch 3, sc in 3rd ch of next ch-5) 20 times, ch 2, join the two sides together with slip st in 3rd ch of beginning ch-5. *Do not turn.*

- **Rnd 28:** Ch 1, hdc in first st, 2 hdc in next ch-2 space, (hdc in next sc, 3 hdc in next ch-3 space) to last space, 2 hdc in last ch-2 space. *You now have* 82 hdc.

- With the opening facing, starting with the left-hand st of the 2 center sts and counting to the left, place st markers in the 11th, 20th, 22nd, and 31st sts.

- Starting with the right-hand st of the 2 center sts and counting to the right, place st markers in the 15th, 16th, 26th, and 27th sts.

- Row 29 will close the top by joining the front, back, and sides together. Attach yarn to the 15th st on the right. Start by crocheting the sts with the st markers in the 15th, 16th, 26th, and 27th together as follows.

- **Row 29 (joining rnd):** Starting with the front side facing, push the right-hand side of the diaper stacker inward toward the center. Yo, insert hook in the 15th, 16th, 26th, and 27th sts on the right-hand side, hdc all 4 of those sts together, working through four layers of sts on front, back, and two inner folded parts together, hdc in next 4 sts (leave the last inner st unused), working through double layer of front and back together, hdc in next 20 sts, push the side panel toward the center, working through 4 marked sts (11th, 20th, 22nd, and 31st), hdc in marked sts, working through four layers of front, back, and two inner folded parts together, hdc in next 4 sts, turn. *You now have* 30 sts.

- **Row 30:** Ch 1, (hdc under frontmost bar of next 5 sts, picot) five times, hdc under frontmost bar of next 5 sts, turn.

- **Row 31:** Ch 1, hdc in each st across, pushing each picot to RS, turn. *You now have* 5 picots.

- **Row 32:** Ch 1, hdc in each hdc across, turn.

- **Row 33:** Ch 1, hdc under backmost bar of each hdc across. Fasten off and weave in ends.

FINISHING

- Cut two strips of double-fold bias tape or ribbon about 14½"/37 cm long. (Check to be sure this length matches the length of the opening on your diaper stacker when it is stretched.) Pin, then sew one length of binding on each side of the opening.

- Cut a strip of double-fold bias tape or ribbon about 22"/56 cm long. Tie into a bow. Pin, then sew the bow by hand at the top of the diaper stacker where the ribbon is.

- Cut two strips of double-fold bias tape or ribbon about 5"/12.5 cm long. Fold in half crosswise and pinch them together. Pin, then sew the binding to the back top corners as hangers.

Optional: Sew a strip of binding to the back (top to bottom) and bottom of the stacker so they don't stretch more than the front.

Bottle Cozies

DESIGNED BY *Carrie Carpenter*

Keep baby's bottles cool when you're on the run. Quick to stitch, these make great shower gifts.

Cozy 1

Cozy 2

FINISHED MEASUREMENTS
5"/12.5 cm high and 7"/18 cm circumference

YARN
Bernat Vickie Howell Sheep(ish), 70% acrylic/30% wool, 167 yds (153 m)/3 oz (85 g), Color 0017 Chartreuse(ish) ⓸

CROCHET HOOK
US F/5 (3.75 mm) *or size needed to obtain correct gauge*

GAUGE
Cozy 1: 19 stitches and 12 rows = 4"/10 cm in double crochet
Cozy 2: 9 stitches and 14 rows = 4"/10 cm in pattern

OTHER SUPPLIES
Yarn needle

CROCHETING COZY 1

- Chain 35.

- Row 1: Dc in 4th ch from hook, dc in next ch, *ch 3, skip next 3 ch, dc in next 5 ch; repeat from * across, ending with dc in each of the last 3 ch, turn.

- Row 2: Ch 3 (counts as dc here and throughout), dc in next 2 dc, *working over next ch-3 loop, work 3 dc in corresponding center skipped ch-st 2 rows below**, dc in each of the next 5 dc; repeat from * across, ending last repeat at **, dc in each of the last 3 sts, turn.

- **Row 3:** Ch 3, dc in next 6 dc, *ch 3, skip next 3 dc, dc in next 5 dc; repeat from * to last 2 sts, dc in last 2 sts, turn.
- **Row 4:** Ch 3, dc in next 6 dc, *working over next ch-3 loop, work 3 dc in corresponding center skipped dc 2 rows below, dc in next 5 dc; repeat from * to last 2 sts, dc in last 2 sts, turn.
- **Row 5:** Ch 3, dc in next 2 dc, ch 3, skip next 3 dc, *dc in next 5 dc, ch 3, skip next 3 dc; repeat from * to last 3 sts, dc in last 3 sts, turn.
- **Rows 6–16:** Repeat Rows 2–5, ending with Row 4. Fasten off.

FINISHING

- Fold piece in half, bringing sides together. Using yarn needle and matching yarn, sew sides together. Weave in ends.

CROCHETING COZY 2

- Chain 33.
- **Row 1:** 2 dc in 3rd ch from hook, *skip next 2 ch, (sc, 2 dc) in next ch; repeat from * to last 3 ch, skip next 2 ch, sc in last ch, turn.
- **Row 2:** Ch 2, 2 dc in first sc, *skip next 2 dc, (sc, 2 dc) in next sc; repeat from * to last 2 dc, skip last 2 dc, sc in next ch.
- **Rows 3–19:** Repeat Row 2. Fasten off.

FINISHING

- Fold piece in half, bringing sides together. Using yarn needle and matching yarn, sew side seam. Weave in ends.

BOTTLE COZIES

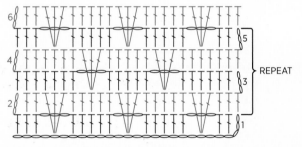

Condensed Cozy 1 Pattern

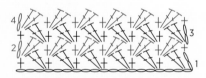

Condensed Cozy 2 Pattern

Pacifier Clip

DESIGNED BY *Andrea Lyn Van Benschoten*

Never again worry about picking up your baby's pacifier from the street, the beach, or a dirty floor. Simply clip this holder to a blanket or clothing — when the pacifier inevitably leaves baby's mouth, it won't go far!

FINISHED MEASUREMENTS
8"/20.5 cm long, excluding clip, and 1½"/4 cm wide

YARN
Patons Grace, 100% mercerized cotton, 136 yds (125 m)/1.75 oz (50 g), Color 62027 Ginger 3

CROCHET HOOK
US F/5 (3.75 mm) *or size needed to obtain correct gauge*

GAUGE
18 stitches and 12 rows = 4"/10 cm in back loop half double crochet

OTHER SUPPLIES
Suspender or pacifier clip, yarn needle

CROCHETING THE STRAP

- Chain 40.
- **Row 1:** Hdc in 2nd ch from hook and in each ch across, turn. *You now have 39 hdc.*
- **Row 2:** Ch 2 (does not count as st), BLhdc in each hdc across, turn.
- **Row 3:** Ch 2, BLhdc in each st across, turn.
- Fasten off, leaving a long tail for sewing.

ATTACHING THE CLIP

- Fold over one short edge through clip; sew closed using yarn needle and tail.
- On opposite short edge, make a 2"/5 cm long loop to hold pacifier; sew in place.

ADDING THE EDGING

- With RS facing, join yarn, *ch 3, sc in next st; repeat from * to clip. Fasten off. Repeat edging on opposite side. Weave in ends.

Little Bunny Mittens

DESIGNED BY *Brenda K. B. Anderson*

These little bunny mittens are worked from the extra-long folded cuff to the fingertip. The ears are made separately, appliquéd with scraps of fabric, and stitched onto the mitten. The nose, mouth, and whiskers are embroidered, and tiny buttons are added for eyes.

SIZE AND FINISHED MEASUREMENTS
To fit 4–5 years: 6"/15 cm hand circumference (excluding thumb) and 4¾"/12 cm hand length (excluding cuff)

YARN
Berroco Vintage DK, 52% acrylic/40% wool/8% nylon, 288 yds (263 m)/3.5 oz (100 g), Color 2106 Smoke (3)

CROCHET HOOK
US F/5 (3.75 mm) *or size needed to obtain correct gauge*

GAUGE
20 stitches and 16 rounds = 4"/10 cm in half double crochet

OTHER SUPPLIES
Four stitch markers, yarn needle, small amount of fabric or felt* for ears, embroidery needle and floss (in pink, black, white, and coordinating with yarn), sewing needle and coordinating thread, tiny black buttons for eyes
*If you use fabric, you will also need Fray Check (found at fabric and craft stores) to keep the cut edges of the fabric from fraying. If you plan to machine-wash often, consider using felt or a fabric that will not fray, as Fray Check may wash out.

PATTERN ESSENTIALS

Hdc dec (half double crochet decrease) Yo, insert hook under front loop only of next st, then from front to back under both loops of following st, yo and pull up a loop through both sts (3 loops are now on hook), yo and pull through all 3 loops.

CROCHETING THE CUFF (MAKE 2)

- Chain 22.

- **Row 1 (RS):** Working in the back bump of each ch across (see page 276), hdc in 3rd ch from hook and in each ch across, turn. *You now have* 20 hdc.

- **Rows 2–18:** Ch 2, BLhdc in each hdc, turn.

- Ch 1, fold the ribbing in half with RS together. Working through double thickness of the front loops of the foundation row and back loops of row just worked, slip st in each st across. *Do not fasten off. You now have* 20 slip sts. Leaving slip st seam on outside of cuff, reposition cuff to work in row ends around. Use st markers to divide the cuff edge into four equal sections.

CROCHETING THE HAND

- **Rnd 1:** Ch 1, working in row-edge sts around top edge of cuff, work 7 hdc between each set of markers for a total of 28 hdc sts around top edge of cuff, removing markers as you come to them. *Do not join.* Pm in the first st of the rnd and move it up as you work the rnds.

- **Rnd 2:** Hdc in each st around. *You now have* 28 hdc.

- **Rnd 3:** Hdc in next 13 hdc, 2 hdc in next 2 hdc, hdc in next 13 hdc. *You now have* 30 hdc.

- **Rnd 4:** Hdc in next 14 hdc, 2 hdc in next 2 hdc, hdc in next 14 hdc; hdc in next st (marked st) to shift beginning of rnd; move marker to following st to indicate new beginning of rnd. *You now have* 32 sts.

- **Rnd 5:** Hdc in next 15 hdc, 2 hdc in next 2 hdc, hdc in next 15 hdc. *You now have* 34 sts.

- **Rnd 6:** Hdc in next 16 hdc, 2 hdc in next 2 hdc, hdc in next 16 hdc. *You now have* 36 sts.

- **Rnd 7:** Hdc in next 17 hdc, 2 hdc in next 2 hdc, hdc in next 17 hdc. *You now have* 38 sts.

- **Rnd 8:** Hdc in each hdc around; hdc in next st (marked st) and following st to shift the beginning of the rnd; move marker to following st to indicate new beginning of rnd.

- **Rnd 9:** Hdc in next 14 hdc, skip next 10 hdc, place second marker in the first skipped st, hdc in next 14 hdc. *You now have* 28 sts, not including the 10 sts skipped for the thumb.

- **Rnds 10–17:** Hdc in each hdc around.

- **Rnd 18:** (Hdc in next 2 sts, hdc dec) seven times. *You now have* 21 sts.

- **Rnd 19:** (Hdc dec, hdc in next st) seven times. *You now have* 14 sts.

- **Rnd 20:** (Hdc dec) seven times. *You now have* 7 sts.

- Fasten off, leaving a long tail. Using yarn needle, run yarn tail through the front loop of each of the remaining 7 sts and pull tight to close the top of hand. Weave in ends.

THE THUMB

- **Rnd 1:** Leaving beginning yarn tail dangling on outside of mitten, pull up loop of yarn in marked stitch at thumb opening, ch 1, beginning with same st, hdc into each of the 10 skipped thumb sts, work 2 extra hdc where thumb meets hand. *You now have* 12 hdc. *Do not join.* Pm in the first st of the rnd and move it up as you work the rnds.

- **Rnds 2–5:** Hdc in each st around.

- **Rnd 6:** (Hdc dec) six times. *You now have* 6 sts.

- Fasten off, leaving long tail. Using yarn needle, run yarn tail through the front loop of each of the remaining 6 sts and pull tight to close the top of thumb. Use beginning yarn tail to stitch any holes closed where thumb meets hand. Weave in ends.

253

THE EARS (MAKE 4)

- Make an adjustable ring (see page 272).
- **Rnd 1:** Ch 1, 6 hdc in loop. *Do not join. You now have* 6 hdc. Pm in the first st of the rnd and move it up as you work the rnds.
- **Rnd 2:** 2 hdc in first hdc, hdc in next 5 hdc. *You now have* 7 sts.
- **Rnd 3:** 2 hdc in first hdc, hdc in next 6 hdc. *You now have* 8 sts.
- **Rnd 4:** 2 hdc in first hdc, hdc in next 7 hdc. *You now have* 9 sts.
- **Rnd 5:** 2 hdc in first hdc, hdc in next 8 hdc. *You now have* 10 sts.
- **Rnds 6 and 7:** Hdc in each hdc around.
- **Rnd 8:** Hdc dec, hdc in next 8 hdc. *You now have* 9 sts.
- **Rnd 9:** Hdc dec, hdc in next 7 hdc. *You now have* 8 sts.
- Fasten off, leaving a long sewing length. Weave in beginning yarn tail at tip of ear.

FINISHING

Note: When adding the ears and facial features, position them on the mittens so that there is a right and a left hand. Use photograph for reference.

- Block all pieces, if necessary.
- Cut a small oval-shaped piece of fabric or felt for each ear, similar in shape but slightly smaller than ear. (If you are using a fabric that might fray, apply Fray Check to all edges of cut pieces and allow them time to dry.) Using embroidery floss and an embroidery needle, whipstitch (see page 276) each appliqué piece to the center of each flattened ear.
- Using pink embroidery floss, create a satin-stitch (see page 276) triangle about ½"/13 mm from tip of mitten for each nose. Using black embroidery floss, outline the two sides of the nose, and create a V-shaped stitch below nose for the mouth, and a vertical stitch that connects center of mouth to the bottom point of nose. Make three long stitches on each side of nose with white embroidery floss for whiskers.
- Using needle and thread, stitch each button to face for eyes.
- Using yarn needle and yarn tails, stitch the bottom edge of each ear to mitten. Slip st the underside of ear to mitten about ½"/13 mm up from where ear connects to mitten. This will keep the ears back and not flopping about.

Baby's First Christmas Stocking

DESIGNED BY *Edie Eckman*

What better way to celebrate Christmas than with a new baby in the house? Fine-weight yarn held doubled creates a light, springy fabric, and since it's made from the toe up, if you run short of yarn, you can just make it shorter. Worked in a cream color, it's just right for baby girl or boy.

CROCHETING THE STOCKING

See chart on page 256.

THE TOE

- With yarn held doubled throughout, ch 4. Join with slip st to form a ring.

- **Rnd 1:** Ch 1, 6 sc in ring, join with slip st to first sc. *You now have* 6 sc.

- **Rnd 2:** Ch 1, 2 sc in each sc around, join with slip st to first sc. *You now have* 12 sc.

- **Rnd 3:** Ch 1, sc in first sc, 2 sc in next sc, *sc in next st, 2 sc in next sc; repeat from * around. *You now have* 18 sc.

- **Rnd 4:** Ch 1, sc in each sc around, join with slip st to first sc.

- **Rnd 5:** Ch 1, sc in first 2 sc, 2 sc in next sc, *sc in next 2 sc, 2 sc in next sc; repeat from * around, join with slip st to first sc. *You now have* 24 sc.

- **Rnds 6 and 7:** Repeat Rnd 4.

- **Rnd 8:** Ch 1, sc in first 3 sc, 2 sc in next sc, *sc in next 3 sc, 2 sc in next sc; repeat from * around, join with slip st to first sc. *You now have* 30 sc.

- **Rnd 9:** Repeat Rnd 4.

- **Rnd 10:** Ch 1, 2 sc in first sc, sc in next 4 sc, *2 sc in next sc, sc in next 4 sc; repeat from * around, join with slip st to first sc. *You now have* 36 sc.

- **Rnd 11:** Ch 1, sc in each sc around, join with slip st to back loop only of first sc.

....
FINISHED MEASUREMENTS
10"/25.5 cm circumference and
17"/43 cm from cuff to toe
....
YARN
Lion Brand Sock-Ease, 75% wool, 25% nylon, 438 yds (400 m)/3.5 oz (100 g), Color 100 Marshmallow (🧶1)
....
CROCHET HOOK
US J/10 (6 mm) *or size needed to obtain correct gauge*
....
GAUGE
15 stitches and 10 rounds = 4"/10 cm in Texture Stitch with yarn held doubled
....
OTHER SUPPLIES
Yarn needle

PATTERN ESSENTIALS

Texture Stitch (multiple of 2 stitches)

Rnd 1: Ch 2 (counts as BLhdc), FLhdc in next st, *BLhdc in next st, FLhdc in next st; repeat from * around, join with slip st to front loop only at top of ch-2.

Rnd 2: Ch 2 (counts as FLhdc), BLhdc in next st, *FLhdc in next st, BLhdc in next st; repeat from * around, join with slip st to back loop only at top of ch-2.

Repeat Rnds 1 and 2 for pattern.

BABY'S FIRST CHRISTMAS STOCKING

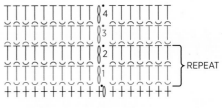

Texture Stitch Pattern

THE FOOT

- **Rnds 1–10:** Work Rows 1 and 2 of Texture Stitch five times. Fasten off.

THE HEEL

- **Row 1:** Skip first 27 sts, standing sc in next st, sc in next 17 sts, turn. *You now have* 18 sc.

- **Row 2:** Ch 1, sc in first 13 sc, turn.

- **Row 3:** Ch 1, sc in first 8 sc, turn.

- **Row 4:** Ch 1, sc in first 8 sc, sc in next st of Row 2, turn. *You now have* 9 sc.

- **Row 5:** Ch 1, sc in first 9 sc, sc in next st of Row 1, turn. *You now have* 10 sc.

- **Row 6:** Ch 1, sc in each sc across, sc in next st of Row 2, turn. *You now have* 11 sc.

- **Row 7:** Ch 1, sc in each sc across, sc in next st of Row 1, turn. *You now have* 12 sc.

- **Rows 8–13:** Repeat Rows 6 and 7 three times. *You will have* 18 sc at the end of Row 13.

- Fasten off, leaving an 8"/20.5 cm tail.

THE LEG

- **Rnd 1 (RS):** Skip first 9 sc of heel, standing hdc in front loop only of next sc, (BLhdc in next sc, FLhdc in next sc) four times, (BLhdc in next hdc, FLhdc in next hdc) nine times, (BLhdc in next sc, FLhdc in next sc) four times, BLhdc in next sc, join with slip st in back loop only of first hdc. *You now have* 36 sts.

- **Rnds 2–21:** Work Rnds 1 and 2 of Texture Stitch pattern 10 times.

THE CUFF

- **Rnds 1–5:** Ch 1, sc in each st around, join with slip st to first sc.

FINISHING

Note: Stocking leg may have biased. If necessary, sc in each sc to center back of leg.

- **Hanging Loop:** Ch 8, slip st in same st, turn. Ch 1, 10 sc in ch-8 space. Fasten off.

- Sew holes closed at corners of heels. Weave in ends.

BABY'S FIRST CHRISTMAS STOCKING

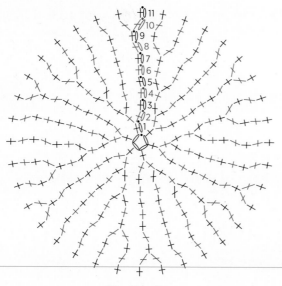

Stocking Toe

Hyperbolic Mobile

DESIGNED BY *Edie Eckman*

Swirling hyperbolic shapes in strongly contrasting colors will entertain your newborn. It is thought that, in the early weeks and months, babies see strong contrasts best, making this black, white, and red printed yarn perfect for this purpose. Just be sure to hang mobile out of baby's reach.

FINISHED MEASUREMENTS
7"/18 cm diameter and 25"/63.5 cm (or as desired) long

YARN
Adrialfil Kimera, 100% Egyptian mercerized cotton, 148 yds (135 m)/1.75 oz (50 g), Color 015 Dumas Fancy 🧶

CROCHET HOOK
US G/6 (4 mm) *or size needed to obtain correct gauge*

GAUGE
Motif 1 = 2¾"/7 cm diameter
Gauge is not crucial in this project.

OTHER SUPPLIES
7"/18 cm diameter wooden hoop or wire circle, yarn needle, clear monofilament, fabric glue or hot glue

PREPARING THE MOBILE

- Glue one end of yarn to inside of hoop. Wrap yarn around hoop, keeping strands parallel and covering the entire hoop. Cut yarn and glue end of yarn to inside of hoop.

- *Ch 75. Fasten off. Weave in ends. Repeat from * two more times.

- Tie each chain to hoop, placing them equidistant from each other. Holding hoop suspended by chains, tie top of chains together in an overhand knot so that hoop hangs straight. Set aside.

CROCHETING THE MOTIFS

MOTIF 1 (MAKE 2)

- Ch 4, join with slip st to form a ring.

- **Rnd 1:** Ch 3 (counts as dc), 5 dc in ring. *Do not join. You now have* 6 sts. Pm in the first st of the rnd and move it up as you work the rnds.

- **Rnds 2 and 3:** 2 dc in each dc around. *You now have* 24 dc.

- **Row 4:** Dc in next dc, hdc in next 2 dc, sc in next 2 dc, slip st in next st. Fasten off.

MOTIF 2 (MAKE 1)

- Ch 4, join with slip st to form a ring.

- **Rnd 1:** Ch 1, 6 sc in ring. *Do not join. You now have* 6 sts. Pm in the first st of the rnd and move it up as you work the rnds.

- **Rnd 2:** 2 sc in each sc around. *You now have* 12 sc.

- **Rnd 3:** *Sc in next sc, 2 sc in next sc; repeat from * around. *You now have* 18 sc.

- **Rnds 4 and 5:** 2 dc in each st around. *You now have* 72 dc.
- **Row 6:** Hdc in next 2 sts, sc in next st, slip st in next st. Fasten off.

MOTIF 3 (MAKE 2)

- Ch 4, join with slip st to form a ring.
- **Rnd 1:** Ch 1, 6 sc in ring. *Do not join.* You now have 6 sts. Pm in the first st of the rnd and move it up as you work the rnds.
- **Rnd 2:** 2 dc in each sc around. You now have 12 dc.

- **Rnds 3 and 4:** 3 dc in each dc around. *You now have* 108 dc.
- **Row 5:** Hdc in next dc, sc in next dc, slip st in next st. Fasten off.

MOTIF 4 (MAKE 2)

- Ch 4, join with slip st to form a ring.
- **Rnd 1:** Ch 1, 6 sc in ring. *Do not join.* You now have 6 sts. Pm in the first st of the rnd and move it up as you work the rnds.
- **Rnds 2–4:** 3 dc in each st around. *You now have* 162 dc.
- **Row 5:** Hdc in next dc, sc in next dc, slip st in next st. Fasten off.

CROCHETING THE CENTERS (MAKE 7)

- Ch 4, 4-dc cluster in 4th chain from ring. Fasten off, leaving a long sewing length.

FINISHING

- Insert yarn tail of one center through center hole of one motif. Sew in place. Repeat for other six centers, placing each in the center of any motif to provide contrasting centers as desired.
- Cut monofilament to different lengths and tie motifs to hoop.

HYPERBOLIC MOBILE

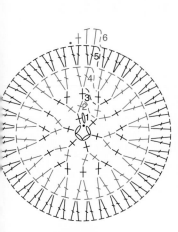

Motif 1

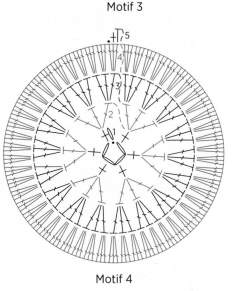

Motif 3

Motif 2

Motif 4

259

Ombré Wrap

DESIGNED BY *Julie Blagojevich*

This generous wrap will come in handy for nursing while away from home. The pattern runs diagonally across the shawl and is worked in a combination of basic stitches.

FINISHED MEASUREMENTS
68"/173 cm wide and 26"/66 cm at deepest point, blocked

YARN
Apple Tree Knits Pure Lace (Jumbo), 100% merino wool, 1,313 yds (1,200 m)/6 oz (170 g), Buttercup Gradient

CROCHET HOOK
US F/5 (3.75 mm) *or size needed to obtain correct gauge*

GAUGE
18 stitches and 14 rows = 4"/10 cm in pattern

OTHER SUPPLIES
Yarn needle, blocking tools

CROCHETING THE WRAP

- Ch 4, join with slip st to form ring.
- **Set-Up Row:** Ch 1, 5 sc in ring, turn. *You now have 5 sts.*
- **Row 1:** Ch 2 (counts as hdc here and throughout), 2 hdc in next 2 sc, hdc in next 2 sc, turn. *You now have 7 hdc.*
- **Row 2:** Ch 2, hdc2tog, hdc in each st across to last st, 2 hdc in last st, turn.
- **Row 3:** Ch 2, hdc in same st, 2 hdc in next st, hdc in each st across, turn. *You now have 9 hdc.*
- **Row 4:** Ch 3, dc in same st (counts as 2-dc cluster), dc2tog, *ch 1, skip next st, 2-dc cluster in next st; repeat from * across, 2-dc cluster in same st as last 2-dc cluster, turn. *You now have 9 sts.*
- **Row 5:** Ch 2, 2 hdc in next cluster, 2 hdc in next ch-1 space, hdc in each st and space across, placing last hdc in top of beginning cluster. *You now have 11 sts.*
- **Rows 6–145:** Repeat Rows 2–5 thirty-five times, turn. *You now have 151 sts.*
- **Row 146:** Repeat Row 2.

OMBRÉ WRAP

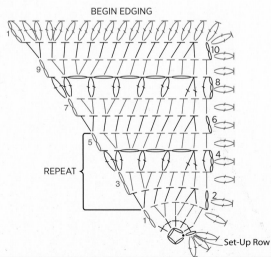

Abbreviated Body Pattern

THE EDGING

- **Row 1:** Ch 3, dc in sa[...] s as first 2-dc cluster), 2-dc cluster in next 2 sts, 2-dc cluster in each st across to bottom point; work a 2nd 2-dc cluster in same st at point, working across other edge of shawl, 2-dc cluster into each row end across to next corner; three 2-dc cluster in the side of the Set-Up Row, turn. *You now have* 303 clusters.

- **Row 2:** Ch 1, (sc, ch 3, sc) in first st, *sc in next st, (sc, ch 3, sc) in next st; repeat from * across, turn.

- **Row 3:** Ch 1, (sc, ch 3, sc) in first ch-3 space, *sc in next sc, (sc, ch 3, sc) in next ch-3 space; repeat from * across, turn.

- **Row 4:** Ch 3, dc in first ch-3 space (counts as first 2-dc cluster), (picot, 2-dc cluster) in same space, *ch 3, skip next sc, sc in next sc, ch 3, (2-dc cluster, picot, 2-dc cluster) in next ch-3 space; repeat from * across, turn.

- **Row 5:** Ch 3, dc in first cluster (counts as first 2-dc cluster), *picot, skip 1 picot, 2-dc cluster in next cluster**, ch 3, sc in next sc, ch 3, 2-dc cluster in next cluster; repeat from * across, ending last repeat at **.

- Fasten off. Weave in ends. Wet block to finished dimensions.

OMBRÉ WRAP

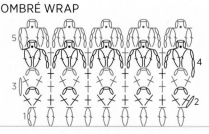

Condensed Edging Pattern

Mom's (or Dad's) Hot-or-Cold Pack

DESIGNED BY *Judith Durant*

This handy little bag is filled with beans and can be used hot or cold to ease sore muscles or soothe a headache. While the little one sleeps, remove this from the freezer or zap it for a minute or two in the microwave, place where you need it, and relax.

FINISHED MEASUREMENTS
Approximately 10"/25.5 cm wide and 5"/12.5 cm tall

YARN
Cascade Heritage Paints, 75% superwash merino wool/25% nylon, 437 yds (400 m)/3.5 oz (100 g), Color 9825 Isle of Skye ❶

CROCHET HOOK
US G/6 (4 mm) *or size needed to obtain correct gauge*

GAUGE
33 stitches (3 pattern repeats) and 20 rows = 4"/10 cm in pattern
Note: Gauge is not crucial, just be sure your stitches are small enough to hold the filling. Hook size used on sample is smaller than yarn manufacturer's recommended size.

OTHER SUPPLIES
Yarn needle, 2 cups small white beans

PATTERN ESSENTIALS

Chevron Stitch (multiple of 11 stitches + 1, add 1 for base chain)

Row 1: 2 sc in 2nd ch from hook, *sc in next 4 ch, skip 2 ch, sc in next 4 ch, 3 sc in next ch; repeat from * across, ending with 2 sc in last ch, turn.

Row 2: Ch 1, 2 sc in first st, *sc in next 4 sts, skip 2 sts, sc in next 4 st, 3 sc in next st; repeat from * to across, ending with 2 sc in last st, turn.

Repeat Row 2 for pattern.

MOM'S (OR DAD'S) HOT-OR-COLD PACK

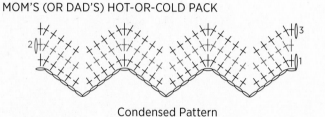

Condensed Pattern

CROCHETING THE BAG

- Ch 90, leaving a tail long enough to sew a short seam. Work Chevron Stitch pattern until piece measures 10"/25.5 cm from beginning. *Do not fasten off.*

FINISHING

- With yarn still attached, block piece to 10"/25.5 cm square. With RS together, join last row to foundation ch with slip st, matching peaks to valleys. Steam seam to flatten, if necessary. Turn RS out and, with long seam positioned along the center back of the tube, sew one short seam. Fill bag with beans as desired (sample uses 2 cups). Sew remaining seam. Weave in ends.

APPENDIX

ABOUT THE DESIGNERS

Brenda K. B. Anderson

Brenda K. B. Anderson's designs have been published in several magazines, including *Interweave Crochet* and *Knitscene*. She is the author of *Beastly Crochet* and *Crochet Ever After*. During the process of working on this book, Brenda became inspired and gave birth to a set of twins!

Annelies Baes

Annelies Baes believes everything is possible in crochet. She likes designing trendy garments with great fit and comfort, as well as accessories. Find her on Ravelry: *www.ravelry.com/designers /annelies-baes-vicarno*. And her website: *www.en.vicarno.com*.

Deborah Bagley

Deborah Bagley learned crochet from her grandmother in 1988, along with her twin sister and mother. In 2012 she and her twin started designing and publishing patterns in their shop, Yarnovations.com. They enjoy making fun and whimsical items. When not crocheting, Deborah enjoys rock climbing, mountain biking, reading, and caring for her wonderful husband and two adorable and active boys.

Sharon Ballsmith

Sharon Ballsmith is an avid crocheter and indie designer, having patterns published in magazines and books since 2010. Always keeping her hooks close by, she loves playing with stitch patterns and dreaming up new designs. You can see more of her designs online at *www.ravelry.com/designers /sharon-ballsmith* and find her on Ravelry as stitchesandstones.

Claudia Barbo

Claudia Barbo's mom taught her to crochet when she was 14. As she became more proficient, she began to experiment with making her own patterns, and started seriously designing about seven years ago. She feels lucky to work at Apple Yarns; many of her designs are for classes or special events. The Baby Mukluks were the 2012 LYS tour pattern for Apple Yarns.

Donna Barranti

Donna Barranti was born in Seattle, Washington, grew up in California, and now lives in north Florida. Her Grandma Hunt taught her to crochet pineapple sachets, but she soon found great pleasure in creating afghans. Donna's most recent design patterns include afghans, shoulder bags, and table runners; they can be found online at Knit Picks (*www.knitpicks.com*) and Ravelry (*www.ravelry.com*).

Dana Bincer

Dana Bincer is one of the twins at Yarnovations. com. After crocheting her first afghan as a teenager, she abandoned crochet to pursue paper crafting for 20 years. In 2012, Dana's twin sister convinced her that crochet was more than just afghans and they've been creating fun and quirky designs together ever since. Dana also enjoys mountain biking, reading, and knitting.

Laura Biondi

Laura Biondi picked up a crochet hook in 2004 and hasn't put it down since! She teaches crochet classes at The Red Thread in Warrenton, Virginia. Laura tries to wear something crocheted every day and shares the joy of crochet with everyone she can. You can visit her Ravelry page, BlackSheepCrochet, to see more of her unique creations.

Julie Blagojevich

Julie Blagojevich has been crocheting since she was eight years old. You can find her designs on the Web at: *www.ravelry.com/designers /julie-blagojevich*, or in her Ravelry store, *www .ravelry.com/patterns/sources/crochetworks*. Her Ravelry group is at *www.ravelry.com/groups /crochetworks*.

Janet Brani

"Looping" off and on since the age of eight, Janet Brani is happily caught up in this new wave of crochet enthusiasm. Her work has been published in *Interweave Crochet*, *Crochet!*, and *Vogue Crochet*. Her printed pattern line is available to the wholesale industry through Deep South Fibers.

Carrie Carpenter

Carrie Carpenter learned to crochet when she was 10 years old. Her designs have appeared in various crochet magazines and books, as well as with yarn companies. She also works as a freelance technical proofreader for craft publishers and designers. When she isn't designing, Carrie enjoys teaching crochet classes at her local yarn shop in Montpelier, Vermont.

Vicky Chan

Vicky Chan is a self-taught designer who lives in Ontario, Canada, with her wonderful husband and two awesome teenage kids. Unleashing her creativity in the summer of 2013, Vicky has been designing and publishing her patterns independently ever since. You can find her at *http://vickychandesigns.wordpress.com* and Ravelry.

Thomasina Cummings

Thomasina Cummings lives with her husband and children in south Wales, UK and has been crocheting since she was a child. She creates patterns for babies, adults, and the home, and her love of textures is evident in her designs. Her current collection can be found on Ravelry at *www.ravelry.com/designers /thomasina-cummings-designs*.

Pam Daley

Pam Daley started designing seriously while going through chemo a few years ago. It was something that allowed her to be creative without depleting what little physical energy she had during those days. Her first designing love was baby things, but she has expanded that love to include socks, gloves, hats, and other accessories for both little ones and grown-ups. Find her designs in her Etsy shop, *www.playingwithfiber.etsy.com*, and her Ravelry shop, *www.ravelry.com/stores /pam-daley-designs*.

Melissa Dallke

Melissa Dallke lives with her husband and five children on a Kansas farm where they raise fiber animals. She has been fascinated with fiber arts her whole life, remembering her grandmother crocheting items for her while growing up. Melissa now sells her own fiber, dyed yarn, and crochet and knit patterns in her Etsy shop, *www.etsy.com /shop/1yarnofatail*.

Sylvie Damey

Sylvie Damey is a French designer living in the beautiful French Alps. Unanimously recognized as "well written and easy to follow," her patterns focus on perfect fit: Instead of using pre-formatted sizing charts, she designs her samples on real-life bodies until the perfect fit is achieved. Follow her crocheting adventures on Facebook: *www.facebook.com/chezplum*.

Tamara Del Sonno

Tamara Del Sonno has enjoyed knitting and crochet since childhood. The loves of her life are her fabulous family, great knitting buddies, and lots of yarns. She's @ClickityChick on Twitter. Clickity Sticks designs are available on Ravelry, Craftsy, or by email at ClickitySticks@aol.com.

Aurelia Mae Delaney

Aurelia wrote this pattern when she was just 13! In high school now, with a focus on music and art, she is looking forward to pursuing an art degree in college. Aurelia recently helped to teach her field hockey teammates to crochet their own hats, and she is excited to have her first professionally published pattern in this book.

Michele DuNaier

After retiring from a career in software design, Michele DuNaier turned her attention to "softwear design." When not designing patterns, she is busy knitting and crocheting for the "Care to Knit" charity group. See all her patterns at *www.ravelry .com/designers/michele-dunaier*.

Judith Durant

Judith has been up to yarny things for more than 50 years. She is editor of the One-Skein Wonders® series and author of several other books about knitting, including *Knit One, Bead Too* and *Increase, Decrease*. Judith is on the web at *www.judithdurant.com*.

Edie Eckman

Edie Eckman writes, designs, and edits from her home base in the mountains of Virginia, yet at the drop of a hat she'll travel to teach knitting and crochet just about anywhere. She is the author of several best-selling books, including *The Crochet Answer Book, Beyond the Square Crochet Motifs*, and *Around the Corner Crochet Borders*. She can be found online at *www.edieeckman.com*.

Beth Graham

Beth Graham loves to learn new things and delights in sharing her discoveries with others. Her patterns appeal to crocheters seeking simple, fun, and innovative projects.

Corley Groves

Corley Groves started knitting when she was about 13. She bought a "learn to knit" set from her school's book fair and took it over to her grandmother's house, where her grandmother spent the afternoon teaching her to knit. She hasn't stopped since! Along the way she has accumulated more yarn than she will use in a lifetime, and she wouldn't have it any other way.

Christy Hagan

Christy Hagan is a crochet teacher, designer, and stay-at-home mom. Throughout the seasons, she is very much inspired by the color and texture combinations found in nature and around her home. A walk outside always sends her inside to get creative with crochet!

Beth Hall

Beth Hall teaches computer technology stuff to support her two-skein-a-day habit. She is a certified Master of Advanced Crochet Stitches and Techniques and a portfolio reviewer for Crochet Guild of America. You can find her on Ravelry as HoosierLady.

Ida Herter

Ida Herter is a homeschooling mom of three kiddos. She enjoys sewing, knitting, and crocheting. Since she picked up her crochet hook again five years ago, she has grown to love creating her own adorable amigurumi designs.

Laura Hontz

Laura Hontz has been crocheting for around 45 years and she loves it! Her fiber collection is legendary with her family and friends. She has been professionally designing crochet patterns for a few years now, and you can find her on Ravelry.

Justyna Kacprzak

Justyna Kacprzak is a crochet designer who is passionate about her job. Having two adorable sons inspired her to start working on baby patterns, apart from her favorite amigurumi. Her website is *www.cuteandkaboodle.com*.

Elizabeth Garcia Kalka

Elizabeth Garcia Kalka is a married mother of four boys. She has two kitties, an obsession with purses and shoes, and more yarn than she can count. She has been crocheting for more than 40 years, and she truly enjoys designing patterns.

Nirmal Kaur Khalsa

After decades of crocheting, Nirmal Kaur Khalsa finally realized she didn't always have to follow directions. In fact, she could let her imagination soar. As a result, her designs run the gamut from simple to complex. She particularly enjoys playing with color and is mildly obsessed with self-striping yarn.

Alla Koval

Alla Koval is a published designer of children's knit and crochet garments and patterns. Her work has appeared in several magazines, including *Crochet!*, *Interweave Crochet*, *Crochetscene*, and *Crochet World*, and in her series of books, Imagical Seasons. Alla Koval Design patterns can be found at *http://mylittlecitygirl.com* and her books can be found at *http://imagicalseasons.com*.

Katherine Larson

Years after her mother taught her to crochet, Kate Larson began designing because she couldn't find patterns for what she wanted to make. She lives in Las Vegas, Nevada, with her husband and two sons.

Ashley Leither

Ashely Leither is the designer and owner of Ashley Designs Corner and has been designing since 2012. She enjoys every moment she gets to be creative!

Reyna Thera Lorele

Reyna Thera Lorele's knit and crochet patterns are featured in her Etsy shop, *www.etsy.com/shop/yiyodesigns*. She blogs about her fiber adventures at *www.yarninyarnout.blogspot.com*. She is also an award-winning author of both fiction and nonfiction.

Gwen Buttke McGannon

Gwen Buttke McGannon lives with her husband and daughter along with their dog. She crochets every day and loves making cute and lovely crochet goods for her Etsy shop, *www.gwengood.etsy.com*.

Diane McKee

Diane McKee fits in crocheting and knitting design around a full-time job. Her stash is mighty and continues to grow unhindered. She lives with her husband and an elderly dog.

Melissa Martinez

Melissa Martinez is a native New Yorker who calls Philadelphia her home. She is an indie knitwear designer who publishes her knitting and crochet patterns under the name Acts of Knittery. Melissa also runs and creates the cloche hats for the Etsy shop ClocheCraze.

Lorna Miser

Lorna Miser began knitting as a child and learned to dye, spin, and design in her 20s. After many years, designs, and books, she is returning to yarn dyeing as Zombie Yarns and will continue designing! Watch for her in magazines and yarn websites, and find her teaching across the country.

Melissa Morgan-Oakes

Author of the best-selling *2-at-a-Time Socks* and *Toe-Up 2-at-a-Time Socks*, Melissa Morgan-Oakes lives in Plymouth, Massachusetts, with her husband and fur-kids, Yoshi and Bradley. She volunteers at Plimoth Plantation, knitting and sewing for Pilgrims. When not toiling over early seventeenth century reproduction garb, she can be found around town with her dogs, or parked in a beach chair on the bay with a good read and a portable knit.

Robin Nickerson

Robin Nickerson's attraction to the world of fiber started when she was a child, and her mom taught her to crochet. After that it was just a hop, skip, and a jump to knitting, spinning, and weaving. She happily immerses herself in yarn while living on the eastern shore of Maryland, near the Chesapeake Bay. She's known as "nickersr" on Ravelry.

LeAnna Nocita-Lyons

LeAnna Nocita-Lyons has been a crocheter since she was 11 years old. Her first design was a scarf for her stuffed animal. LeAnna lives on Vashon Island, Washington, with her husband and four cats.

Tanja Osswald

Tanja Osswald is a crochet designer from Hagen, Germany. She enjoys inventing and developing new techniques, playing with yarn, construction, and ideas. Designing is what her mind does when it relaxes. Thus, her creative designs are unlike the mainstream perception of crochet or knitting. She is currently enjoying an exploration of slip stich crochet. Her innovative patterns can be found on Ravelry.

Linne Peters

Linne Peters loves to work with her hands crocheting, knitting, sewing, cooking, and gardening. In addition to those activities, she is a jogger. She lives in south Seattle, Washington, with two teenaged children, husband Jim, one cat, and two guinea pigs.

Anne-Michelle Phelan

Anne-Michelle Phelan grew up in a small village beside the sea in County Wexford, Ireland, filling her summers with sand and her winters with wool. Never not making, she keeps a hook close by and fills her dreams with adventures of yarn.

Anastasia Popova

Anastasia Popova is an accomplished crochet designer with works published in numerous books and magazines. Anastasia passes her crochet expertise on to others through her classes, ranging from instructions for complete beginners to advanced students.

Linda Rommerdahl

Linda Rommerdahl is a military brat: born in an Air Force family, enlisted in the Coast Guard, met and married a Coastguardsman, retired from the Coast Guard Reserve. She is the mother of three adult children, grandmother to one grandson. She has been crocheting for 40 years, knitting for two. She can be found on Facebook at Makings of a Yarntrepreneur.

Annalee Rose

Annalee Rose has been a crocheter for over 40 years. She enjoys trying new designs in luxury yarns, as well as creating her own designs. Also an avid knitter, there's rarely a time when she doesn't have a hook or needles in her hands. She has taught crochet classes at her LYS (Local Yarn Shop) for a number for years.

Bronislava Slagle

Bronislava Slagle started knitting and crocheting when she was 10 years old. Nowadays, she publishes her knit and crochet designs on her blog. She also started making "knit & crochet along" video tutorials for her "HandMadeRukodelky" YouTube channel, where she has acquired a very faithful following. Once a week she teaches knitting and crocheting at Black Rock Public Library in Bridgeport, Connecticut. This year one of her designs was published by *Knit Picks*.

Melinda Slaving

In her 10+ years at Storey Publishing, Melinda Slaving has worked on every one of the books in the One-Skein Wonders series. But she's never been as excited about a book as she is for this one, since her first child is due in April of 2016.

Marcia Sommerkamp

Marcia Sommerkamp is pleased to be included in her third One-Skein Wonders book as a contributing designer. She also sells designs on Ravelry as Marcia Sommerkamp Designs; produces product for three vendors; and has become a crazy cat lady, raising or caring for 13 strays (at last count). She is eagerly awaiting her first grandchild on June 4, 2016.

Gwen Steege

A confirmed fiber fanatic since childhood, Gwen Steege edits books on crochet, knitting, spinning, weaving, and dyeing, and has contributed designs to several books in the One-Skein Wonders series. She shares her passion for fiber in her book, *The Knitter's Life List* (Storey, 2011). She lives in Williamstown, Massachusetts.

Kristen Stoltzfus

Kristen Stoltzfus has been designing since she was 19, and her designs have been featured in several magazines and by several yarn companies. She lives in the hills of Idaho with her large and varied family, loving life.

Andrea Lyn Van Benschoten

Andrea Van Benschoten is a professional member of the CGOA and has designed patterns for publishers and yarn companies in both the United States and England. Her fiber arts work has been on display at Lafayette College, the Catskill Fly Fishing Center & Museum, and Peters Valley Craft Center. She lives in New Jersey with her husband, Glenn, and her cockatiel, Mendelssohn. Her website is *www.alvbfiberart.com* and her blog is *www.thefiberforum.com.*

René E. Wells

René Wells's Grandma Kay taught her the joy of fiber when she was seven years old. Now she is a Granny teaching others. She is published in *Luxury Yarn One-Skein Wonders*®, *Sock Yarn One-Skein Wonders*®, *Crochet One-Skein Wonders*®, and *One-Skein Wonders*® *for Babies.*

Kate Wood

Kate Wood learned to crochet at the tender age of 30 and has done little else since. You can find her on Ravelry as tinypantswood.

Some of the props used in the photos for this book can be found at the following Etsy shops:

CANVAS BASKET *(see page 138)*
LITTLE HEN STUDIO
www.etsy.com/shop/littlehenstudio

GREEN CAMERA *(see pages 42–43)*
LITTLE MISS WORKBENCH
www.etsy.com/shop/littlemissworkbench

GLOSSARY

2-dc cluster Yarnover, insert hook into stitch indicated and pull up a loop, yarnover and pull through 2 loops on hook, yarnover, insert hook into same stitch and pull up a loop, yarnover and pull through 2 loops, yarnover and pull through all 3 loops on hook.

3-dc cluster Yarnover, insert hook into stitch indicated and pull up a loop, yarnover and pull through 2 loops on hook, (yarnover, insert hook into same stitch and pull up a loop, yarnover and pull through 2 loops) twice, yarnover and pull through all 4 loops on hook.

4-dc cluster Yarnover, insert hook into stitch indicated and pull up a loop, yarnover and pull through 2 loops on hook, (yarnover, insert hook into same stitch and pull up a loop, yarnover and pull through 2 loops) three times, yarnover and pull through all 5 loops on hook.

5-dc cluster Yarnover, insert hook into stitch indicated and pull up a loop, yarnover and pull through 2 loops on hook, (yarnover, insert hook into same stitch and pull up a loop, yarnover and pull through 2 loops) four times, yarnover and pull through all 6 loops on hook.

adjustable ring Leaving a 6"/15 cm tail, form a loop in the yarn and hold it in your left hand with the working yarn over your index finger (figure 1). Draw the working yarn through the loop so you have 1 loop on the hook. Work the appropriate number of build-up chains for the first stitch (figure 2), then work stitches into the ring as

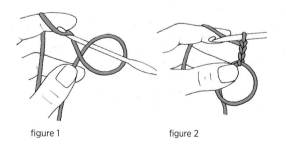

figure 1   figure 2

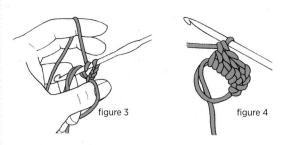

figure 3   figure 4

instructed (e.g., single, double, or treble crochet), working each stitch over the loop yarn and the tail yarn (figure 3). When you've crocheted the last stitch, separate the tail from the loop and pull it up to close the loop (figure 4). You may leave an open hole in the center or pull it up tightly to close the ring.

back loop vs. front loop The back loop is the one farther away as you look at the work. The front loop is the one closer to you.

back loop   front loop

back post vs. front post

To work a back post stitch, insert the hook from back to front to back around post of stitch indicated.

To work a front post stitch, insert the hook from front to back to front around post of stitch indicated.

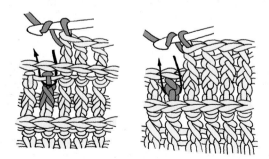

back post   front post

BLdc (back loop double crochet) Work 1 double crochet in the back loop only.

BLdc2tog (back loop double crochet 2 stitches together) (Yarnover, insert hook into back loop only of next stitch and pull up a loop, yarnover, pull through 2 loops) twice, yarnover and pull through all 3 loops on hook.

BLhdc (back loop half double crochet) Half double crochet in the back loop only.

BLhdc2tog (back loop half double crochet 2 stitches together) (Yarnover, insert hook into back loop only of next stitch and pull up a loop) twice, yarnover and pull through all 5 loops on hook.

BLsc (back loop single crochet) Single crochet in the back loop only.

BLsc2tog (back loop single crochet 2 stitches together) (Insert hook in back loop only of next st, yarnover and pull up a loop) twice, yarnover and pull through all 3 loops on hook.

BL slip st (back loop slip stitch) Slip stitch in the back loop only.

BPdc (back post double crochet) Yarnover, insert hook from back to front to back around post of stitch indicated and pull up a loop, (yarnover and pull through 2 loops on hook) twice.

BPdc2tog (back post double crochet 2 together) (Yarnover, insert hook from back to front to back around post of next stitch indicated and pull up a loop, yarnover, pull through 2 loops) twice, yarnover and pull through all 3 loops on hook.

BPhdc (back post half double crochet) Yarnover, insert hook from back to front to back around post of stitch indicated and pull up a loop, yarnover and pull through 3 loops on hook.

BPsc (back post single crochet) Insert hook from back to front to back around post of stitch indicated and pull up a loop, yarnover and pull through 2 loops on hook.

dc (double crochet) Yarnover, insert hook into stitch or space indicated, yarnover and pull up a loop, (yarnover and pull through 2 loops) twice.

dc2tog (double crochet 2 together) (Yarnover, insert hook into next stitch or space and pull up a loop, yarnover, pull through 2 loops) twice, yarnover and pull through all 3 loops on hook.

dc3tog (double crochet 3 together) (Yarnover, insert hook into next stitch or space and pull up a loop, yarnover, pull through 2 loops) three times, yarnover and pull through all 4 loops on hook.

dc4tog (double crochet 4 together) (Yarnover, insert hook into next stitch or space and pull up a loop, yarnover, pull through 2 loops) four times, yarnover and pull through all 5 loops on hook.

dc5tog (double crochet 5 together) (Yarnover, insert hook into next stitch or space and pull up a loop, yarnover, pull through 2 loops) five times, yarnover and pull through all 6 loops on hook.

dtr (double treble crochet) (Yarnover) three times, insert hook into stitch or space indicated and pull up a loop (yarnover and pull through 2 loops on hook) four times.

esc (extended single crochet) Insert hook in next stitch and pull up a loop, yarnover and pull through 1 loop, yarnover and pull through 2 loops.

esc2tog (extended single crochet 2 stitches together) (Insert hook into next stitch and pull up loop, yarnover and pull through 1 loop) twice, yarnover and pull through all 3 loops.

fdc (foundation double crochet) Begin with slip knot on hook, chain 3, yarnover, insert hook in 3rd chain from hook, *yarnover and pull up a loop, yarnover and pull through 1 loop *(chain made)*, (yarnover and pull through 2 loops) twice *(double crochet made)***. For each subsequent fdc, yarnover, insert hook under 2 loops of chain at base of stitch just made; repeat from * to ** for desired length.

fhdc (foundation half double crochet) Begin with slip knot on hook, chain 3, yarnover, insert hook in 3rd chain from hook, *yarnover and pull up a loop, yarnover and pull through 1 loop *(chain made)*, yarnover and pull through all loops on hook *(half double crochet made)***. For each subsequent fhdc, yarnover, insert hook under 2 loops of chain at base of stitch just made; repeat from * to ** for desired length.

FLdc (front loop double crochet) Double crochet in the front loop only.

FLhdc (front loop half double crochet) Half double crochet in the front loop only.

FLhdc2tog (front loop half double crochet 2 together) (Yarnover, insert hook into front loop only of next stitch or space and pull up a loop) twice, yarnover and pull through all 5 loops on hook.

FLsc (front loop single crochet) Single crochet in the front loop only.

FL slip st (front loop slip stitch) Slip stitch in the front loop only.

FL slip st 2 tog (slip stitch 2 together in front loops only) Insert the hook into the front loop of each of the next 2 stitches, yarnover, pull through all loops on hook.

FPdc (front post double crochet) Yarnover, insert hook from front to back to front around post of stitch indicated, yarnover and pull up a loop, (yarnover and pull through 2 loops on hook) twice.

FPhdc (front post half double crochet) Yarnover, insert hook from front to back to front around post of stitch indicated, yarnover and pull up a loop, yarnover and pull through 3 loops on hook.

FPsc (front post single crochet) Insert hook from front to back to front around post of stitch indicated and pull up a loop, yarnover and pull through 2 loops on hook.

FPtr (front post treble crochet) (Yarnover) twice, insert hook from front to back to front around post of stitch indicated and pull up a loop, (yarnover and pull through 2 loops on hook) three times.

fsc (foundation single crochet) Begin with slip knot on hook, chain 2, insert hook in 2nd chain from hook, *yarnover and pull up a loop, yarnover and pull through 1 loop *(chain made)*, yarnover and pull through 2 loops on hook *(single crochet made)***. For each subsequent fsc, insert hook under 2 loops of chain at base of stitch just made; repeat from * to ** for desired length.

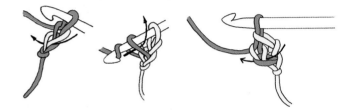

hdc (half double crochet) Yarnover, insert hook into stitch or space indicated and pull up a loop, yarnover and pull through all 3 loops on hook.

hdc2tog (half double crochet 2 together) (Yarnover, insert hook into next stitch or space and pull up a loop) twice, yarnover and pull through all 5 loops on hook.

hdc3tog (half double crochet 3 together) (Yarnover, insert hook into next stitch or space and pull up a loop) three times, yarnover and pull through all 7 loops on hook.

picot Chain 3, slip stitch in 3rd chain from hook.

reverse hdc (reverse half double crochet) Half double crochet from left to right (right to left for lefties), as follows: with right side facing and keeping hook pointing to the left (to the right for lefties), yarnover, insert hook into stitch indicated and pull up a loop, yarnover and pull through 3 loops.

reverse sc (reverse single crochet) Single crochet from left to right (right to left for lefties), as follows: With right side facing and keeping hook pointing to the left (to the right for lefties), insert hook into stitch indicated and pull up a loop, yarnover and pull through 2 loops.

sc (single crochet) Insert hook into next stitch or space indicated, yarnover and pull up a loop, yarnover and pull through 2 loops on hook.

sc2tog (single crochet 2 together) (Insert hook into next stitch or space and pull up a loop) twice, yarnover and pull through all 3 loops on hook.

sc3tog (single crochet 3 together) (Insert hook into next stitch or space and pull up a loop) three times, yarnover and pull through all 4 loops on hook.

slip st (slip stitch) Insert hook into stitch or space indicated, yarnover and pull through all loops on hook.

standing hdc Beginning with a slip knot on the hook, yarnover, insert hook into stitch or space indicated and pull up a loop, yarnover and pull through all 3 loops on hook.

standing sc Beginning with a slip knot on the hook, insert hook into stitch or space indicated and pull up a loop, yarnover and pull through both loops on hook.

tr (treble crochet) (Yarnover) two times, insert hook into stitch or space indicated, pull up a loop — *(4 loops on hook)*, (yarnover and pull through 2 loops on hook) three times.

trtr (triple treble) (Yarnover) four times, insert hook into stitch or space indicated and pull up a loop (yarnover and pull through 2 loops on hook) five times.

V-st (V-stitch) (Double crochet, chain 1, double crochet) in 1 stitch or space.

OTHER TECHNIQUES

Felting Place item in a pillowcase and close it with a rubber band. Place the pillowcase in washing machine with a pair of jeans to increase the agitation. Set the washing machine to the hottest temperature and lowest water level. Add a small amount of soap and begin the wash cycle. Before the cycle ends, stop the machine and check the felting progress. If more is needed, reset the wash cycle and continue. It's important to check the felting progress often, about every 5 to 10 minutes, to ensure you get the desired size. Measure the dimensions at each check, and as you near the desired size, check more frequently. Air dry.

Pompom Cut a square of cardboard a little larger than the size of the pompom you want to make. Make a slit down the center, stopping just past the center point.

1. Center a 12"/30.5 cm piece of yarn in the slit, leaving both ends hanging.

2. Wrap yarn around the cardboard to desired thickness of pompom. Cut the end of the yarn.

3. Tie the wrapped yarn tightly together with the piece of yarn that's hanging in the slit.

4. Cut the wrapped yarn along both edges of the cardboard.

5. Remove the cardboard, fluff up the pompom, and trim any uneven ends.

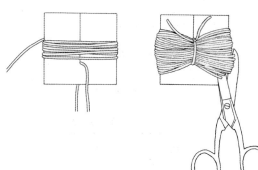

Satin stitch With yarn threaded on a yarn needle, bring yarn from wrong side to right side at one edge of the shape you are stitching (figure 1). Insert needle from front to back at opposite edge of the shape, then bring it from back to front along the design edge directly next to where the yarn originally exited (figure 2). Continue in this manner until shape is covered with thread.

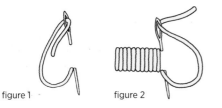

figure 1   figure 2

Whipstitch Holding the two pieces to be joined together, *insert threaded needle from back to front through one stitch on each piece and pull through; repeat from * until the pieces are joined.

Working in back bump of chain Insert hook into back bump of crochet chain and work stitch as indicated.

YARN WEIGHTS WITH RECOMMENDED HOOK SIZES AND GAUGES

STANDARD YARN WEIGHT SYSTEM	TYPES OF YARN	RECOMMENDED HOOK SIZE IN METRIC (US) TERMS	RECOMMENDED GAUGE IN SINGLE CROCHET, OVER 4" (10 CM)	UK/NA/AU EQUIVALENTS
0 LACE	Fingering, 10 count crochet thread, laceweight	Steel hooks 1.75 mm and smaller		1–3 ply
1 SUPER FINE	Sock, fingering, baby	2.25–3.5 mm (B/1 to E/4)	21–32 sts	3–4 ply
2 FINE	Sport, baby	3.5–4.5 mm (E/4 to 7)	16–20 sts	5–8 ply
3 LIGHT	DK, light worsted	4.5–5.5 mm (7 to I/9)	12–17 sts	8 ply
4 MEDIUM	Worsted, afghan, Aran	5.5–6.5 mm (I/9 to K/10.5)	11–14 sts	10–12 ply
5 BULKY	Chunky, craft, rug	6.5–9 mm (K/10.5 to M/13)	8–11 sts	12–16 ply
6 SUPER BULKY	Bulky, roving	9 mm (M/13 and larger)	5–9 sts	16–20 ply

Adapted from The Craft Yarn Council's Standards & Guidelines for Crochet and Knitting and Ravelry's Standard Yarn Weights.

ABBREVIATIONS

beg begin(ning)

BLdc back loop double crochet

BLdc2tog back loop double crochet two together

BLhdc back loop half double crochet

BLhdc2tog back loop half double crochet two together

BLsc back loop single crochet

BLsc2tog back loop single crochet two together

BL slip st back loop slip stitch

BPdc back post double crochet

BPdc2tog back post double crochet two together

BPhdc back post half double crochet

BPsc back post single crochet

ch chain

dc double crochet

dc2tog double crochet 2 together

dc3tog double crochet 3 together

dc4tog double crochet 4 together

dc5tog double crochet 5 together

dtr double treble crochet

esc extended single crochet

esc2tog extended single crochet two together

fdc foundation double crochet

fhdc foundation half double crochet

FLdc front loop double crochet

FLhdc front loop half double crochet

FLhdc2tog front loop half double crochet two together

FLsc front loop single crochet

FL slip st front loop slip stitch

FL slip st 2tog front loop slip stitch two together

FPdc front post double crochet

FPhdc front post half double crochet

FPsc front post single crochet

FPtr front post treble crochet

fsc foundation single crochet

hdc half double crochet

hdc2tog half double crochet two together

hdc3tog half double crochet three together

k knit

p purl

pm place marker

RS right side of work

sc single crochet

sc2tog single crochet 2 together

sc3tog single crochet 2 together

slip st slip stitch

st(s) stitch(es)

tr treble crochet

trtr triple treble crochet

WS wrong side of work

yo yarn over hook

SYMBOL KEY

⊂⊃ = chain (ch)

◠ = chain (ch) when stitch is worked in chain rather than space

⬭ = extended chain (exch)

• = slip st (sl st)

+ = single crochet (sc)

T = half double crochet (hdc)

† = double crochet (dc)

‡ = treble crochet (tr)

⧻ = double treble crochet (dtr)

⁒ = reverse single crochet (reverse sc)

⁀T = reverse half double crochet (reverse hdc)

⊥ = foundation single crochet (fsc)

⊥ = foundation double crochet (fdc)

+ = Back Post single crochet (BPsc)

J = Front Post half double crochet (FPhdc)

C = Back Post half double crochet (BPhdc)

J = Front Post double crochet (FPdc)

C = Back Post double crochet (BPdc)

J = Front Post treble crochet (FPtr)

X = X-stitch (X-st)

∨ or ⋁ = V-stitch (V-st)

⩗ = beginning V-stitch (beg V-st)

⩔ = Corner V-stitch (Corner V-st)

= various shells

= lacy shell

= large shell

= corner shell

= fan

∧ = half double crochet 2 together (hdc2tog)

⋀ = double crochet 2 together (dc2tog)

⋀ = double crochet 3 together (dc3tog)

= Cluster stitch (CL) over 3 sts

= Cluster stitch (CL) over 4 sts

= Cluster stitch (CL) over 7 sts

⋀ = treble crochet 2 together (tr2tog)

⋔ = Back Post double crochet 2 together (BPdc2tog)

◖ = puff stitch (puff st)

⑂ = 2-dc cluster

⑃ = 3-dc cluster

= beginning 5-dc cluster (beg 5-dc cluster)

= 5-dc cluster

= beginning cluster (beg cluster)

⩔ = first corner

⩕ = second corner

= beginning star stitch (beg star st)

⋏ = star stitch (star st)

⬭ or ⬭ = picot

= circle-fringe

⌢ = worked in back loop only

⌣ = worked in front loop only

⌃ = worked under backmost bar of hdc

⌄ = worked under frontmost bar of hdc

◠ or ⬭ = surface crochet

◎ = adjustable center ring

✳ = stitch marker

⟷ = direction of work

INDEX

activity book
Zip, Snap, and Button It!, 182–86
All Grow'd Up Skirt, 149–150
Anderson, Brenda K. B., 69–71, 119–122, 252–54, 266
April Showers Cape, 126–27
Autumn Beanie, 46–47

Baby Crocs, 62–63
Baby Duomo Cap, 38–40
Baby Mocs, 58–59
Baby Mukluks, 66–67
Baby Ringle, 11–13
Baby's Bath Set, 162–63
Baby's First Christmas Stocking, 254–56
Backpack, Max's, 236–38
Back's Where It's At Bolero, The, 78–81
Baes, Annelies, 73–74, 110–16, 266
Bagley, Deborah, 246–48, 266
Ballsmith, Sharon, 224–26, 266
Barbo, Claudia, 66–67, 266
Barranti, Donna, 152–54, 266
Bath Set, Baby's, 162–63
beanies. See hat(s)
bears
Benjamin Bear, 170–73
Ellie Bear, 180–81
Beg 5-dc cluster, 193
Beg cluster, 224

Beg dc2tog (beginning double crochet 2 together), 36
Beg V-st (beginning V-stitch), 51
Benjamin Bear, 170–73
berets. See hat(s)
bibs
Bib Trio, 154–57
Little Star Bib and Washcloth, 152–54
Ribbed Baby Bib, 160–61
Sweet Pea Bib, 158–59
Bincer, Dana, 76–78, 188–190, 239–242, 266
Biondi, Laura, 19–21, 33–34, 180–81, 266
Blagojevich, Julie, 128–29, 226–28, 260–62, 266
Blanket Pattern, 230
blankets
Baptism Blanket, 229–230
Christening Cloud, 213–15
Cotton Play Mat, 211–12
Flouncy Edged Blanket, 218–220
Grey Coverlet, 226–28
Ivory Dreams Blanket, 216–17
Kitty Kat Lovey, 175–77
Sweet Baby James, 224–26
Vaya con Dios Stroller Blanket, 221–24
Bluebell Sacque, Vintage, 102–5
Bolero, The Back's Where It's At, 78–81
bonnets. See hat(s)
booties
Baby Crocs, 62–63

Baby Mocs, 58–59
Baby Mukluks, 66–67
Bumpy Bootees, 67–69
Christening Bootees, 54–55
Little Hearts Bootees, 60–61
Monster Bootees, 64–65
Pompom Bootees, 55–57
Teeny Tiny Socks, 69–71
Boot Toppers, Sunshine, 71–72
Bottle Cozies, 249–250
Boy's Cardigan, 110–13
Braided Headband, 40–41
Brani, Janet, 44–45, 71–72, 266
Bumpy Bootees, 67–69
Bunny Buddy, Granny, 188–190
Bunny Hat, 19–21
Bunny Mittens, Little, 252–54
Burp Cloth, 166–68
Buttoned-Up Diaper Cover, 141–42
button loop, 100
buttons, sewing, 91

Cady's Cowl, 243–44
Camouflage Cap, Pink, 13–14
Cape, April Showers, 126–27
caps. See hat(s)
cardigans
Boy's Cardigan, 110–13
Floral Lace Cardigan, 123–25
Rosetta Cardigan, 113–16
Summer Kisses Cardigan, 85–87

Carpenter, Carrie, 216–17, 249–250, 267
cat
  Kitty Kat Lovey, 175–77
  Owl and the Pussycat, The, 191–92
Chan, Vicky, 123–25, 267
Chevron Stitch, 264
Chevron Pattern, 149
Christening Bootees, 54–55
Christening Cloud, 213–15
Christmas Stocking, Baby's First, 254–56
Circle-fringe, 224
Cluster, 243
Cocoon, Snuggly Wave, 209–10
Corner shell, 213
Corner stitches, 88, 224
Corner V-st, 221
Cotton Play Mat, 211–12
Coverlet, Grey, 226–28
Cowl, Cady's, 243–44
Cozies, Bottle, 249–250
Crocodile Ruffle, 138
Crocodile Stitch, 28–29, 63
Crocodile Stitch Pixie Hat, 27–29
Crocs, Baby, 62–63
Cuddly Snuggly Elephant, 196–99
Cummings, Thomasina, 85–87, 267

D
Dad & Me Necktie Shirts, 76–78
Dad's Diaper Bag, 239–242
Daley, Pam, 40–41, 54–55, 267
Dallke, Melissa, 267
Damey, Sylvie, 60–61, 78–81, 267

Dc7tog, 56
Delaney, Aurelia Mae, 175–77, 267
Del Sonno, Tamara, 17–18, 267
Dewdrop Flower Pin, 244–45
Diaper Bag, Dad's, 239–242
diaper covers
  Buttoned-Up Diaper Cover, 141–42
  Ruffled Diaper Cover, 138–140
Diaper Stacker, 246–48
doll clothes
  Squiggle Twins, 44–45
Dolly, Pocket, 202–4
Drawstring Pants, 146–48
dresses
  Pretty in Pink, 89–92
  Prism Pinafore, 100–101
DuNaier, Michele, 102–5, 130–33, 267
Durant, Judith, 36–38, 146–150, 162–63, 218–220, 229–230, 263–64, 268

E
Eckman, Edie, 67–69, 100–101, 134–36, 154–57, 254–56, 254–59, 268
Effie Effalump, 186–88
elephant
  Cuddly Snuggly Elephant, 196–99
  Effie Effalump, 186–88
Ellie Bear, 180–81
Exch (extended chain), 14, 178, 211

F
fan, 102
felting, 275
Fish, Goldie the Bouncing, 200–201
Floral Lace Cardigan, 123–25
Flouncy Edged Blanket, 218–220
Flower Pin, Dewdrop, 244–45
Flower Power Beret, 48–50
FPtr2tog (front post treble 2 together), 206

G
Goldie the Bouncing Fish, 200–201
Graham, Beth, 38–40, 268
Granny Bunny Buddy, 188–190
Grey Coverlet, 226–28
Groves, Corley, 138–140, 268

H
Hagan, Christy, 126–27, 268
Hall, Beth, 42–43, 268
Handsome Boy's Vest, 95–97
hat(s)
  Autumn Beanie, 46–47
  Baby Duomo Cap, 38–40
  Baby Ringle, 11–13
  Bunny Hat, 19–21
  Crocodile Stitch Pixie Hat, 27–29
  Flower Power Beret, 48–50
  Heart Squared Hat, 25–26
  Hope Beanie, 34–35
  Little Tam, 36–38
  Morgan Beanie, 10–11
  Pink Camouflage Cap, 13–14

hats (continued)
    Queen Anne's Lace Beanie,
      50–52
    Shine Bright, Day or Night,
      30–32
    Snowflakes Hat, 22–24
    Spring Petals Bonnet, 17–18
    Squiggle Twins, 44–45
    Toddler's Watch Cap, 42–43
    Wee Little Hat and Mittens,
      15–16
    Winter's Night Hat, A, 33–34
    Zucchini Sleep Sack and Cap,
      206–8
hat sizing, 21
Hdc dec (half double crochet
    decrease), 252
Hdc shell, 224
Hdc under backmost bar, 247
Hdc under frontmost bar, 247
HdcV-st, 114
headbands
    Braided Headband, 40–41
    Shine Bright, Day or Night,
      30–32
Heart Squared Hat, 25–26
Herter, Ida, 170–73, 268
Hontz, Laura, 25–27, 97–99, 268
Hope Beanie, 34–35
Hot-or-Cold Pack, Mom's (or
    Dad's), 263–64
Hyperbolic Mobile, 257–59

J

In the Woods Vest, 93–95
Ivory Dreams Blanket, 216–17

J

jackets
    Justin's Jacket, 134–36
    Pistachio Gelato Jacket,
      130–33
    Vintage Bluebell Sacque,
      102–5
Jumper Top, 128–29
Justin's Jacket, 134–36

K

Kacprzak, Justyna, 22–24,
    64–65, 93–95, 268
Kalka, Elizabeth Garcia, 13–14,
    211–12, 268
Khalsa, Nirmal Kaur, 117–18, 268
Kimono Shell Sweater, 97–99
Kitty Kat Lovey, 175–77
Koval, Alla, 50–52, 244–45, 269

L

lace, babies and, 212
Lacy shell, 213
Large Shell, 131
Larson, Katherine, 46–47, 269
Leg Warmers, Mommy & Me,
    73–74
Leither, Ashley, 10–11, 34–35, 269
Little Bunny Mittens, 252–54
Little Hearts Bootees, 60–61
Little Miss Felted Purse, 234–35
Little Pegasus, 193–96
Little Star Bib and Washcloth,
    152–54
Little Tam, 36–38

Lorele, Reyna Thera, 206–8,
    213–15, 269
Lovey, Kitty Kat, 175–77

M

Martinez, Melissa, 48–50, 269
Max's Backpack, 236–38
McGannon, Gwen Buttke, 234–
    35, 243–44, 269
McKee, Diane, 166–68, 269
Melissa Dallke, 200–201
Miser, Lorna, 106–9, 158–59,
    191–92, 269
mittens
    Little Bunny Mittens, 252–54
    Wee Little Hat and Mittens,
      15–16
Mobile, Hyperbolic, 257–59
Mocs, Baby, 58–59
Mommy & Me Leg Warmers,
    73–74
Mom's (or Dad's) Hot-or-Cold
    Pack, 263–64
Monster Bootees, 64–65
Morgan Beanie, 10–11
Morgan-Oakes, Melissa, 186–87,
    269
Moss Stitch, 111
Mukluks, Baby, 66–67

N

Necktie Shirts, Dad & Me, 76–78
Nickerson, Robin, 221–24, 269
Nocita-Lyons, LeAnna, 236–38,
    269

O

Octagon Pants, 143–45
Ombré Wrap, 260–62
Openwork Pattern, 226
Osswald, Tanja, 11–13, 270
Owl and the Pussycat, The, 191–92
Owl Puppet, 177–79

P

Pacifier Clip, 251
pants
    Drawstring Pants, 146–48
    Octagon Pants, 143–45
Pegasus, Little, 193–96
Peters, Linne, 58–59, 270
Phelan, Anne-Michelle, 27–29, 270
Pick Up and Knit, 144
piggy toy
    Lil' Miss Lilly, 174–75
Pin, Dewdrop Flower, 244–45
Pinafore, Prism, 100–101
Pink Camouflage Cap, 13–14
Pinwheel Vest, 106–9
Pistachio Gelato Jacket, 130–33
Play Mat, Cotton, 211–12
Pocket Dolly, 202–4
pompom, 34, 57, 275
    Pompom Bootees, 55–57
Popova, Anastasia, 89–92, 174–75, 270
Pretty in Pink, 89–92
Prism Pinafore, 100–101
Puff st (puff stitch), 51, 178
Puppet, Owl, 177–79

purses
    Little Miss Felted Purse, 234–35
    Put-and-Take Purse, 232–33
Pussycat, The Owl and the, 191–92
Put-and-Take Purse, 232–33

Q

Queen Anne's Lace Beanie, 50–52

R

Reversible Sweater, 87–89
Ribbed Baby Bib, 160–61
Rommerdahl, Linda, 143–45, 270
Rose, Annalee, 95–97, 270
Rosetta Cardigan, 113–16
Ruffle, Crocodile, 138
Ruffled Diaper Cover, 138–140

S

sacks. See sleep sacks
Sacque, Vintage Bluebell, 102–5
safety
    lace, babies and, 212
    sewing buttons, 91
    tie length, 24
    toy, 172
Satin stitch, 276
Scfl (single crochet in the frontmost loop), 119
Seed Stitch, 117
Shell Stitch, 74, 90, 102, 131, 158, 213

Shine Bright, Day or Night, 30–32
Shirts, Dad & Me Necktie, 76–78
Six-Button Vest, 119–122
Skirt, All Grow'd Up, 149–150
Slagle, Bronislava, 177–79, 270
Slaving, Melinda A., 164–65, 270
sleep sacks
    Snuggly Wave Cocoon, 209–10
    Zucchini Sleep Sack and Cap, 206–8
Snowflakes Hat, 22–24
Snuggly Wave Cocoon, 209–10
Soap Mitt Pattern, 163
Socks, Teeny Tiny, 69–71
Sommerkamp, Marcia, 30–32, 270
Spring Petals Bonnet, 17–18
Squiggle Twins, 44–45
Star St (star stitch), 153
Steege, Gwen, 62–63, 141–42, 182–86, 202–4, 209–10, 232–33, 270
stitches. See also glossary
    Beg 5-dc cluster, 193
    Beg cluster, 224
    Beg dc2tog (beginning double crochet 2 together), 36
    Beg V-st (beginning V-stitch), 51
    Blanket Pattern, 230
    button loop, 100
    Chevron Pattern, 149
    Chevron Stitch, 264
    Circle-fringe, 224
    Cluster, 243
    Corner shell, 213

stitches (continued)
Corner stitches, 88, 224
Corner V-st, 221
Crocodile Stitch, 28–29, 63
Dc7tog, 56
Exch (extended chain), 14, 178, 211
fan, 102
FPtr2tog (front post treble 2 together), 206
Hdc dec (half double crochet decrease), 252
Hdc shell, 224
Hdc under backmost bar, 247
Hdc under frontmost bar, 247
HdcV-st, 114
Lacy shell, 213
Large Shell, 131
Moss Stitch, 111
Openwork Pattern, 226
Pick Up and Knit, 144
Puff st (puff stitch), 51, 178
Satin stitch, 276
Scfl (single crochet in the frontmost loop), 119
Seed Stitch, 117
Shell Stitch, 74, 90, 102, 131, 158, 213
Star St (star stitch), 153
Soap Mitt Pattern, 163
Star St (star stitch), 153
surface chain, 166
Texture Stitch, 255
Towelette Pattern, 163
Tr2tog (treble crochet 2 together), 230
V-st (Dc, ch 1, dc), 28, 46, 90, 131, 211, 218, 221
V-st (Dc, ch 2, dc), 51
Wave Stitch Pattern, 209

Whipstitch, 276
working in back bump of chain, 276
X-st (X-stitch), 85, 93
Stoltzfus, Kristen, 55–57, 82–84, 271
Stroller Blanket, Vaya con Dios, 221–24
Summer Kisses Cardigan, 85–87
Sunshine Boot Toppers, 71–72
surface chain, 166
sweaters. See also cardigans
Kimono Shell Sweater, 97–99
Reversible Sweater, 87–89
Sweet Baby James, 224–26
Sweet Pea Bib, 158–59

T
tams. See hat(s)
teddy bear. See bears
Teeny Tiny Socks, 69–71
Texture Stitch, 255
tie length for safety, 24
Tiny Tango Vest, 82–84
tips
hat sizing, 21
lace, babies and, 212
sewing buttons, 91
tie length, 24
toy safety, 172
Toddler's Watch Cap, 42–43
Towelette Pattern, 163
toys
Benjamin Bear, 170–73
Cuddly Snuggly Elephant, 196–99
Goldie the Bouncing Fish, 200–201

Granny Bunny Buddy, 188–190
Kitty Kat Lovey, 175–77
Lil' Miss Lilly, 174–75
Little Pegasus, 193–96
Owl and the Pussycat, The, 191–92
Owl Puppet, 177–79
Pocket Dolly, 202–4
Zip, Snap, and Button It! 182–86
toy safety, 172
Tr2tog (treble crochet 2 together), 230

U
Unforgettable Vest, 117–18

V
Van Benschoten, Andrea Lyn, 15–16, 251, 271
Vaya con Dios Stroller Blanket, 221–24
vests
Handsome Boy's Vest, 95–97
Pinwheel Vest, 106–9
Six-Button Vest, 119–122
Tiny Tango Vest, 82–84
Unforgettable Vest, 117–18
In the Woods Vest, 93–95
Vintage Bluebell Sacque, 102–5
V-st (Dc, ch 1, dc), 28, 46, 90, 131, 211, 218, 221
V-st (Dc, ch 1, dc), 51

W

washcloths
  Little Star Bib and Washcloth,
    152–54
  Waves and Patchwork
    Washcloths, 164–65
Wee Little Hat and Mittens,
  15–16
Wells, René E., 87–89, 160–61,
  271
Whipstitch, 276
Winter's Night Hat, A, 33–34
Wood, Kate, 193–99, 271
working in back bump of chain,
  276
Wrap, Ombré, 260–62
wristlets
  Shine Bright, Day or Night,
    30–32

X

X-st (X-stitch), 85, 93

Z

Zip, Snap, and Button It!, 182–86
Zucchini Sleep Sack and Cap,
  206–8

INDEX TO PROJECTS BY YARN WEIGHT

0-lace

Christening Cloud 213
Grey Coverlet 226
Jumper Top 128
Ombré Wrap 260

1-sock

Baby Duomo Cap 38
Baby Ringle 11
Baby's First Christmas
 Stocking 254
Baptism Blanket 229
Bib Trio 154
Bumpy Bootees 67
Buttoned-Up Diaper Cover 141
Cady's Cowl 243
Dad & Me Necktie Shirts 76
Drawstring Pants 146
Floral Lace Cardigan 123
Handsome Boy's Vest 95
Mom's (or Dad's) Hot-or-Cold
 Pack 263
Pocket Dolly 202
Pompom Bootees 55
Prism Pinafore 100
Queen Anne's Lace Beanie 50
Reversible Sweater 87
Ribbed Baby Bib 160
Spring Petals Bonnet 17
Teeny Tiny Socks 69

2-sport

Baby Crocs 62
Baby Mukluks 66
Boy's Cardigan 110
Burp Cloth 166
Flouncy Edged Blanket 218
Goldie the Bouncing Fish 200
Hyperbolic Mobile 257

Kitty Kat Lovey 175
Little Star Bib and Washcloth . .152
Monster Bootees 64
Put-and-Take Purse 232
Snuggly Wave Cocoon 209

3-DK

All Grow'd Up Skirt 149
The Back's Where It's At Bolero 78
Braided Headband 40
Christening Bootees 54
Crocodile Stitch Pixie Hat 27
Effie Effalump 186
Heart Squared Hat 25
Kimono Shell Sweater 97
Little Bunny Mittens 252
Little Tam 36
Mommy & Me Leg Warmers . . . 73
Pacifier Clip 251
Pistachio Gelato Jacket 130
Rosetta Cardigan 113
Six-Button Vest 119
Snowflakes Hat 22
Summer Kisses Cardigan 85
Sunshine Boot Toppers 71
Tiny Tango Vest 82
Vaya con Dios Stroller Blanket .221
Vintage Bluebell Sacque 102
Waves and Patchwork
 Washcloths 164
Wee Little Hat and Mittens 15

4-worsted

April Showers Cape 126
Autumn Beanie 46
Baby Mocs 58
Baby's Bath Set 162
Bottle Cozies 249
Cotton Play Mat 211

Cuddly Snuggly Elephant 196
Dad's Diaper Bag 239
Dewdrop Flower Pin 244
Diaper Stacker 246
Flower Power Beret 48
Granny Bunny Buddy 188
In the Woods Vest 93
Ivory Dreams Blanket 216
Justin's Jacket 134
Lil' Miss Lilly 174
Little Hearts Bootees 60
Little Miss Felted Purse 234
Little Pegasus 193
Max's Backpack 236
Morgan Beanie 10
Octagon Pants 143
The Owl and the Pussycat 191
Owl Puppet 177
Pink Camouflage Cap 13
Pinwheel Vest 106
Pretty in Pink 89
Ruffled Diaper Cover 138
Squiggle Twins 44
Sweet Baby James 224
Sweet Pea Bib 158
Toddler's Watch Cap 42
Unforgettable Vest 117
Zip, Snap, and Button It! 182

5-chunky

Bunny Hat 19
Ellie Bear 180
Hope Beanie 34
Shine Bright, Day or Night 30
A Winter Night's Hat 33
Zucchini Sleep Sack and Cap . . 206

6-bulky

Benjamin Bear 170

Welcome to the World of One-Skein Wonders®

The best-selling One-Skein Wonders books each come with 101 unique projects for using those spare skeins or giving you a reason to buy more! From scarves and shawls to home dec accessories and outfits for baby, there are so many fabulous projects in each book, you'll want to buy them all!

These and other books from Storey Publishing are available wherever quality books are sold or by calling 1-800-441-5700.
Visit us at *www.storey.com* or sign up for our newsletter at *www.storey.com/signup*.

Ready to expand your crochet creativity?

Edie Eckman has the motifs and techniques to inspire your next project. These best-selling crochet books offer hundreds of beautiful ideas and problem-solving guidance you need to make your projects special and successful.